Mister Rogers' How Families Grow

Berkley Books by Fred Rogers and Barry Head

MISTER ROGERS TALKS WITH PARENTS
MISTER ROGERS' PLAYBOOK—
INSIGHTS AND ACTIVITIES FOR PARENTS AND CHILDREN
MISTER ROGERS' HOW FAMILIES GROW

by Fred Rogers and Clare O'Brien

MISTER ROGERS TALKS WITH FAMILIES ABOUT DIVORCE

Mister Rogers' How Families Grow

by Fred Rogers and Barry Head

With Drawings by Jim Prokell

BERKLEY BOOKS, NEW YORK

MISTER ROGERS' HOW FAMILIES GROW

A Berkley Book/published by arrangement with Family Communications, Inc.

PRINTING HISTORY
Berkley trade paperback edition/November 1988

ISBN: 0-425-11268-3

PRINTED IN CANADA

10 9 8 7 6 5 4 3 2 1

To
MARGARET McFARLAND,
once again,
with our
love, thanks and respect,
and to
OUR FRIENDS AND COLLEAGUES
at
Family Communications, Inc.
who help us in many ways
both seen and unseen

CONTENTS

CONTENTS

INTRODUCTION

Showing how families grow is quite different from telling how they grow; and showing is what we've tried to do here: We want to provide you with glimpses of grownups and children living together as they work out who they are—to themselves and to one another.

The material in the book is based on weekly newspaper columns called *Insights Into Childhood*. In these we've attempted to capture moments looking in on children in their infinite diversity. Yet children, unique as each child is, also share a great deal by just being children. Adults, of course, share the same things because they, too, were children once, and no matter how big or old we get, echoes of our childhoods still resound throughout our lives. In that sense, the "insights into childhood" we have written about are as much insights into our own childhoods as into our children's.

We've come to think of this book as "insights into families" in the same way. Families are of infinite diversity and yet share so much in common; and, as we look in on someone else's family, we're likely to glean insights not only into that family's workings but also into the workings of our own.

How Families Grow is largely a collection of people's feelings and memories, and people beyond numbering have generously volunteered their experiences in the hope that a little light shed from their lives might further illuminate the lives of others. The word "illumination" brings us in the most natural way to the mention of our very dear friend and teacher, Margaret McFarland. A great deal of the material here grew out of Dr. McFarland's own lifetime of personal and clinical experiences in human development—not only with children but also with the adults those children become—and her wisdom and compassion have illuminated many, many lives.

One thing this book makes clear is that growing isn't always easy, but we feel that the people you'll meet here also suggest that the struggle to grow is a worthwhile undertaking. Their experiences reinforce the belief that life is worth living. May what they have generously shared with us be an inspiration to you as you now share in how these families grow.

FRED ROGERS
BARRY HEAD

INTRODUCTION

PART 1:

THE WORK
OF GROWING

The Lay of the Land

Does it make a difference where a child grows up? I don't mean in what kind of family or what kind of home. I mean where in the sense of geography and topography—what a child could see looking out a window.

There was once a little girl who was born and grew up in the French port city of Marseilles. When she was a baby, her parents would take her with them for walks along the waterfront. Before long, she was able to toddle around them as they sat on a bench in a park overlooking the harbor. No doubt there were many times when she stared intently—as toddlers do—at all the goings on, coming to associate the sights and sounds and smells she'd known since infancy with all the activities that make up the life of a bustling port: A sudden plume of steam from a ship's smokestack brought a loud toot behind it, and there were what must have been the piercing flares of welding torches that made her squint, the jolting sounds of hammering and riveting, the smells of paint and tar mixed with the salt air. . . .

The child's name was Gisele, and as she grew, the waterfront became her favorite place to be, the place she'd go to play with friends and the place she'd go alone to think and wonder what the world was all about. As with all children, that "world" seemed to go on filling more and more space. First, there had been the tiny world of her crib and the closeness of her parents' bodies. Then, there had been the world of a room, and then a house, a street, a neighborhood that stretched down to the harbor.

"And then one day there was the horizon beyond," Gisele recalled later on, "but I realized that even the horizon wasn't the limit of the world, because ships would leave the piers and vanish, while others appeared as dots out there and came steaming home, growing huge again as they neared the shore. I spent hours and hours watching ships coming and going, wondering where to? And why? And for how long? I wrote one of my first poems about that. It had a refrain in it that in English would have been something like this:

"There must be lots to be done out there,
To be done beyond the horizon,
Beyond the setting sun!"

When she was eighteen, Gisele left home to travel and work all over the world. She finally made her home in Pittsburgh, Pennsylvania, where I met her. She went on traveling . . . and writing poetry, too. She was endlessly curious about the world, about what else there might be out there, "beyond the setting sun."

If any of us could follow the strands of our lives back to their beginnings, we'd probably be surprised how much we've been influenced by the first worlds we discovered beyond our cribs and homes. Dr. Margaret McFarland, chief consultant in early childhood development to *Mister Rogers' Neighborhood*, grew up in Pittsburgh, and she has speculated on how growing up in that city might affect a child. To begin with, she notes that Pittsburgh is a city where many people live on steep hillsides. This could suggest that small children there learn a lot about striving and persistence as they struggle up the slopes—just as they could also learn about self-control and restraint as they're toddling down.

Pittsburgh is also a city of rivers and tunnels and bridges. Going into a long tunnel, a child might feel that he or she had dropped from light into dark, or that the world had dropped away altogether. But time after time, there comes the sudden reemergence into the light, along with the discovery that the world is still there after all. This repeated experience might have particular meaning for children who worry about evening darkness, about going to sleep. Will I awake? Will the light come back? Will the people I love still be there? Tunnels might signify something else, too: that there *can* be man-made solutions even to large obstacles and that ways can be found *through* difficulties. The concrete and steel bridges that span the rivers and join neighborhoods together, Dr. McFarland surmises, might be representations for a child of the emotional bridges that we all need to connect with one another. As we grow, we have to learn to bridge gaps of *many* kinds—from the gaps left by someone's absence to the more prosaic need to bridge paragraphs.

The rivers themselves offer messages, and not only through the movement on their surface. In Pittsburgh, grandparents and parents often take their children fishing along the riverbanks. How could a child not come to realize that surfaces often conceal more than they show, that there are wonderments to be found beneath the surfaces of things . . . and people?

We all have to grow up somewhere. It might be amidst the peaks of the Rockies, or among the cornfields of the Midwest, or deep in the canyons of a skyscrapered city, or, like Gisele, along some coast with a far horizon. Fewer and fewer people nowadays end up where their lives began, but wherever circumstances or choice take us, I have little doubt that, wherever we go, the earliest landscapes of our lives will still be with us.

Of course, families have a sort of topography to them as well—and no two the same. We grow up with different numbers and kinds of relatives, some of us with many and some with few. From very early on we're aware of how those other people in our lives get along with one another, and as we grow, we come to get along with each of them in different ways. With some we feel secure and comfortable. With others we may be unsure and uneasy. Siblings and cousins may make us competitive. Uncles and aunts may constrict us with limits that are more confining than those our mothers and fathers set . . . or they may permit us freedoms our parents won't allow at home. Children can find some grandparents scary, while other grandparents will remain in their grandchildren's memories with a special love unlike any other.

Day-to-day family life has its peaks and valleys, with times that rush along like white-water rivers, and times that seem as still as a summer lake. Occasionally an emotional earthquake will send everything into an upheaval and rearrange the landscape of our lives into new, unfamiliar patterns.

So it goes. For most children, though, one of the most constant shaping forces of their early lives—almost as significant as the influence of parents—is that of brothers and sisters. In fact, parental influence and sibling influence are always closely intertwined as children in the same family grow together. That's true all life long, but never more so than at life's beginning. Infancy is a particularly special time for many reasons. Living it and having to let it go is bound to be a significantly formative experience for the sequence of children in any family.

For a first child the time of infancy has special qualities. In a family of several children, the first child is the only one who will have the sole attention of the parents. A firstborn is the only one who can say—and feel!—"my" parents in the sense of "mine alone." A firstborn is the only one who can be told, "Your mom wasn't a mom and your dad wasn't a dad until you came along." That's something children can like to hear again and again. And the child who brought a husband and wife the new identity of becoming parents can have unique importance to those parents. It's not that firstborns become preferred or loved more than the other children in a family. It's just that parents can't ever again experience the very same feelings they had when they first grew from being a couple into being a family.

The birth of a younger brother or sister means, for firstborns, having to let go of the prized time of infancy. The limelight now belongs to the second child. This letting go can be especially hard for firstborns, as many parents know, harder than for any subsequent child, because the first experience they have as family is one of unshared attention. Even though second children may be, for a time, the new focus of their parents' care, they have to share their parents' attention and love with the older sibling right from the beginning. But at least they're "the baby of the family," and the way a second child can relish and protect that position can often add to the upset a first child may already feel over being displaced. First and second children so often have difficult and quarrelsome times trying to work things out!

If a third child comes, it's then the second child who has to let go. Someone else has become the baby of the family. The older child, however, has become the oldest and is still the first. And it's common for the oldest to latch on to the new baby (just as the second child may do with a fourth child, if there is one) and become a little "parent" to it, almost adopting it as his or her own.

Does this mean a second child is bound to feel left out?

Certainly not . . . unless the parents withhold their attention and love, but that's not usually the case. In fact, a special closeness between a first and a third child may be matched by special feelings of closeness between a second child and his or her parents.

There's a family we know in which there are three girls. The middle child is now in her twenties, and to her, being the middle child meant seldom having new clothes. She got her older sister's hand-me-downs, but by the time she was done with them, they were usually too worn to pass on to her younger sister—who got new ones of her own. But what delight and meaning this middle child found in the new clothes her parents did give her!

As she grew, she became a little more introspective than her sisters, a little more of a loner and dreamer. Today she is a writer of poetry and prose, and she is finding rare and wonderful gifts to give the world.

No one can say this young woman is who she is simply because she is a middle child. The most anyone can say is that the "topography" of her family contributed to the person she has become so far . . . and we need to keep in mind that's something that can be said about all of the rest of us as well.

There's nothing unusual about children's difficulties with sharing their close caregivers; the chances are we all did. What could be more natural than for a child who has begun to grasp the who's who of his or her family to move on to an urgent concern over who's *whose?*

"My mommy says . . ." "When my daddy gets home . . ." Just about anyone who has spent any time around young children has probably heard similar phrases that suggest the feelings of ownership that preschoolers can feel toward the grown-ups they love.

It's a significant sign of growth when a child begins to use "my," "your," "his," and "her" correctly. It not only shows an awareness of individuality—or being separate from other people—but it also shows a developing awareness that certain things and people in this world belong together.

Belonging *together,* though, is very different from belonging *to,* particularly when it comes to people. After all, people aren't "belongings," but that's an understanding that takes some time to grow. From a young child's point of view, a favorite adult may indeed seem to be a belonging—and the most important belonging of all!

One little girl, three years old, knew she was soon to have a baby brother or sister, and she knew right where the baby was. Pointing to her mother's tummy one day, she asked, "And who's going to be that baby's mother?" For that three-year-old, her mommy was hers! Like most children, she was probably going to have some difficult feelings to cope with once the baby arrived. It's hard to learn to share the people you love, and the more you care for them, the harder it can be.

Preschoolers are sometimes jealous of the time that their parents spend with each other. For instance, have you noticed how often, when parents are sitting together on a sofa, their three- or four-year-old will wriggle up in between? There's affection in that act, that's true—a search for cozy togetherness. Yet, it's an example of how complex affection can be: You can be almost sure that part of the motivation is a child's need, when parents show too many signs of "belonging" to each other, to assert his or her own feelings of ownership.

As for friends—just whom they belong to often gets to be a source of problems as well. Can my friend really be your friend at the same time? Particularly a "best" friend? How suddenly those best friendships shift, and how bitterly children can feel when they do! It's almost as if they feel they've been robbed.

Whom does the teacher in school belong to? You can see children wrestling with that question as they begin transferring their feelings of parental ownership to the other important adults in their lives. How disdainful and resentful children can be of another child who seems to have special claims on a teacher's attention! How quickly a once-favored teacher can fall out of favor by showing that special attention to someone else!

There's no easy way through the conflict between caring and sharing, and it's a conflict that comes early into every child's life, often before words can be much help. Later on, talking about these feelings can be helpful, but feeling secure in another person's love grows best through weeks and months and years of feeling that security. Fortunate children, even as they come to realize that the people they love can love others, too, learn day by day that love does not have to be an "either-or" kind of thing, or a "more or less" kind of thing.

When that three-year-old wondered who would be the new baby's mommy, she was in her own way asking, "What is love?" With the birth of her brother or sister, I hope she found the chance to understand that while "my" mommy became "our" mommy, her mother's love for her was still hers in a very real sense: something no one could ever take away.

Discovering Ourselves

One of the ways love may have been different for us back when we were little is that it probably took on a far more tangible, concrete form for us then than it does today. That form could have been just about anything... so long as its appearance had some close association with the *people* we were coming to love.

It might, for instance, look like a chair. Chairs have backs... and arms... and legs. If I didn't know better, I might be inclined to look under a chair to find the seat; our seats are usually underneath us. But then I can understand the logic: We put our backs against the back of a chair, our arms on the arms, our legs where the chair's legs are, and we put our seats on the seat.

All the same, it seems to me that that's adult logic. If a very young child could tell us what he or she thought the parts of a chair were, I wouldn't be surprised to hear that child call the seat a lap. After all, we don't put just our seats in a chair; we put our laps there, too.

Laps often have a deep and special importance for a child. Children usually spend a lot of time there. Laps are closely associated with nursing and feeding. They're warm, safe places. In the earliest days and weeks of life, a child in a lap, leaning up against a caregiver's body, may hear a lot of internal sounds that became familiar during the nine months before birth. And laps, along with breasts and necks and shoulders, may come to represent for children one of the closest points of physical contact they can have with the caregivers they are growing to love.

One child, whenever his mother would go out and leave him with a babysitter, regularly toddled over to the chair he most associated with his mother and clambered up into its . . . lap. For him, there seemed little doubt that it was the closest thing he could have to his mother's actual body. Once there, he'd comfort himself during his worry and sadness over her departure by rocking himself (as his mother had often done while she sang to him) and sucking his thumb in a recreation of the nursing times he and his mother so often shared.

He knew where he was—even if everyone else thought he was sitting on a seat!

There's something else that I've seen toddlers do many times, and you may have seen it, too: A mother or father will take the toddler's older brother or sister up onto the lap to look at a book or share a hug, and the toddler will come tottering across the room and protest, complaining loudly and tugging at the parent's knees or the older child's legs.

"That's my place!" the toddler seems to be saying. "Mine!" The same thing can happen when a new baby is the one who gets to sit in the lap—sometimes, it must seem, almost all the time. If parents can seem like possessions to a young child, then a parent's lap may become one of the most intimate and prized possessions that one child can take away from another.

Those kinds of possessions are hard to let go, even to share. Many adults find that they have a favorite chair in the house, or from the perspective of the child in them, a favorite "lap." It can be hard to have a stranger or even a friend unwittingly take that place. That can be particularly true if the chair once belonged to a beloved parent or grandparent, once held a loving lap that held us, too.

When we recognize that feeling in ourselves, we're coming close to experiencing how a young child may feel when a special lap has been usurped. We may chide ourselves and chide our children over what can seem a small matter, but we need to remember that for all of us for a time, laps and love may have been almost one and the same. And where love is concerned, small matters can seem large indeed!

The puzzle of who we are, what all has contributed to the ever-unique and ever-changing being that is you and that is me, can be only partially solved in anybody's lifetime: There are far too many pieces, and new ones get added all the time. But just as chairs can mean laps that mean love, tangible objects can also represent parts of who we feel we are—parts of our "identities."

Did you ever have trouble throwing away or giving away an old coat? Or did you ever lose something that really hurt to lose? When that happens, often the only way we have to explain our feelings of—yes, grief—is to say that the object that's gone had "sentimental value."

"Grief" is a word we usually use for the loss of someone we loved, and as we grow older, we tend to use less intense words for the loss of things. We may only say we feel "sad," but even though that sadness generally passes a great deal more quickly than our sadness over the death of a loved one or the end of a loving relationship, both are forms of grief.

What are the most painful things to lose? For most of us, I believe, they're things that represented people—a family heirloom, a grandparent's diary, a piece of embroidery made by a parent, a scarf that a friend always wore. When things like that get lost, we may feel as though a part of ourselves has gone, because those people were part of who we are. Any time we feel that we've lost a part of ourselves, it's going to hurt . . . really hurt.

Understanding how closely people and things and self are blended together in early childhood may help explain the fierce possessiveness children can sometimes show over objects that to us are just "things." As babies grow into toddlers, there's a kind of "hatching" they have to grow through. Little by little, they emerge from a feeling of oneness with their closest caregiver into a sense of themselves as a separate human being.

And even as that is happening, they are moving out into a world of things that, at first, can seem a physical part of the new and separate human being they are becoming. I remember a mother recounting with puzzled concern about how her normally calm, loving little boy had one day thrown an ungovernable tantrum when she threw his "sucky blanket" into the washing machine. His screams and tears seriously alarmed her.

What was wrong with him, she wondered?

Another parent told of a toddler who kicked up a terrible fuss whenever a visiting child was put in his crib—even at times when he didn't want to be in it himself.

How does a parent best teach a child to share, to be generous?

I've come to believe that in the early years, when children are hatching and moving out into the world, parents need to protect their children's sense of self in every way they can. We can generally count on that sense of self to change in its own good time so that people and things take their appropriate places as parts of our children's growing identities. But for that to happen, children need a secure sense of identity to begin with, even if, for a while, that means our accepting their

MISTER ROGERS' HOW FAMILIES GROW

blankets and teddies and cribs as real parts of who they are—things with real "sentimental value."

It may be hard for us to understand our children's possessiveness over little things, but their feelings are a natural and necessary part of growing. Strange though it may seem, those children who learn early on that not everything in life has to be shared, often become adults capable of sharing with others the most precious things their lives have to offer.

It's not surprising that parents may become concerned when their child's close attachment to an object continues far beyond the age when most children have let such objects go or have even forgotten about them. But in deciding what to do about these attachments, I believe it's important to keep in mind that there's a transition going on that isn't yet complete—that the child has yet to replace his or her relationship with an object with relationships with people. Time, all by itself, may complete that transition. Patient understanding and encouragement may ease it, and caring, professional help can often speed it up.

If we abruptly cut the process short, however, we can be sure that a child will be left with unfinished business that will have to be resolved at other times and in other ways.

There was a boy of eleven who still had a cherished panda bear— well-worn by then, but no less loved for that. His panda was a constant companion, and he talked to it. Like many children who have such a special toy animal, he told it his secrets, his happy thoughts and his sad ones, too. Panda was comforting to him. In fact, the boy felt that, in its own way, Panda could talk to him as well.

To his parents, eleven seemed too old to be making so much of a stuffed toy, and they tried to get their son to give Panda away.

When he steadfastly refused, his mother told him one day, "Well, if you won't give your panda away, it will have to go into the attic." And that's where Panda went.

The loss of his friend was hard for that boy to accept. Later, he confided to an adult whom he trusted. "You know," he said, "I still go up to the attic sometimes and talk to Panda. It's different now, though. Panda can't seem to talk back." Panda's silence, it seems to me, was eloquent nonetheless—an expression of the boy's conflict between his love for Panda and his love for his mother on the one hand, and his fear of his mother's disapproval on the other.

It's commonplace for children, toward the end of their first year, to adopt some object and carry it everywhere as though it were part of themselves. This tends to happen just when children are trying to understand the boundary between their feelings on the inside and what their senses tell them is the reality on the outside. These objects seem to help children bridge that gap; they are part of the inside world and the outside world at the same time. For most children, these objects gradually take their proper place, physically, in the outside world, but even when they do, they can continue to have a great deal of emotional meaning. These meanings, and the objects themselves, stay with us on some level, whether we've forgotten them altogether or whether they've simply become distant memories.

A middle-aged friend of mine told me how he recently opened a cedar chest in his mother's basement and came across a teddy bear that had been special to him for years when he was little. "Feedme," he'd called it, because its mouth opened and you could drop dry food down a tin chute and take it out again through a zipper in the teddy bear's back.

"I thought Feedme had long since been thrown out," my friend told me, "and finding him there after more than forty years gave me quite a start. He gave me a problem, too: What to do with him now?

"My boys are grown, and even if they had little kids, Feedme would be far too ratty and moth-eaten to pass on. Yet I couldn't bring myself to bag him up and toss him out.

"I thought about it, and although in some ways it seemed silly to keep him, I thought: 'Why do violence to yourself?' So I'm taking Feedme home.

"He is part of myself—part of the child I was and part of the man that child has become. You know something? It feels good to be able to say hello to that child again!"

As the eleven-year-old we mentioned and his panda grow older, I hope there will come a time when they, too, for real or in memory, can "go home" together again.

A Matter of Time

There's no way we can go back and fully understand the world the way we once did as little children, or see the world the way our children are seeing it now. Children and parents will always have misunderstandings about the meanings of lots of things beside pandas. It sometimes seems surprising that we manage to communicate with our children—and they with us—as well as we do. Even as basic a notion as *time* is radically different for children and adults, while for all of us at any age, change seems to be the only constant.

One way to begin to grasp that difference between Adult Standard Time and Children's Standard Time is to go back even farther to Infant Time. At that young age time, of course, had no meaning at all. Light and dark did . . . but only because our eyes were sometimes open and sometimes shut. Pain and pleasure did . . . but only because we were sometimes full and sometimes empty. Discomfort and comfortableness did, too, depending on whether we were messy or clean . . . or whose arms were holding us.

If you close your eyes in a quiet place, and if you can let go of your thoughts, of everything except the feelings of your body, you may be able to get closer to how an infant perceives its world. It's a time of life when all experience is "now," a now in which the images change like pictures projected on a wall moving ever so slowly in and out of focus . . . with a sound track that grows and fades in volume . . . with a room temperature that gradually rises and falls. It's perpetual change, but a perpetual *now* of all our senses.

The regular workings of our body, and the repeated forms of care we get, slowly enable us, as infants, to develop a sense of the patterns and rhythms in our ever-changing "nows." Memory begins to come into play and tells us that we've felt hungry before, and so we come to have a past.

Memory also tells that someone has repeatedly brought us comfort in that past, and so maybe they will again. That expectation brings with it a future.

Even as children learn to tell time, from clocks or watches, their bodies, or their senses, continue to regulate their days (as ours do, too, much more than we may realize). At the end of a morning in school, for instance, one seven-year-old turned to a classmate and asked, "What time is it? My stomach tells me it's lunchtime!"

But what a long way we have to go from these first childhood perceptions of time to Adult Standard Time when we may find ourselves saying, "I'd better leave at 3:45 today because yesterday I left at 4 o'clock and only just made the 4:35, and I've got so much to do tonight for tomorrow's meeting!"

For young children, concepts of time first form around events. It may be time to get up; time for breakfast, lunch or supper; time for a nap; and, of course, time for certain television programs. Abstractions such as half an hour don't have much real meaning until children's lives begin running by a clock—for instance, the clock that's on the wall in school. What's more, we grown-ups don't make time's preciseness any easier to understand when we insist on saying, "I'll be with you in a second" or "In a minute!" "Why does it always take you hours to get dressed?"

In our clockwork world, it can take practice for adults to change over every so often to Children's Standard Time, but doing so can be worth the effort, since many of the misunderstandings, and subsequent reminders, about time that go on in any family arise from parents and children not being in the same time zone. "Can't we go yet?"—when it's asked for the third or fourth time—may test a busy parent's patience. The chances are that "I've already told you! We'll go about 3:30!" won't satisfy the young questioner.

Nor will "We'll go when the little hand's between the three and the four, and the big hand's on the six."

On Children's Standard Time, the best Estimated Time of Departure might be better understood as: "We'll go just as soon as your brother gets home from school."

"Mommy," a four-year-old asked, walking hand in hand with her mother down the long airport corridor, "if I walked backward, could I get to yesterday?"

That kind of "time" question can delight a parent with its whimsy and yet startle with its simplicity and logic, its ability to reveal to us the child we were—and still are. Haven't we all, at all ages, wondered where yesterday went, where yesterday is now? Some of us may even want yesterday back, just as some of us may dread the coming of tomorrow.

Why does everything *always* have to change? We've all asked this question at some point or another. The chances are that no one was able to answer fully that question for us when we were little, and there won't be many parents who can find a satisfactory answer for their children. All we know is that as time passes, everything does change. At its root, however, the question reflects a concern not so much about time itself but about stability. So where can we find the stability we all—adults and children alike—seem to need?

I believe there's no time in life when stability is more important than it is in early infancy. That's because there's no other time when the world is so new, so unfamiliar, so seemingly in constant change and no other time when we have so little experience to bring to understanding that world.

Can't *anything* be trusted not to change? For some children, the answer, happily, is yes: the constancy of care. There may be more caring faces at one time than at another, and their ways of providing care may take different forms and change as our early needs change, but the fact that we are cared for *doesn't* have to change. And if, in those early years, it doesn't change, babies can grow to be children who can care for themselves and then to be adults who can care for others.

With the help of a constant caregiver, a baby may find stability in a regular cycle of body functions and in the recurring hurts of hunger, and in the predictable relief from discomfort. It isn't long before babies begin finding out that their hands and feet belong to them and that they have bodies of their own, but as they learn to creep and crawl and toddle, they learn, too, that their very own bodies are changing all the time.

The early, deep sense of the constancy of care may be our most important resource in coping with the perpetual changes in the world around us and in our lives. As children experience the sometimes unsettling transitions of day to night, summer to winter, they need to know that even in the darkness and cold, there will be care until light and warmth return.

Infants need to know that as their bodies change in dramatic and even alarming ways, people will care for them. Dr. Margaret McFarland remembers how a young neighbor brought her the first of her teeth to fall out. Dr. McFarland knew that tooth would have great personal value for the little girl; it was, after all, part of her body, and she was at an age when body parts have an intense importance for children.

"Do you want me to keep it?" Margaret asked, and when the little girl said yes, they put it carefully in a little cup in a special place. That girl visited her again and again to make sure that her tooth was really safe, and Dr. McFarland made sure that it *was* safe until long after that girl and her family had moved away. Margaret knew that taking care of that tooth was a way of taking care of that child right then, and I have no doubt that such care helped that child learn that there could be people beyond the family who knew how to care for children and their feelings.

Children need to know, too, that when accidents happen, there will be care to help stop the pain. They need to know the same thing about times of emotional pain: I have no doubt that the children who are most likely to adjust well to divorce—who come to find a new growth and strength through a divorce—are those children who find they can count on constancy of care from *both* parents, from grandparents, and from others as well.

Constancy of care. Perhaps that's all we can hope to find that doesn't change. But what a lot that is! Without it, we may spend the years of our lives trying to walk backward to yesterday or trying to halt our steps toward tomorrow. But when we know that care is there, life can seem well worth living, even in the rough-and-tumble, ever-changing *now*.

Language and Laughter

As we grow, the care we get from those who love us comes more and more through words. Nothing, of course, ever replaces the nourishment of a hug, but language certainly provides "food for thought," even though it's often also fodder for further misunderstandings.

A friend of ours remembers that, when he was four or so, he heard his older sister being told to "watch her tongue." Curious, he went off to his room and tried to watch *his*. "To begin with," he recalls, "I found it was a hard thing to do and made you go cross-eyed. And then I couldn't figure out for the life of me what was meant to happen when you did watch it."

There must be thousands of times during childhood when children misunderstand what they hear. Our mind has a way of making sense— any kind of sense—out of what our ears and eyes bring to it. When what comes in is new or unfamiliar, or undefined, the mind will do its best to match that information with something it already knows. This striving to shape the unfamiliar into the identifiable can be seen in a child's inclination to impose on the seeming formlessness of treetops and clouds, faces or animal shapes that he or she knows.

The same thing happens with unfamiliar words and meanings. Just the other day, a colleague, who is slightly hard of hearing, was working with the radio droning in the background. He was astounded to hear a commercial message having to do with "Mozart's hairline." "I couldn't imagine what that was all about," he said, "so I asked someone else in the room. At first I got a blank look . . . and then a guffaw. It had been an ad for Ozark Airlines."

Many of children's misunderstandings may arise the same way—by fitting the unclear into what's already understood. I'm told that children have thought that the carol, "Silent Night," was about someone called "Round John Virgin." My sister used to say as part of her nighttime prayer, "the pirates and the glory forever and ever. . . ." But there's another frequent source of children's misunderstandings, and that's their tendency to take what we say literally. How can they do otherwise when they're just beginning to put words together? At the same time that their parents may be telling them, "Say what you mean," those parents, themselves, aren't saying what they mean at all.

Does "We'll go in a minute" really mean that sixty-second period of time parents may be helping their children to understand? What do you suppose a child imagines when a grown-up talks about being "all ears" or "all thumbs"? Or having "to keep your eyes peeled"?

Phrases about body parts, particularly, are likely to be misunderstood because body parts are of such urgent concern to very young children. One of their major concerns is whether body parts really and truly hold together, or whether they can break off like parts of a toy. When an adult talks about "losing" an arm or a finger, a child may understand that it simply got lost. And hearing about "losing" a husband or a child may be a frightening thought for children when fears about separation from those they love are another natural source of anxiety. It's not the fear of death that may be so upsetting; it's just that it seems so easy for people to get lost from one another.

Death, though, *is* the subject of many misunderstandings, perhaps because adults often have a hard time talking about it simply and directly. Saying that "Grammy went to sleep and never woke up" may seem like a gentle way to break the news of a close relative's death, but it has led to nighttime fears for many children who begin worrying that if they let themselves go to sleep, *they* may never wake up either. A very clear instance of children's literal understandings is the story of the child who was terrified to go to the funeral home to see "Grandpa's body laid out" . . . but who was vastly relieved once he approached the open casket because he could see that Grandpa's *head* was still there as well . . . not just his body.

Sometimes it's our misunderstandings as well as our children's that

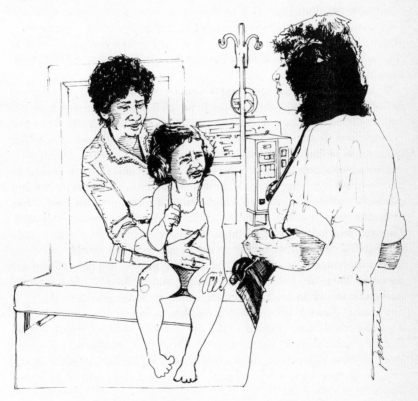

"It's okay, honey, they're just going to blow it up."

THE WORK OF GROWING   17

contribute to the confusion or anxiety. When one little girl was having her blood pressure taken for the first time in a doctor's office, her mother was so eager to let her daughter know the procedure wouldn't hurt that that's where she focused her intended reassurance. But the more she tried to be calming and factual, the more terrified her little girl became. "It's all right, honey," that mother insisted again and again as the nurse struggled to get the cuff on the girl's arm, "they're just going to blow it up. That's all, just blow it up!"

When we're trying to tell a child something that's very important, and that child just can't seem to understand, it could be helpful for us to listen with a child's ear—with a child's words. As we do, we adults will be learning more about who we are, and in the best possible sense we'll be watching our tongues.

It seems to me that one of the slipperiest kinds of communication for us human beings (of *any* age!) is humor. I thought about that this morning as I smiled at the beauty of the summer day. Where, I wondered, does a smile come from? If, for instance, we imagine a child who somehow grew up among animals and never remembered seeing a human face . . . would that child ever smile or laugh? If you think the answer is yes, when do you suppose those smiles and laughs would begin? What do you think would make them happen? A cat chasing its tail? A monkey slipping on a banana peel?

I don't have the answers, and I'm not even sure that anyone does. But when I think about it, it seems to me that inborn or learned, smiles and laughter have deep origins. Certainly, the range of things that some people find funny—and other people don't—confirms again the uniqueness of each individual.

I watched a little baby smiling the other day, and she was smiling at her mother. At times she was clearly smiling in response to her mother's smiles. She was copying a facial expression, but more than that, she was echoing a feeling that her mother's smile imparted. Through smiles, the two of them were expressing the pleasure they were giving one another by their very presence in this world.

At other moments, though, the mother put on a mock-solemn expression. Then her baby stopped smiling and studied her face intently as though trying to read unfamiliar words that were written there. If the mother stayed solemn for more than a few moments, her baby would suddenly give a quick smile and a burst of kicking and waving . . . and then just as suddenly stop and study her mother's face again. She was obviously trying to make her mother smile. As soon as she succeeded, her little body relaxed, she smiled, too, and even broke into hiccuppy laughter.

As I watched, that baby's behavior suggested that a smile and a laugh are two quite different things. A smile is something of warmth and pleasure. Would our imaginary "animal child" ever have smiled at the dawn of a new summer day? That kind of smile can depend on how we feel about ourselves at the time: even beauty around us can cause anguish if, through contrast, it intensifies sad, sour, or fearful feelings we're having about ourselves. And what is it that's most likely to make us feel *good* about who we are? I believe it's the reassurance we get from the smiles (and other expressions) of the humans we love that we, ourselves, are both lovable and loved. It's as though the beauty of a summer dawn could arouse in us the awareness of our own beauty—an awareness that was given to us by others when we were very young.

Laughter, on the other hand, may have a lot to do with the release of tension. That baby grew solemn when her mother's smile vanished. Where had that expression of warmth and pleasure gone? Was it gone forever? And then suddenly it returned, bringing laughter or relief. You can see the same thing in peekaboo games when the loved face seems to disappear . . . and then comes back. Somewhat older children, under the tension of sad or solemn occasions, can upset their parents with fits of the giggles. It may even be that one of the reasons "sick" jokes spring up so fast around tragic events and circumstances is the need to relieve the tension that can come with looking at sadness too squarely.

Of course what we consider funny is a matter of cultural and personal values, too. What provokes laughter in one culture may evoke compassion or disgust from another. The things that move our children to laughter later on in their lives are likely to be similar to the things they saw us laughing at while growing up.

Parents may find their children funny when they try to do things that grown-ups are supposed to do—using a long word (a little bit wrong) or mimicking an adult gesture or tone of voice. Children can feel miffed at times like that; no one likes to be laughed *at*, not even adults who may feel equally miffed when children laugh as Mom trips and stumbles or Dad spills his soup in his lap—the kinds of things little children often do.

Laughing *with* someone else, of course, is the best kind of laughter, and the difference between laughing *at* and laughing *with* is something children often need their parents' help in understanding. Times when families laugh together are among the most precious times a family can have.

But humor, especially between adults and children, can, indeed, backfire. "When I was five or so," a friend told us, "I remember an uncle asking me, 'Do you know what your belly button's for?' 'No,' I said, because I honestly didn't. 'Well,' he said, 'it holds your body together. If you unscrew it, your bottom will fall off.'

THE WORK OF GROWING 19

"That idea seems funny to me now, but back then I thought he was serious, and for ages I was terrified to let anyone near my belly button!"

Do you know how it feels when someone tells a joke that everyone finds funny—everyone, that is, but you? In fact, the joke may seem worse than not funny; it may hurt.

Well, all of us bring "inner dramas" to whatever we see and hear. A certain song may evoke such poignant memories that it can make us cry at the very same time it makes someone else want to dance. A television program about, say, divorce, might be a spellbinding story of intrigue for one family, while, for another, it might be too painful to watch.

Early childhood is a time when inner dramas are developing particularly rapidly and strongly, and it's also a time without the emotional protections that adults develop as they grow.

Young children feel very directly, and they hear and understand very literally. Most children, in their early years, really want to believe the adults they love . . . and fortunate children can. The healthy capacity to doubt comes to them later.

And yet, many grown-ups, with the best intentions, unwittingly tease and joke with children in ways that can trigger real alarm because the "joke" happens to hit one of early childhood's concerns.

One of the most common of children's fears is that their bodies can come apart just like a toy that breaks and can't be mended. No wonder our friend didn't find his uncle's joke about his belly button funny at all! And then there's the old joke of pretending to pinch off a child's nose and making your thumb look like the nose you've just pretended to take off. Or telling children to stop making faces because, if the wind changes, their faces will stick forever in a funny shape. When we're unsure about our bodies and how they work, this kind of teasing can be truly frightening—all the more so because in our early years we're also likely to be unsure of what is real and what is pretend. Body-threatening jokes can backfire because of both of these childhood uncertainties.

Does that caution mean parents shouldn't ever be playful with their children's bodies? Of course not! The miraculous human body is made for enjoying play, and the countless healthy body games that exist in all the world's cultures can help children understand just how miraculous their bodies really are.

These words of caution are meant only to urge you to keep in mind that humor can affect people differently at different ages. Not everyone, for instance, finds clowns funny. A grown-up friend of mine took his niece to a circus not long ago—the first circus he'd been to in longer then he could remember. "I found I had a strong and unpleasant reaction to the clowns," he told us. "My niece loved them, but I was uncomfortable with them the whole way through. Why do you suppose that was?"

I asked my friend whether he could remember how he felt about the clowns in the circuses he went to when he was little, but he couldn't recall. We had a letter from a mother, though, telling us about her son who was terrified of clowns—even on television. That boy may not feel comfortable with clowns when he grows up, either. But what was it about clowns that was frightening to him, his mother wanted to know?

Like with so many concerns, if that boy's parents are able to find the cause of his fears, help him talk and play about them, his feelings about clowns may change. He may even come to think them funny. But finding the cause of children's fears is seldom simple.

Part of my friend's early concern about clowns might stem from the fact that costumes of any sort can be scary for some young children—particularly facial makeup that distorts human features into weird shapes and colors. Before children can enjoy makeup and masks and such, they need to feel sure about what's real underneath . . . and to be able to understand that what's real *is* still there under the makeup and *will* still be there when the makeup comes off. (Indeed, parents who suddenly change their facial appearance with a new hat, hairdo or eyeglasses, or by suddenly shaving off a beard, may find themselves surprised by the temporary alarm these alterations can produce.)

Also at issue could have been the boy's anxieties about self-control.

Striving for many kinds of self-control is a big task of early childhood —whether it's control over movements, thoughts or feelings. Children count on adults to help them keep their expressions of anger in bounds, to help them avoid hurting themselves, to help them understand what's real and what isn't. It can be very frightening for young children to see adults so out of control. And that's what clowns are—adults who not only look grotesque, but who also are clearly out of control as they take pratfalls that look real, assault one another with real-looking anger. What's more, the injuries they pretend to nurse seem very real.

There's another aspect to clowning, though, and I sometimes wonder if it may not be the one that contains the real reason for clowns' sad smiles: "Clowning around," as children do, is often a cover-up for anxious feelings, a way of coping with uncomfortable situations.

One of the commonest occurrences that can bring out the clown in a child is the arrival of strangers. I can see it now: John and Mary Smith are expecting a visit from elderly, dear friends of Mary's parents—people John and Mary hardly know. "These are special friends of Grandma's," they tell their four-year-old son, Nicky, "and we want you to be on your *best* behavior! Okay?" Nicky nods, already feeling the tension in the air.

Well, you can finish that story for yourself, but it's going to be an unusually mature and secure four-year-old who can carry off that meeting to his or her parents' complete satisfaction! For many children, the visit will be marked by scoldings, such as, "Nicky! Stop interrupting!" "Nicky! Can't you sit still?" "Nicky! Stop showing off!" "Nicholas! For heaven's sake stop *clowning around!*" If things get sufficiently tense, the clown may really break loose, and the visit may even end in anger and tears.

Insecurity: Perhaps that's what makes the clown's smile such a sad one. It can be insecurity about who and what we are, or insecurity about who loves us and why. It's my experience that children who can talk to their caregivers about these kinds of things are seldom the ones who need to clown around. It's children who have no one to trust with their feelings who may start clowning early . . . and grow into adults who go on clowning all life long.

Reaching Outward

Human growth, at least as we understand it, appears to be a paradoxical thing. On the one hand, each new stage in a person's emotional development depends on the outcomes of all previous stages, so there's some logic and even inevitability about the progress of our development. At the same time, though all our experiences shape our destiny, they don't determine it. We live with the unexpected as well as with the expected, the influences upon our lives are uncountable, and there are always chances to do some repair to the emotional damages of a disadvantaged childhood, just as later circumstances may mitigate the benefits of an advantaged one.

All I feel certain about is that *all* our past experiences count and in some way contribute to how we deal with—and what we make of— each new experience we encounter. Nothing is lost. Like it or not, we grow like onions grow, layer upon layer, or like a tree ring upon ring, outward from its core. Certainly, among our most formative experiences are our earliest ones, the ones we can't remember but around which all others gather. Some of these significant experiences may occur even before our birth, but those are hard ones to assess. Clearer by far are the thousands of experiences infants encounter from the moment of birth as they reach out to their new world with all their senses.

In an old home movie taken when I was a toddler, there's a scene in which I'm in my grandfather's arms. He's trying to put his hat on my head, but each time he does, I snatch it off and throw it down. There must be scenes like that in countless home movies everywhere: Putting a large hat on a small child is such a typical kind of adult play, and snatching it off is such a typical toddler response!

Talking with Dr. McFarland the other day, we came to the subject of what she likes to call "hungry hands." Mine were certainly "hungry" in that movie scene. They couldn't wait to get hold of that hat—and get rid of it. What was remarkable was that my hands could do so. Only a few months before, I would not have been able to put together the feeling that I didn't like the hat on my head, the intention to take it off, and the coordination needed for my hands to do so. A few months before that, I wouldn't have known even what or where my hands were to begin with.

In most babies, you can see an awareness of their hands begin at about three months old. At first, their hands, often clenched into fists, move around in a random way. The fists fly open and clench shut randomly, too. But then there comes a moment when, as their hands pass in front of their eyes, they stop. It's almost as if the eyes were stopping the hands. When that happens, a new circuit has been completed between eye, hand, and *mind*.

When you think about all we do later on in life, the opening of that circuit becomes a major milestone in our development. Soon, a baby's two hands meet and explore one another, learning how to squeeze one another and let go. Of course the hungry mouth wants to get hold of them, too, and that new eye-hand-mind circuit makes it possible. It makes it possible for the hands to bring just about anything else within reach up to the mouth for exploration as well.

Suddenly, parents have to become very careful of what's around. It seems obvious to most parents to keep dangerous things away from those hungry hands, but it's easy to overlook the importance of feeding those hands with things that are not only safe but also varied and interesting in shape and texture. This hunger of the hands is an urgent outreach to the world. It's one of the earliest forms of curiosity and exploration, of discovery and pleasure.

It's a beginning of very important learning.

If children at this age come to feel that the outreach itself leads to the disapproval of their loved caregivers, they may grow up believing, in some deep corner of themselves, that there's something "bad" in reaching out. If that notion takes root in early childhood, the experts tell us, its uprooting can be a long and painfully difficult task.

Toddlers' hands seem to have an appetite that can't be satisfied! When we caution toddlers or forbid them to reach out and touch certain things, they may be able to restrain themselves as long as we're right there, close by. Their own self-control is only just beginning to grow, though, and as soon as our backs are turned, they may seem to "disobey." (That's true for children's explorations of their own body parts, too.) It's not disobeying, however, and there's nothing stubborn or willful or bad about the insistent hunger of their hands.

I can't remember exactly how my parents coped with my own hungry hands as I grew, but there must have been some encouragement because I know that those hands have gone on being hungry all my life—hungry for writing, for piano playing, for working puppets. For others, that hunger may be for making and building, for sign language, for computation, or for scientific research. But whatever the outcome, I believe it depends to a great extent on the healthfulness of the diet those hands were given when they were small.

Not all outreach is as obvious as the outreach of a baby's hands. What, for instance, are the first *smells* you can remember?

Most people find that a hard question to answer, as though those earliest smells weren't held in memory the way, say, our early experiences with touch, sight, and sound were. I just asked a grown-up friend, and he couldn't answer, but then when I asked, "Are there any smells you come across nowadays that take you way back to childhood?," he was able to come up instantly with an example.

"A certain kind of floor or floor wax," he said. "At my grandmother's house, when I was little, there was a wooden staircase, and it always had the same smell. Every now and then I'll come across that smell somewhere, and that's where I'll be: back at my grandmother's. And it brings a feeling, too—a strong feeling of safety and comfort."

That friend thinks his memory of that smell goes back to when he was about four or five, but the chances are it goes way back before that; being four or five is most likely when he can recall a *visual* memory of the staircase to go along with the smell. But he visited, at his grandmother's, he told me, off and on right from birth.

There's one category of smells that suggest that our ability to remember smells is active from the very beginning: Several parents have told me that the smells associated with *their* infants gives them a certain pleasurable reassurance. Some have said it's the smell of the nursery room where their baby sleeps. Others have been more specific and mentioned the smells of baby oil and talcum powder, and even the odor of diapers. Those, of course, are the smells they, themselves, were smelling when they were tiny babies.

At the beginning, those smells must have seemed to come from our earliest caregiver rather than from ourselves, and in part, of course, they did. At changing time, the smells of oils and powders came most strongly when the caregiver's face was close, when that person's hands were upon us, or voice was soothing in our ears. At that time, we didn't know who or what we were; we were everything, and everything was us. It was only little by little that we began to differentiate between those things that belonged to our own bodies, and other things—and people—that didn't. And as our sense of our own separate and distinct selves began to "hatch," the things that told us we were *we*, including smells, took on great importance.

One three-year-old became greatly upset when his mother decided the time had come to wash his "sucky blanket." To her, the blanket was soiled and smelly, little better than a rag. For that little boy, though, the blanket was a vital bridge between himself and the world—something that wasn't a part of his body, yet gave him his own feelings on his own skin as he rubbed it against his face and gave him, too, the repeated reassurance of his own smells. When the blanket came out of the washing machine feeling different and smelling of soap powder, it must have seemed that he'd lost part of himself, and it wasn't until he had broken it in again with his own body smells that he was able to find comfort from his blanket once more.

Along with learning that *we* had our own smells, we learned that "mother" had distinct smells of her own, not only her natural body smells but also smells that came from where she went and what she did. We learned, too, that "father" brought with him yet another set of smells. In those early understandings may lie significant parts of our later understandings of *female* and *male*. There also may lie some of the origins of deep, unconscious associations we may have with kitchens and gas stations, farms and factories, cityscapes and countrysides, barber shops and beauty parlors—with any of the places and occupations that generate the smells that rub off on the people we love.

Yes, "the nose knows," and it knows a lot more than we think it does. In fact, perhaps more keenly than any of the other senses, it serves as a reminder that the child we once were is still very much alive within us—not only the child but the toddler, baby and infant as well.

If you doubt the strength and vitality, the *immediacy*, of that child within us, you might ask yourself what makes the year's various holidays resonate so strongly in most of us. Even a friend of ours who "took a holiday from the holidays" this year admits that as the winter season unfolded, there was little he could do to control his old, familiar tremors of anticipation, mystical joy and unaccountable sadness. He felt, he said, "at the mercy of his senses."

It seems that if we grew up participating in holiday rituals, no matter how seemingly small, we're going to be dealing with lots of leftover feelings all life long, whether or not we choose to go on celebrating as we did when we were little—or even choose not to celebrate at all. Why should that be?

To understand why, I believe we have to look back once again to our earliest associations. We need to remember that in infancy, it was our senses more than our minds that governed our feelings. When we saw a bottle or smelled food, that would tell us that soon we'd have the pleasure of feeling full. When we felt the wetness of a diaper around us, we knew that soon we would start feeling cold and uncomfortable. When we saw the world getting dark, we would start to fear the separation from loved ones that bedtime would bring. And when we heard our mother's voice, or some music in a room nearby, we felt comforted again that we were not really alone.

The rituals that have grown up around the holidays tend to call strongly on our senses and the earliest associations that came with whatever our senses told us. Many of us think quickly of food when we think of the year's holidays. Food is so closely tied to nurturance and love, to good smells and tastes, and good feelings of satisfaction. (Some children have even been known to associate the whiteness of snow with the whiteness of milk—and to find an exuberant delight in snow that was hard for their parents to understand.)

Warmth was pleasurable to us when we were little, too, and the winter holidays, for many of us, bring sharp contrasts between warm hearths, warm hugs, and warm laps, and the coldness of the season outdoors.

There's contrast as well between darkness and light. The lighting of the candles at Channukah drives away the darkness, and a friend of ours who's grown up now remembered his most powerful memory of early Christmases: the moment when the church was made dark . . . one candle was lit . . . and then another from the first . . . and the others from those . . . until everyone was holding a lighted candle and the church was light again.

Holiday songs and carols often bring strong feelings from long ago. Way before we could understand the words or hum the tunes, we may have felt through the music the closeness, security, and comfort that came with our first hearing—in a parent's arms or tucked in a gently rocking cradle.

Our feelings about the holidays, and the feelings and sensations they evoke, say so much about the way human beings grow: little by little from the inside out, always changing, always whole, always unique. I'm not surprised that our friend found it so difficult to give up a holiday—"to take a holiday from the holidays." The season was calling out to the child within, and he might just as well have tried to take a holiday from the person he has become . . . or to put it another way, to take leave of his senses.

Rituals, Magic, and Reality

Remembering back to our childhoods we can often find many memories of rituals that gave us pleasure. Holiday rituals stand out in many people's minds, but the chances are that there were plenty of others, too—some of which may have brought us close to the realm of magic. One friend of mine remembers how his mother and he crowded against the dark window pane of his bedroom so they could watch the first star come out. "Star light, star bright, first star I've seen tonight, I wish I may, I wish I might, get the wish I wish tonight," they'd chant.

Another friend remembers a grandfather who would make a wish whenever he was lucky enough to catch sight of the very first sliver of a new moon. To make that wish come true, he recalls, you had to stand with your back to the moon, look at it over your left shoulder and spit once.

I often talk with children about how wishing doesn't make things come true, about magical thinking, and about the difference between reality and fantasy. Does that mean, some parents have asked me, that all these little rituals are "bad" for children? Should they be avoided or debunked right from the very start?

Rituals that are part of your family tradition and that you remember fondly from childhood are certainly not "bad" for your children! But there is cause for caution, because some situations can sometimes be harmful to a child's healthy emotional growth.

Children do wish for things, and if they wish for something terrible to happen to someone they love and it does happen, they may be left with deep-seated and long-lasting feelings of responsibility and guilt. They need to know that even scary, mad wishes will not make things come true, and it's that part of wishing that I think children do need to understand right away. In the same way, children need to know from the start that monsters and superheroes, ghosts and goblins and witches, are only pretend. There's a big difference between letting children go on believing that fearful things are real and in letting them believe in fantasies that are kind and loving.

When are children ready to learn the truth? A viewer of the *Neighborhood* wrote: "I'm eleven years old, and I have a little sister. She believes in the tooth fairy, so don't tell her who is the real tooth fairy.

That is the parents' job to tell them there is no tooth fairy, or let them find out for themselves." I feel that boy was giving us good advice: It's up to each family to decide how much they want to make of kind fantasies, and how long they want to keep them going.

Generally, there comes a time when a child will ask, "Is there really a tooth fairy?" Many parents have found it helpful to ask in reply, "What do you think?" One child once answered, "I guess I don't really think so . . . but I'd like to think so." What she was saying was that she was now ready to know the truth. Her father told her that the way she felt was just the way most people feel—and that was why lots of people like to pretend about the tooth fairy . . . even when they know that it's "somebody else."

Parents often fear that their children will be terribly disappointed when they learn that their magical fantasies are just that—fantasies. I don't believe that the disappointment is likely to be a very serious one. And when children learn the truth about who made a special wish come true, or who gave them a special gift, they learn something much more important than just "the facts." They learn that kindness and love, far from being "magical," are available from the real people in their lives, and that it takes real people to give them.

The whole issue of the difference between fantasy and reality, between what's real and what's pretend, is such an important one for young children! It's easy for us to assume that our children will pick it up as they go along, sort of "by ear." Well, eventually most children probably would, but without parents' help—such as in reassuring children that wishes *cannot* make things come true—many aspects of fantasy can make childhood a scary time. If we are in touch with our own childhoods at all, most of us will probably recognize that childhood fears can linger under the surface of our adult lives, rearing up now and then in strange and surprising ways.

Understanding what's real and unreal about children's fears isn't easy. It may be helpful to think about those fears as having three parts.

The first part is what the child seems to be afraid of—for instance, a monster in the bedroom closet. The monster, of course, isn't real.

The second part is the feeling of fear itself. That *is* real, very real.

The third part is the cause of the fear. We can be sure that's real, too, even if we don't know what it is. It's whatever the monster in the closet represents. It could be the anger of a loved parent, or perhaps a child's own anger that he or she fears might get out of control. It might be many things, but whatever it is, it's *real* and we need to take it seriously. We need to listen carefully, to reassure.

The kind of well-intentioned reassurances that start out "Don't be

MISTER ROGERS' HOW FAMILIES GROW

silly, honey, there's no monster in the closet" are *not* likely to be helpful. It's one thing to pooh-pooh an unreal monster, and quite another to pooh-pooh a very real fear, and there's never anything silly about being afraid.

People who work with children find that their fears often take widely-shared fantasy forms. We came across one of those forms the other day in a letter from a mother who wrote: "Just last night my four-year-old son woke up at midnight crying and with his heart pounding like crazy. Once again he'd had a dream about a skeleton, and skeletons seem to frighten him a whole lot."

That's not the only letter we've had about skeletons. In fact, I've come to believe that skeletons are one of those widely-shared images that crop up among children everywhere. The skeleton is a powerful symbol in the myths and legends and art of cultures all over the world, and when a symbol seems to be that universal, it's a good guess that it's origins lie somewhere in those early-childhood concerns that are universal as well.

The sight of a real skeleton can be unnerving for any of us. If you've come across one in an art studio, a science class, or a medical setting, it might have given you at least an eerie shiver to think that there is such a thing inside you . . . and that that skeleton had once been inside a living person . . . and, of course, that one day that's all that might be left of *your* body. Real-life skeletons can bring us face-to-face, suddenly and sharply, with the fact of death.

Though skeletons are likely to be associated in some way with death in children's minds as well, a four-year-old's notion of exactly what death is will almost certainly be a far cry from our own: It will depend on experience, talk in the family, and the unique nature of each child's capacity for fantasy. At the same time, the general idea of death will, for most children, carry with it some sense of separation—a time when pets or people go away and don't come back. Fears about separation from early caregivers is *certainly* one of those childhood "universals"!

Other kinds of separations, though, may be quite a different matter. For instance, when a younger brother or sister is born, separating from that little intruder might seem like a thoroughly *good* idea—so long as it's the intruder who goes away. It was interesting, in the letter from that mother about her four-year-old's dreams, to read about another "skeleton" dream her son had had the day before the one she first mentioned: "He woke up frightened," she recounted, "because he dreamed an alligator was eating his two-year-old sister into a skeleton." It's likely those two dreams on those consecutive nights were closely related. How trusting that boy is to be able to share them with his mom! All she had to do was listen and her four-year-old was telling what was foremost in his inner life. Had she called his dream "nonsense," he might never have shared another, ever.

Two other "universals" among young children seem to be, one, a time of anxiety about the wholeness and solidness of their bodies, inside and out; and, two, the way children use play as a way of mastering their fears about scary things. These two came to mind when a friend recalled an early, fierce attachment to one of his first Halloween costumes—a costume of a skeleton. He wore it even when it had become far too small for him; he just didn't want to give it up. No one can know for sure, but the sight of his "bones" on the *outside*, all in place and well-connected, might have given him a little better idea and greater confidence about how things were put together on the *inside*. What's more, pretending that *he* was a skeleton, able to control what that skeleton did, including just how scary it became, may have helped him understand that moving, talking kinds of skeletons were only make-believe, like his costume, after all.

The images that visit different children in their dreams or that they may use in their play are sometimes uncannily similar. It may be a long time before we fully understand where they come from or what they represent. Perhaps all we can hope to do is to remind ourselves that these images do come from somewhere *real*, and they do represent *real* things. If we can do that much, we may be better able to give these symbols (and the minds that conjure them up) the caring attention they deserve as children strive to work out who they are, where they are, and what they mean to all the other people around them.

Learning to Get Along

The room was crowded, but in the crowd there was one standout: a four-year-old who was marching around the edges with a scowl, chanting, "Too much pee-pul! Too much pee-pul!"

Do you know the feeling?

From the time we're born, babies tend to find other human beings a stimulating sight. Some babies, by nature, are more sensitive to faces than others, but few babies greet a face with no reaction at all. That's not surprising; as babies we're completely dependent on what other people do to and for us. Most of what we are learning then about ourselves and our world comes through other people, and part of what we have to learn as we grow is how to adapt to these people while still remaining the individuals we are.

The way that process unfolds in our earliest years will have a lot to

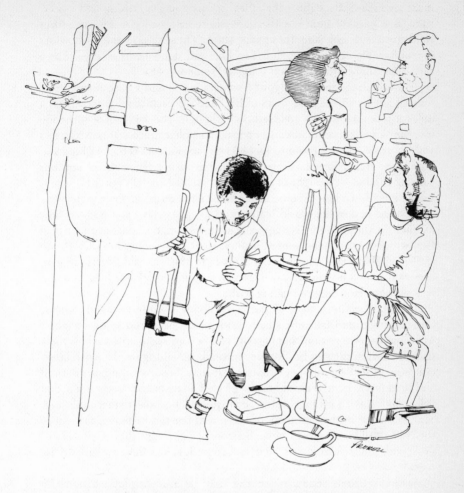

"Too much pee—pul! Too much pee—pul!"

do with how it continues during the rest of our lives, and that process
can't be hurried.

There's a common occurrence among babies that suggests how little
sense, if any, they have of individuality: If two babies are in the same
room together and one begins to cry, the other will often start howling,
too. It's hard to know why this happens. The second baby may be
echoing the first baby's sound of alarm, or may even feel an actual part

THE WORK OF GROWING   31 of the first baby's crying as though he or she were the one doing it. It must seem to little babies that they are part of everything and everything is a part of them. At that age, there's no way a baby can either think or even feel something like this: "There's someone else who's uncomfortable and crying, but I'm fine and don't need to cry." For a tiny baby, there's just no such thing as "someone else"!

The understanding that "you're someone else and I'm someone else" unfolds slowly in the first years of life, and for each child it moves on a different timetable. By toddlerhood, though, the sight of a someone else you love is usually already exciting and pleasurable. It may cause a sudden rush across a room to hug a knee, accompanied by laughter and babbling. Many parents have seen how arousing the sight of another toddler can be—the sight of a someone else like me! To parents' alarm, that can lead to a loss of self-control and a rush across a store or street as though the rest of the world had ceased to exist. Have you noticed how frequently these impulsive approaches to strange children end up in the two of them staying some distance apart and staring intently at one another? That stare can be very similar to the one toddlers may give themselves in a mirror. It's as if they're trying to work out how much of a "someone else" they're dealing with.

Toddlers' excitement and curiosity about themselves and others, though, suggests that most small children are prepared to be sociable. That may be one reason that parents can become concerned when their preschoolers appear to be "loners" instead, unwilling to play with other children. It just doesn't seem natural. It may, however, be both natural and necessary. Until a child has developed a reasonably secure sense of self, playing with other children can quickly become overstimulating. Time alone or in the company of loved and trusted caregivers is where this self-confidence grows best, because it's through their early closeness with these caregivers that children develop the capacity to be social.

As a child feels ready, he or she may be able to play contentedly alongside another child . . . then with another child . . . and then, by four or five or so, with a small group of children. These steps in growth and development don't, of course, occur in a neat and tidy sequence or at predictable intervals. What parents are most likely to notice are signs of *unreadiness* for certain kinds of sociability. Those signs—tantrums, fights or a chant of "too much pee-pul!"—don't have to mean a child is antisocial. What they're most likely to be are a child's way of saying, "What I need instead of a lot of someone elses right now is more time to get to know me!" In the heat of overstimulation, a child may crave a private, secure place to cool down—a familiar crib or a special hiding place in a closet or behind a sofa.

The need for solitude is a real and deep need for humans of all ages—even for babies. In one family we know, the parents bombarded their baby daughter with toys that rattled and tinkled and jiggled and spun, toys of all shapes and colors and textures. It seemed as though that baby hardly had a waking moment without intense outside stimulation of one kind or another.

Her parents were well-meaning; they wanted to encourage her to develop and learn in any way they could. But that baby, like almost all babies, needed time to get used to all the new things she was finding in her new world. Even without her parents' efforts to stimulate her, that world is plenty stimulating enough! She needed times that were quiet, times of solitude, and she let her parents know it. When she'd had enough, she'd turn away from them and the toys they brought. When they still insisted she pay attention, she'd close her eyes and go to sleep.

It can be hard for parents to have their babies turn away from them. When a mother finds her baby turning away from her face, it can even seem like rejection. But faces, for babies, tend to be even more stimulating than toys, and a baby who can avoid overstimulation by turning away for a time may already be showing a healthy coping skill that will be useful all through life.

The kind of solitude we're talking about goes by many names. It may be called "quiet time," or "down time," it may be criticized as "day-dreaming" or "woolgathering" (particularly in school!), or it may be promoted later on as "meditation" or "deep relaxation." But whatever it's called, it's a time to ourselves, away from outside stimulation, during which inner turbulence can settle, and we can become more familiar and more comfortable with our feelings.

Solitude is not loneliness, nor does it mean that a child has to go off alone. In fact, very young children usually find it hard to be all by themselves for a long length of time. Oftentimes, the best times of solitude occur while someone they love and trust is nearby, even in the same room. They may need the reassuring presence of an adult in order to let go, to feel their feelings, to think back over an event that troubled them, or to think ahead to a new challenge. It's the same kind of comforting "solitary togetherness," the companionship in silence, that spouses and old friends sometimes provide one another.

When I see a baby quietly staring at his or her own hands... or a toddler off in a corner putting something into a cup and then taking it out, over and over again... or a preschooler lying in the grass daydreaming... I like to think that they, in their own ways, are learning the uses of solitude, one of which, certainly, is finding in times alone the courage to go on growing.

THE WORK OF GROWING   33

Parents often turn to pets for help in encouraging their children to "get along." It may be that there's an only child in the family, and so a pet appears to be a ready-made companion. When our children get their first pets, though, we need to make sure we don't let them get overburdened by a responsibility they may not be ready for yet. The care of any living thing—plant, pet or person—is a special kind of responsibility, and parents may have to be strong partners to their children in those kinds of early nurturing relationships. What's for sure is that the arrival of a pet adds yet another dimension to the many layers of caring (and confusion!) of family life.

"We grew up with pets of all kinds," recalls a friend of ours who was one of two children. "It got to be a family joke that when Mom would get mad at Dad, he'd find a reason to cuss at my older brother, who'd pick a fight with me, who'd get grumpy and growl at the dog, who'd chase the cat, who'd go and stare hungrily at the goldfish. By the time the family anger trickled down into the aquarium, it was usually about over."

Pets can represent many things to children, and children can learn a great deal about themselves and their world as they become the givers —as well as the receivers—of care.

"When our daughter's first gerbil came into the house," a mother tells us, "Joanne was about three and seemed to think it was just another toy. She'd take the top off the cage and try to grab the gerbil the way she'd try to grab a ball or spoon. I don't know how long it really took, but it seemed like only a few days before she began to understand that a gerbil could hurt, just the way she could. Little by little she began to understand more: that the gerbil had its own ideas about what it wanted to do, that it had to be kept confined for its own safety, and that it had to have food and water . . . that we had to *give* it food and water because it couldn't get them for itself. We never made a big deal of it, but I know that somewhere inside she was also coming to understand more about the care we were trying to give her."

By having a pet in the house, a child can also gain the chance to practice being the person in control. A small child's world is peopled by large grown-ups who may seem to have all the power, who make all the decisions and who set all the limits. As you watch children play, you can often see them creating situations where they are clearly in charge. It may be building a block building in a very definite way—and then deciding when to knock it down. Or a child may practice "being in the driver's seat" literally—taking a toy truck and making it go where he or she wants it to. "I'll make the decisions for once," they seem to be saying, and having that opportunity is something all children yearn for and need.

With a small, live creature, of course, it's not only control but also the limits of control that a child can learn to understand. Children can make a dog or cat get off the sofa. They can be the ones to decide when a pet gets a biscuit for a reward. They may be able to restrain an animal on a leash, or pick it up and take it where they want it to go. They may even be able to dress a pet in a T-shirt or make it wear a hat. But pets, such as cats and dogs, have ways of making their limits unmistakably, and sometimes painfully, clear. In their own ways, they announce that they have feelings, too—that they can feel sad or feel mad as well as feel happy and cooperative. As they do so, they help children understand more about their own feelings and the many ways grown-ups respond to them.

My own friend and companion, when I was little and didn't yet have a sister, was Mitzi, a brown, wire-haired mongrel. We played and had long "conversations" during which she heard many of my secrets and shared my joys and sadnesses. We ran in the fields and huddled together through thunderstorms. I gave a great deal of myself to Mitzi, and she faithfully reflected that self back to me, helping me learn more about who I was and, in those early days, what I was feeling. When she died, she went on teaching me—about loss and grief... and about the renewal of hope and joy.

Children don't need pets in order to grow in healthy ways. Certainly not. But for those who have them, pets can bring children one of their earliest chances to transfer the getting of care to the giving of care, and then to transfer that care from animals to people. When we see our children beginning to transform our love for them into love for other creatures and other humans, we can really tell they're growing!

Phases and Stages

How much easier raising children would seem if they only grew according to fixed schedules and predictable timetables! There are, of course, broad guidelines that suggest times by when most children develop certain abilities and skills, but there are always exceptions to even these general rules.

Nor is growth a steady march forward toward some clear finish line beneath a banner that proclaims: "ALL GROWN UP!" Growth occurs in fits and starts; in steps backward as well as forward; from the inside and on the outside; up, down, and sideways.

All the same, while children are moving through phases and stages at their own rates and in their own ways, they encounter common growth tasks. Most children, for instance, need to learn to turn over, sit, crawl, stand, walk, run, climb. These are clear, physical tasks that are easy for parents to watch.

Other tasks aren't so immediately obvious. Children need to learn to tolerate the absence of those they love. We've talked already about children's need to learn the difference between real and pretend. Another of children's important growth tasks is learning to recognize and express their feelings. Often it will be their successes and failures in mastering these tasks that will trigger "phases" in behavior—phases of confidence, frustration, cooperativeness, solitariness, stubbornness, or defiance. We can't always hope to understand just what's going on and why, as our children shift from phase to phase, any more than our children may understand it. All we may be able to do is remind ourselves that something important to growth *is* going on . . . and try to provide the kind of consistent, firm and loving care within which these urges toward growth can unfold safely and without undue anxiety.

Take, for instance, a phase in toddlerhood when children seem to feel they're capable of almost anything, almost omnipotent. We were there once, too, but we've most likely forgotten how it was to feel we were the belly button of the universe—at least the known universe of our families. Everything revolved around us. Laugh, and people made a fuss of us. Squawk, and people came running, learning the word "no" made people really jump. If we were hungry, they'd feed us; cold, and they'd clothe us; sleepy, and they'd find us a place to lie down . . . and keep watch over us.

We were *it!*

And for a while, we thought we could do just about anything we took a notion to do—for instance, set off down a flight of stairs. One parent remembers how fast he ran to *his* toddler at a moment like that. He got to the head of the stairs just in time to offer his son a hand. The boy was furious. "NO!" he shouted. "Me do it all by my lone!"

In those days, if we closed our eyes, we thought no one could see us. If our parents "bought" a new baby at a hospital, well, we'd make them take it back to that store in a hurry! If we were a boy, Mommy was ours to marry one day. If we were a girl, then Daddy would marry us. Wishes, it seemed, could make things come true—perhaps even mad, scary wishes we later wished we hadn't wished in the first place.

Little by little, we had to come to terms with *not* being omnipotent after all. Accidents that hurt told us it wasn't so. The limits our parents set and kept for us showed us we couldn't always have our way. The dawning awareness of all we couldn't really do must have brought many disappointments, but the chances are that it brought relief as well. On the one hand, we had to accept that Mommy and Daddy were already married, and though we could love them and be loved by them, we could never be their lovers. On the other hand, we could feel free to wish and pretend about anything we liked without having to fear the consequences.

How difficult it all must have been to sort out, and we certainly didn't sort it out overnight! Most likely, our first attempts led us to the decision that if *we* weren't omnipotent, then it must be Mom and Dad who were. Realizing our own limits and frailties and vulnerabilities, we may have needed to believe that our parents could give us anything, make our wishes come true, make anything happen, and protect us from all harm. Casting them as the omnipotent ones in our lives would be at least second best.

Then we had to learn that we couldn't even have second best, either. A friend of ours, who grew up with a loving but stern and authoritarian father, remembers vividly an event that happened when he was six or so. He was out driving with his father, and his father was pulled over for speeding. In his father's humble compliance with the state trooper's orders, he found the first real blow to his fantasy of his father's omnipotent authority. "That moment," our friend recalls, "ranks right up there with being told there was no Santa Claus!"

One of the ironies about omnipotence is that we need to feel it, and then lose it, early in life in order to achieve a healthy, realistic, yet excited, sense of potency later on. A young child's elation at the discovery of "*Me*, and all I can do!" will come early if it comes at all. This discovery needs to be nurtured and encouraged, just as surely as parents need to find loving ways to help their children understand its realistic boundaries.

Margaret Mahler, a renowned expert of early childhood psychology, spoke of young children's "love affair with their world." The best and longest-lasting love affairs, it seems to me, are those where neither partner feels omnipotent but where each partner gains added potency from the other. So it is with children and the world. The world can't give everything, and a child can't have everything. But the world certainly has much to bring to children, and many of the finest gifts in return for this bounty come from the loving adults that children can become.

Three letters from young friends lead to some more thoughts about phases and the work of growing. The first letter came from a boy who was too young to write, so he dictated it to his mother:

"I don't pick up my toys. I just cry and cry and cry some more. I just don't like to pick up my toys."

For some reason we can't know, that boy was having trouble with family rules. As I thought about his letter, I began imagining myself back to his age when the notion of "I" was new and urgent—someone with a will of my own, with my own likes and dislikes, with new kinds of control and mastery over my body and the objects in my world, and with a new ability to speak up for myself to the people around me.

Imagining that time felt good. It felt exciting. It made me feel I wanted to assert that new self. But then I could also imagine trying to assert that self in a world where all the rules and decisions were made by grown-ups telling me what to do and when to do it . . . and what not to do and when not to do it. What place was there for my new self?

Imagining those restrictions didn't feel good. In fact, it made me feel angry and even more determined to resist doing those things I didn't like to do—such as picking up my toys. I could imagine being angry—and afraid of that anger. Could I control it? What would it do?

Would it make someone I loved angry at me? And if it did, would that person stop loving me? That felt worse. It made me feel scared. I could imagine feeling like crying, and yet, still not wanting to let go of the me I had strived so hard to become.

The second letter came from a girl who was just old enough to write for herself. Here's part of what she wrote:

"Do you ever have trouble with your boys when you tell them to clean their room? Do they obey you and clean up their rooms right away, or do they not want to do it when you ask them to? You know, when I'm in the mood to clean my room, I clean it. But when I am grumpy, I don't want to."

Here, it seemed, was a girl who had grown into the "sometimes I do, but sometimes I don't" time of life. How confusing that might be at first! Imagining back again, I could remember myself wondering who on earth I was, that "I" I had just recently become. Here I'd been working on asserting my self in the grown-up world when all of a sudden there seemed to be two selves—the glad-to-clean-up one and the grumpy-don't-want-to one. And how about the self who was sometimes happy and the self who was sometimes sad, or the sometimes angry, sometimes loving one? As I imagined myself wrestling with that puzzle, I could feel myself wanting, more than anything, someone I loved whom I could hug and talk with about it all.

The third letter came from an older girl. We'd written to each other before. Here's what she said:

"Your last letter showed me how much I really have grown as you said—inside and out. I really had not noticed that I am getting too big for some things, and as I thought about it, I found I was glad I was growing, but thinking I'm not really a baby anymore made me want to cry."

For this girl, growth had resulted in a self that was whole and yet capable of feeling two ways at the same time about the same thing—a self capable of feeling the full bittersweetness of life that came from letting go of the old to take hold of the new. What a significant stage of human development!

That these children had been able to reach out and trust me with thoughts that were so important to them suggested that they'd already learned to trust their closest caregivers. All children certainly need the trusting part of love as they make the often perplexing journey that is growth. Families will find their own solutions to the day-to-day problems of picking up toys and cleaning up rooms. My hope is that sharing these children's letters will help us parents, as we care for our own children, recall the days when once we were little, too.

Can you remember, for instance, how hard it was at ten to accept diligent practice as a necessary part of learning?

Dale is ten. He's full of curiosity about how things work, and there are lots of things he wants to learn to do. But for Dale, his mother tells us, "practice" is a bad word:

"His dad and I have tried to help him realize that most things are accomplished through hard work and patience—that you can't simply pick up a pencil, bat or flute and automatically write, play ball, or play beautiful music. But we don't seem able to get the point across. If things don't come easily for him, he backs off and goes on to something else."

It seems to me that there are two separate issues here, and they can be particularly hard to deal with when they get rolled into one as they are here. They're not just childhood issues, either!

The first issue is coping with the frustration we may feel when we can't be good at something as quickly as we'd like to be. For children (and often for grown-ups) a major cause of this frustration is having unrealistic expectations of what we can achieve. Parents can be very helpful to children who are trying to learn a new skill by breaking that skill down into manageable parts that a child can reasonably expect to master. For a four-year-old, for instance, trying to put a ten-piece puzzle together can be a very frustrating experience, resulting in that child losing interest in the puzzle and, like Dale, "going on to something else." But a child of that age could feel a real sense of satisfaction and achievement by trying to fit two pieces together . . . then three . . . and gradually more. A small child who is used to mastering manageable challenges can grow into an older one who can take, say, the "puzzle" of being a good ballplayer and put that together piece by piece, too.

Even working on a manageable task, however, is likely to take some persistence, some willingness to try and try again. That's the other issue I see in practicing: How to help children keep trying at a feasible task until they can do it.

Practicing between piano lessons becomes a source of confrontation in many families, and it's a good example here. The two most common ways I've seen parents try to get their children through fifteen-minute practice sessions are "No, you can't go out and play until you've done your practicing!" and "If you practice fifteen minutes each day this week, we'll do something special on the weekend." While children do need to learn that certain tasks have to be done, and while they can be encouraged to do them with appropriate rewards, neither approach, it seems to me, places much value on the fact of practicing or the pleasure of achievement. They risk making practicing a necessary chore without much meaning in itself.

But there's another approach parents might want to consider. Suppose you've set up a schedule for your child that's (1) back from school, (2) a snack, and (3) fifteen minutes at the piano.

Those fifteen minutes might be a time you set aside for yourself, too, for some household task you can do wherever the piano is—perhaps shining shoes or sorting the laundry. It could become a time for being together, for expressing pleasure in your child's small but real achievements, for offering encouragement when necessary, and for providing help when it's needed.

It could be a time of companionship and support, and just your availability and willingness to be there could turn what otherwise may seem senseless drudgery into three of the most important things in all children's lives: The sense that what they are doing is worthwhile; the sense that they, themselves, are capable and worthwhile; and the belief that they hold the ability to give pleasure to the people they love.

Some children are curious, others indifferent. One child is active, another sluggish. Mary wants to learn new skills, Johnny couldn't seem to care less. Parents wonder and worry and marvel, and well they might: A young child's growing relationship to people and the world is truly a wonderful, worrisome and marvelous thing! As the letters we receive tell us, parents often rejoice that their children—almost before those children know the alphabet or can count to twenty-six—are "highly motivated" or, on the other hand, parents become concerned that they've given birth to an "underachiever." Those are popular words these days, but they need to be kept in perspective.

I believe that the roots of motivation lie in the earliest interactions between an infant and his or her first, closest caregiver. Think for a moment how an eagerness to read—to cite just one example—might grow and flourish:

If a mother is an infant's first, close, loving and constant caregiver, the sound of her voice will almost immediately become for that child one of the earliest safe and trustworthy attachments to an unfamiliar world. Not only is a mother's voice part of her face when she is present, but it can also be a reminder that she is still *somewhere* even when she's out of sight—a reassurance that she will come back again.

When mothers pick up a book to "read" to their toddlers, they often pick up their toddlers as well and create for them a cozy haven on their laps, against their bodies. It's a place of caressing touches, of warmth, of loving looks, familiar smells—a place that's filled with the sound of the mother's reassuring voice. In the intimacy of reading together at this early age, what does a book mean? Words and pictures, of course, but how little significance they can have compared to the *sensations* that this thing called "book" brings with it!

Here's a common occurrence, one that may be familiar to you: A toddler starts a fuss when his or her mother is clearly about to leave the house. Standing at the screen door, the toddler (to the dismay of an inexperienced babysitter?) launches into a howling tantrum as the mother gets into the car and drives out of sight. And when the mother is gone, what happens next? The toddler wanders back into the room, picks up a book, clambers into a favorite chair, and proceeds to "read," mumbling nonsense syllables and randomly turning the upside-down pages.

It's obviously not the content of the book that matters; it's the attempt to recreate a *feeling*, a feeling that Mother is there even when she isn't.

If parents don't understand this true meaning of first books, they may overemphasize things like putting the right names on letters or getting the names of animal pictures correct. It's true that the desire to please by getting things right—and getting a smile and a hug—is another important and healthy part of motivation, but what parents need to consider carefully is their reaction to their children's getting things *wrong* at this age: Does this thing called "book" suddenly become something that brings sharp disapproval, something that threatens what really counts—the good feeling of being together? Do books become something to avoid or even fear?

Little by little, the content of books does begin to matter. That loving voice begins to read stories out loud, stories that in themselves evoke strong feelings and that in turn combine with feelings about the voice itself. And then we begin to read for ourselves. How we feel about reading in solitude is likely to have a lot to do with how we felt about books at the very beginning. Some grown-ups can "curl up beside the fire with a good book," finding once again the warmth and reassurance of childhood and perhaps hearing, through some inner ear, a loving voice that can no longer be heard for real. Other grown-ups find no joy in books, feel no warmth about them and hear no voice.

There are certainly many factors that affect motivation other than interactions in early intimacy, but I do believe good feelings about the world and what it offers take root through earlier good feelings about the first important people in our lives. A love of learning has a lot to do with learning that we're loved.

We met a father the other day who talked with wonderment about his eleven-year-old daughter, Sheila. It seemed that his daughter just couldn't get enough of what life had to offer. "I remember when she was nine," he told us, "how we became concerned about the number of activities she was taking on. She was into riding ponies, dancing, playing the guitar, swimming in competitions—you name it. One day her mother and I sat down with her and suggested she let up on a few of her interests and concentrate on a couple of her favorites. No way. She shook her head, looked us straight in the eye, and said, "I want to do it *all!*"

Was she highly competitive? we wondered. "Not really," her father told us. "She enjoys competitions, but when she loses, she's philosophical about it. She just seems to thrive on all the things there are to be done."

Curious about the roots of all this enthusiasm, we asked what life had been like for Sheila when she was younger. She was the fourth of five children, it turned out, and she grew up on a horse farm in New Jersey. The family was closely-knit and working the farm was a full-time job in which all the children were expected to share.

Now I've seen enough of farm life to know that the city-dweller's romantic notion of country living is usually far from the facts; it can be as backbreaking and heartbreaking as any other kind of work. All the same, it can bring with it something we all need if we are to feel the fullness of life: a deep-rooted sense that we have a place in the order of things. Perhaps it's easier to feel the rhythms and urgencies of life when we're surrounded by the continuum of birth and growth and death, and when our labor makes a difference in the outcomes of the seasons—what grows, what is harvested, what animals are born and thrive. That we and the earth are organically part of one another is bound to take longer for children to understand when the world they first come to know is one of subways and elevators, artificially controlled climates, and food that comes out of cans and cellophane wrappers.

We wondered, too, about Sheila's earliest days in school. "For her first three years in the small school she went to—kindergarten, first and second grade—Sheila had the same teacher, and she was fantastic," her father told us. "She was a caring, loving, down-to-earth woman who seemed as full of curiosity about life as Sheila herself was. She knew how to set limits, and she had high expectations for her children, but I think that was because *she* had high expectations from life and knew that self-discipline is an important part of our becoming all that we can be . . . and finding the joy that comes with that becoming. She loved Sheila and Sheila loved her. She was a remarkable woman, and those first school years certainly played an important part in the way Sheila has come to look at life."

That's something else we all need in order to feel the fullness of life—not only a sense that we belong on our planet, but also that we belong in other people's lives, that we are loved, lovable, and capable of loving. For most children, this begins in the intimacy of the immediate family, but it's a crucial moment for all children when they move *beyond* the home. Will they find that the world is full of other caring people worth caring about? A child's first teacher is so often the first, beyond-the-family person who confirms (or doesn't confirm!) that things like curiosity are good, that life is rich in opportunity, and that the trust first learned at home can be extended to, and received by, others as well.

It's true that young children already bring a great deal with them from home when they arrive at the schoolhouse door. Certainly what Sheila brought with her—and had confirmed by her teacher—was the joy in life and security in love that her mother and father had first given her. "But we don't all grow up in 'perfect' families," you may be thinking. No, we don't. In fact, *none* of us does, and Sheila's family wasn't perfect either. As her father talked, it was clear that that family was as full of human imperfections as any other.

As it happens, Sheila's parents are separated right now. Naturally, they worry about how their difficulties will affect their children. Their children *will* be affected, of course, each in his or her own way. But feeling sadness and feeling anger are also part of feeling the fullness of life. "Doing it *all*," as Sheila probably knows by this time, means taking the rough with the smooth. Yet I believe it's children like her—who have already grown to feel that life is worth living and people are worth loving—who are the ones most likely to go on rejoicing in life even through times that are hard.

THE WORK OF GROWING   43

Discovering Our Uniqueness

There's an indivisible wholeness to our feelings about ourselves, our feelings about the world, and the way the world seems to make us feel. We all have our ups and downs, our better days and our worse ones, but most of us have a fairly consistent "center of gravity" that is either toward the optimistic and positive, or, by contrast, toward the pessimistic and negative. No one is totally one or the other, of course, but we can usually feel definite differences of degree among the people we know.

That center of gravity begins to coalesce, I believe, immediately after birth—from the moment an infant sees the fact of his or her existence reflected with pleasure or displeasure in the caregivers' eyes. Throughout children's early years, though, one of the most consistent and powerful shapers of a child's optimism or pessimism is how he or she sorts out the puzzle or being uniquely different among fellow humans who nonetheless have so much in common.

A friend reports watching a mother and her five-year-old son playing in the park. They were making rubbings of leaves. First, they made rubbings of leaves from several different kinds of trees—a birch, a maple, and an oak. The mother commented on how different the leaves were from one another.

Then they made rubbings of several leaves from the same tree. Again, the mother commented on their differences. "You know," she said to her son as they took a break for a picnic lunch, "no two leaves in this world are exactly the same. But every leaf needs soil and water and sun and air . . . and a tree to grow on. So they're all alike in some ways, too!"

That story made us think of a time when we were chided by a father for the frequent emphasis we put on the value of uniqueness in human beings. He was a thoughtful and a caring man, and we listened carefully to his criticism—which went something like this:

"It's beneath your dignity to call someone 'special' just because he or she likes a particular shade of yellow, for instance. That's picayune; and if that's all uniqueness consists of, someone who has no virtues at all may still be able to say, 'I'm unique!' Is that what you want?

"When I look at my children, I can see all sorts of things that make them different from one another—and from everyone else in this world, for that matter. Big deal! I think you'd do better to concentrate on arousing children's curiosity, creativity, and self-reliance, on building their capacities for realistic pride."

That father had a point: Each of us is unique, and many of the things that make us so are small things. And he was right that for someone to know he or she is unique is not enough—neither for a child nor a grown-up. But it's not just that knowledge that we try to get across when we talk with children and adults. Far from it. What matters most is how children feel about that knowledge once they do begin to realize that they are different from everyone else. It matters, it seems to us, because how each one of us comes to feel about our individual uniqueness has a strong influence on how we feel about everyone's uniqueness—whether we grow into adults who rejoice in the diversity of the world's people or into adults who fear and resent that diversity.

There's even more to it than that, though. Uniqueness and their feelings about it can't take on full meaning in children's lives unless they also come to understand how much we are all alike. Finding out that we are one of a kind could be a lonely and frightening thing without the reassurance of knowing that we belong to humankind . . . and that all humans laugh and cry about many of the same things; that all have similar hopes and fears; that all have many of the same needs; and that those needs are best met by other human beings who can love us for both our similarities and our differences.

It's a child's earliest caregivers who lay the groundwork for any child's understanding of "I" and "you" and "we." It's a slow understanding, and one that comes as much through the facial expressions and actions of a mother with her newborn, as it does through the words and games of a parent and child playing with leaves in the park.

We'll go on emphasizing that understanding again and again, because we believe that children who gain the fullness of that understanding are the ones most likely to develop the curiosity, creativity, self-reliance, and pride that the father who wrote us seems to value so much.

A child's going off to school is one of the truly significant moments in a family's life. It's a time of excitement, but it's often a time of difficulty, too, as children encounter the world beyond the confines of the family and in it find new images of themselves.

Recently, a grandmother reminded us just how hard a time this can be. "We have a four-year-old adopted granddaughter. She was born in Southern India and came into our family at the age of six months. Lately she has become very concerned about the color of her skin and wishes that she could have white skin like her mother. She is very unhappy about the difference, especially because the children at school ridicule her with remarks about her skin color and exclude her from their play. I'm sure you can imagine how painful this is for all of us."

Not every child will be brought face-to-face with his or her differences as directly as this little girl, but all children will, to some degree, find that going to school brings them new awarenesses of the ways they are unique. Having to deal with that uniqueness is a growth task children share no matter what their differences, and it's seldom an easy task for the very reason that grandmother mentions: At her granddaughter's age, it's natural for children to long to be like the people they love and the new friends they meet.

They can't, of course, be exactly like those people—not even when they grow up. But in helping children learn that this is so, their earliest caregivers (and that certainly includes teachers) can often best begin by talking about the ways that all people are similar even if not the same. All people share many of the same feelings, have many of the same hopes, and suffer many of the same disappointments. And everyone

"My daughter dreams of being Cinderella . . . but never of being black."

MISTER ROGERS' HOW FAMILIES GROW

needs to feel lovable and capable of loving. Those seem to be common roots that humans share, and feeling good about this is an important step toward a child's good feelings about his or her uniqueness and the diversity of others.

A black mother told us that her biological daughter was having a hard time struggling with her racial identity within a predominantly white society. "My little girl dreams of being Cinderella, and she dreams of being rich," she told us. "But," she added, "she never dreams of being black. I wish I could explain to her that her inward beauty is more important than being accepted by the people around her." That's something I believe most of us would wish our children to believe, but it's a belief that can grow only through the loving care of parents at home, teachers in school, and parents and teachers working together in a shared concern for the children in their care. Moving beyond the family into school may bring hardships to children, but it brings opportunities as well. As that black mother said of her daughter's age and her struggles, "Now is a good time to let the truth reach the heart."

We're all so much alike . . . and yet we're all so different! The mail we get tells us that again and again. On the one hand, these letters give us a great feeling of kinship, which I think is something we all long—and need—to feel. And at the very same time, these letters tell us that each writer and each family is unique in many ways, too. I find myself rejoicing at the endless variety of human beings, and that's partly, I know, because all the ways we're different from one another tell me that it's all right for me to be different in my ways, too.

A mother wrote to tell us that she is a vegetarian and that her four-year-old daughter is choosing to eat that way as well. This mother worries that when her daughter starts in school, this "difference" may cause trouble. . . .

Another mother is concerned that the family surname—an unusual, hyphenated Hebrew name that comes from centuries of proud tradition—will make life difficult for her son when he goes to school.

Two other mothers wrote: One is alarmed that peer-group pressure is stifling creativity and individuality in her children, who are feeling driven to compete and conform. The other is distressed by the possibility of her children's school adopting school uniforms as a dress code. Uniforms would, she believes, breed conformity.

What fine examples these are of the tug-of-war we play all our lives to be accepted as part of a group while still remaining our individual selves!

These parents' problems are real. I, myself, don't eat meat, and I know that my preference can sometimes make life difficult. My middle name, McFeely, was sometimes the object of jokes when I was young, but it, too, was a name my family was proud of. Though many people would consider my clothes "traditional," I feel comfortable in what I wear, and I wouldn't want to be told to dress in a different way. (Of course many school-age children like to wear exactly what their friends are wearing.)

These concerns, or concerns like them, will always be part of our lives. They seldom have neat or easy solutions. How can you "solve" a tug-of-war? In that kind of contest, the way to win is to become strong enough to cope with the stress and strain . . . and go on tugging.

It's the people who feel strong and good about themselves inside who are best able to accept outside differences—their own or others'. We help children develop this ability every time we affirm how special they are to us for being themselves. The gift of self-confidence is given to children by their earliest caregivers, and what an important and long-lasting gift it is! Children who have received that gift are likely to be the ones who can be teased about their names and their preferences without feeling "put down" or diminished inside. They're also the children who can conform in their behavior and their appearance when they have to (as we all have to from time to time) without feeling that they are compromising who they are.

They're also, I believe, the children who can grow into adults (and parents) who rejoice that they live in a world of unique individuals and at the same time share with their neighbors the hopes, fears, sadnesses and joys that human beings have in common.

There are some differences we share with others, such as differences of culture, tradition or ethnicity. Other differences are ours alone and can indeed make us feel lonely if they're allowed to.

If you went to visit some friends to see their new baby girl, and you saw she had a large birthmark on the side of her face, what would be your first words? Suppose the baby were your baby. What would be your first thoughts? And if you were that child, how do you suppose you'd feel about yourself as you grew?

We'll each find our own answers to those hard questions (if we can find answers at all), but the chances are that wrestling with them will bring us insights into how we react to feelings of disappointment and grief, and the degree to which most of us harbor hopes for perfection of many kinds.

Feeling imperfect can hurt. I remember hearing a made-up story of a little boy who was crying his heart out because, as he wailed, "I'm put together all wrong!" His mother asked him what he meant. "I can tell I'm all wrong, Mom," he said, "because my nose runs and my feet smell!"

We can laugh at the absurdity of a joke, but there's often truth in what seems at first to be ridiculous. There was a very real little girl sitting in a real day-care center one afternoon, and her tears weren't made-up at all. "I hate myself! I hate myself!" she was sobbing. "Why on earth do you say that?" asked a concerned caregiver. "Because my little fingers are crooked!" the child explained.

The longing for perfection can be a double-edged incentive for children—and for the adults they grow up to be. While it can push some people into grasping more than they thought they could reach, it is bound to bring others a sense of disappointment and failure when their expectations of reaching perfections fall short—as they are bound to do.

Whether that desire for perfection works for us or against us may well depend on our earliest experiences. Already in infancy, babies find ways to bring pleasure to their caregivers—by their smiles, their attempts to imitate and to learn. Babies sense their caregivers' expressions of approval, and disapproval.

Through these intimate exchanges, babies gain their first sense of self-worth—or worthlessness. They catch the profound message of how the most important people in their life feel about them. For many parents, the birth of a child with an obvious blemish or disability can come as a grievous disappointment, as can even the birth of a child of the "wrong" sex. Whenever our fondest hopes are dashed, it's natural to grieve the loss of what might have been. And allowing ourselves to feel that grief may be one of the best ways to come to accept our disappointments and then begin finding new hopes for a different future.

No child is "perfectly" whole in mind, body, spirit, ability . . . nor can any child meet all of a parent's hopes and expectations. Yet there is a wholeness to each and every child, a wholeness that is unique and that brings with it a unique set of possibilities and limitations, a unique set of opportunities for fulfillment.

We all are born and grow with our own kinds of "crooked little fingers." Being perfectly human means having imperfections. All the same, most of us strive mightily to be perfect in the eyes of those we love. What those eyes tell us—as infants—are the most important messages we get about the value of being who we are.

Securing Our Identities

There's a story a mother told me once about a day when she left her five-year-old daughter in her own mother's care. The plan was for grandmother and granddaughter to go off to a local playground and swimming pool with a picnic lunch, and so this mother dropped her daughter off in sneakers, jeans, and a T-shirt—her long, dark hair in barrettes—and with a little bag with a towel, swimsuit, and hairbrush.

But somewhere along the way the plans changed. "Debbie and I decided it would be more fun to go shopping instead," the grandmother explained at the end of the afternoon. The mother was aghast. There was Debbie decked out in new shoes, knee socks, a corduroy jumper . . . and a pageboy haircut. Grandma stood there smiling, expecting approval and gratitude. The mother glared at her and shouted: "How could you have dared do that without asking me!" And then she seized her daughter and her belongings and stalked off to the car where Debbie, naturally, burst into tears.

"The clothes, of course, weren't the issue," Debbie's mother explained. "It was the haircut. With Debbie's hair short like that, I felt I was picking up a different child. Where was my little girl?"

Well, there are certainly lots of issues to think about in that story, and parents and grandparents who read it may find many things to talk about! There's one, though, that might escape notice, and that's the relationship between haircuts and identity. We may tend to see that issue as one that's more common to adolescence, but it's a real one in early childhood, too.

It can even be one reason why some children may get upset when it's time for a haircut. The more common ones are certainly important to understand and deal with—the fear of sharp scissors, the fear that hair-cutting will hurt, having to sit up high and sit still, the fear of being tilted backward and of the soap that may get in the eyes during a shampoo, the itchy hair that can get stuck in the collar. But it's also a fact, strange as it may seem to us, that children often worry that they'll be someone different when the haircut is over.

A child's sense of identity grows slowly and for several years isn't likely to be very secure. It's easy to think that the reason for Debbie's tears was simply that she was upset at seeing her mother and grandmother angry at one another, and that's likely to be part of what made her cry. But it may not have been the full reason. I wonder if Debbie, in her new hairdo, might not have been feeling that she was someone different—someone her grandmother now loved but someone her mother didn't love anymore. After all, it seemed that she was the cause of her mother's anger.

Usually it's parents who make the decisions about how their children's hair is to be cut, and what we decide is most likely to be determined by what gives us pleasure. Young children, in turn, see that pleasure in our eyes and can feel good about themselves for being a source of delight to the grown-ups they love. There will come a time, though, as healthy development continues, when the way children feel about themselves will be just as important to them as how they think we feel about them. That's when parents can expect to encounter opposition where there was none before, along with firm and even angry statements of likes and dislikes, I WILLs and I WON'Ts.

It's seldom easy for parents to give a child the priceless gift of his or her own identity. It can mean giving up part (but certainly not all) of the identities they, the parents, have assumed. Debbie's mother and grandmother may have learned more about that as they worked on resolving their conflict. And it may be helpful to all of us to remember that although the struggle for identity is one of life's truly important battles, the arenas of that struggle are often as ordinary as the barber's or hairdresser's shop.

In another story we heard, a mother was out in the park with her twin two-year-old sons who looked the same, were dressed the same and sat side by side in the double stroller, when a passer-by stopped . . . as passers-by had so many times before. And as had happened time and again as well, the passer-by said: "My, aren't they cute! Are they twins?"

"No," answered the mother, exasperated by such familiar words, "they're a pair of identical strangers."

Most of us would probably have asked the same question, as if we had to confirm the seemingly miraculous evidence of our eyes. We all know identical twins exist and aren't even that uncommon, and yet there's something about the apparent duplication of a human being that evokes deep feelings within us. It's the stuff of folk tales, legends, myths, drama, science fiction. With talk nowadays about "cloning," it may be part of science itself.

A friend of ours remembers being told, when he was little, that somewhere on this earth, among the billions of earth's people, there was an exact replica of himself. Because that information had come from a supposedly trustworthy friend, he believed it for a time. "I was entranced by the notion that somewhere there was another *me*," he remembers. "I longed to find him, but at the same time I know I was afraid to find him, too." I suspect that many of us were told the same thing; it's just the sort of rumor that passes like wildfire among children. But even if we never heard that tale, we're likely to have had the same fantasy—and the same feelings. Those feelings may still be within us when the arrival of twins makes us confront the puzzle of "double identities" for real.

The fact of twins can be a puzzle for everyone—parents, relatives, friends, strangers . . . and the twins themselves. When a wife becomes pregnant, she and her husband naturally expect to have *a* child. It is possible that they may go on expecting *a* child all the way to the delivery room, as happened to neighbors of ours. "I'm still adjusting," the mother told us, even now that her boy and girl are six months old. "I expected one child. When all of a sudden there were two, I seemed to feel I had given birth to a 'double child' rather than to two separate children. Having a boy and a girl probably made this adjustment easier for me than for a mother of identical twins, but I still feel a sense of *oneness* about my babies. I wonder if I always will."

Many parents do. That feeling of having a "double child" may be part of the reason some parents dress their twins alike, have them sleep in the same crib, try to feed them at the same time, and attempt to treat them in other ways as much alike as they can.

Other people's attitudes tend to confirm this "oneness." Friends and relatives often refer to "the twins" as though referring to a single unit rather than to two individuals, each with a name of his or her own . . . and each with distinct characteristics. Strangers, like that passer-by in the park, are struck by the fact of *twinship* so forcefully that similarity is what they feel bound to talk about rather than difference.

As twins grow up, they will be affected by the attitudes of those around them—just as are all children. And just as all children are, twins are separate and unique individuals who need constant reaffirmation of the value of their uniqueness. It is certainly true that twins can have a special closeness to one another—through shared circumstance and shared experiences, and in the case of identical twins, through their closely-shared genetic heritage. But twins can also grow to have specially angry distance between them—a distance that can last a lifetime. It may seem like a contradiction, but whether twins grow to be partners or adversaries may have a lot to do with how strongly their differences were understood and supported by the caregivers they had when they were little.

A sense of individual identity is one of the greatest gifts that parents can give a child. If that gift is not given, children will have to fight for their identities instead, and when twins have to fight each other for identity, they may, indeed, grow up to be "identical strangers."

Our search for identity has a lot to do with choice-making. Who we feel we are influences the choices we make, and the consequences of those choices often give us new insights, surprises and even shocks about who we really are.

What to eat. . . . What to wear. . . . Whether to go or stay. . . . What kind of picture to draw. . . . What shape of block building to build. . . . Whether to say yes or no. . . . From our earliest years, there are always decisions to make. Later on, our decisions may seem more important: what to buy, where to live, what career to pursue, whom to marry, how to raise our children. Yet, it's good to keep in mind that whatever age we are, the choices we have seem important to us, and that the feeling we have no choices, no matter how young or old we are, can be a source of sadness and despair.

Another thing that makes the choices of early childhood especially significant is that the kinds of choices we make when we're older—and our feelings about choice-making in the first place—grow out of our first experiences with choosing.

Have you ever known someone who just can't seem to make decisions? One acquaintance of ours comes to mind, a woman who finds it easier to live with bare walls than to choose pictures to hang on them. For her, it's as though there's only one right answer, and faced with all the possibilities, she feels sure her choice is likely to be wrong.

We didn't know her when she was little, but choice-making can be particularly hard for very young children when there are too many choices to choose from, or when making a choice may result in disapproval or anger from the grown-ups they love. Asking a child, "What do you want to wear today?" is so open-ended a question that it may invite a child to make a choice that is clearly inappropriate and has to be overruled. Instead, it may be more helpful to offer limited choices such as "Would you like to wear your red sweater or your blue one, your brown pants or your green ones?" That way, a child is presented with realistic alternatives where there is no question of "right" or "wrong."

When parents help their children learn that there are such things as limited, realistic choices, they're giving them an approach to choice-making that will be valuable throughout life. By avoiding situations that confront a child with right-wrong decision-making, they can help their children learn to make choices with confidence and with the knowledge that although some choices will work out better or worse than others, there will always be the opportunity to make new ones.

But why not avoid all these problems by making our own, grown-up decisions for our children until they're grown-up enough to make them for themselves?

For some parents, that might seem the easier path to take. But I wonder how likely a child is to become a realistic and optimistic choice-making adult without having grown through manageable choices offered by loving caregivers.

We all have a deep-seated need to feel we have some control over what happens in our lives. That need was with us as soon as we began feeling our individuality. Most children are well on their way toward that feeling by the time they're one year old, and even then, in some one-year-olds, they're probably starting to wonder just how much choice they have in this world.

Part of feeling good about ourselves is feeling that we have the chance to do what we want to do and to be what we want to be. As we grow older, we'll find out more about what's realistic for us and what isn't. But if we grew, from our earliest years, with the sense that there are always choices to be made, we may be able to let go of some of our hopes without despair, accept some of our mistakes with composure, and go on choosing new roads to fulfillment.

Parents naturally hope that as their children grow into choice-makers, they will somehow acquire good judgment along the way, making better rather than worse choices as they grow. Like most characteristics that we grow to have in adult life, the seeds of good judgment probably take root very early. They start their growth as off-shoots of the judgments that the loving adults in our early life provide before we're able to make those judgments for ourselves.

Just the other day at a friend's house, I watched a toddler reach for a little vase on a table. Before touching it, though, he paused and looked to his mom for an "okay" or "not okay." That toddler needed his mother's judgment.

The limits we set for our children on what to eat, where to play, what to wear, and when to go to bed, all reflect our best judgment and give our children a basis for making their own judgments about these things later on.

Even very young children may sometimes challenge our judgments. "Why do I have to do it?" they may ask about something we've told them to do. Most parents, at one time or another, have probably replied in exasperation, "Because I said so!" That answer, though, isn't very helpful in helping children understand how and why judgments get made. Parents certainly don't need to bargain with their children, but the more we can talk about the limits we set, the more our children are likely to come to understand that those limits are there out of loving concern for their safe and healthy growth.

Moral judgments follow quickly on the heels of the practical ones our children learn from us. What they come to feel is "good" and "bad" is sure to reflect what we've let them know about our own judgments. People come to many different conclusions about what's right and what's wrong; our value systems are part of our traditions and our culture, and they're part of what makes each of us a unique human being. And here is one of the most important things we can help our children learn about judgments: Making judgments and passing judgments are two very separate things!

I would hope for a child that he or she grow up with the good judgment to respect people's differences, with the belief that people's differences are not matters on which we need to pass judgment, and with the feeling inside that it's good and right, not bad and wrong, to be different.

Whether or not a child is able to make these kinds of judgments depends, I believe, on that child's appreciation of his or her own differences. How people come to feel about their own uniqueness is very likely to influence how they feel about everyone else's uniqueness. It's likely to make a big difference about whether they grow into adults who rejoice in the diversity of the world's people, or into judgmental adults who may even fear and resent that diversity.

A child's earliest caregivers are the ones who let a child know through facial expressions, words, and actions whether or not it's okay to be different—to be the separate and unique individual each one of us is meant to become. That's a judgment our children begin picking up from us in the very first weeks of life.

And I believe that the children who feel loved and valued for their uniqueness are the ones most likely, later in life, to see judgments as things to be made for ourselves rather than passed on others.

PART 2:

CHILDREN AT WORK

Working Things Out

Work makes the world go round, the saying goes, but we'd quickly add that, in childhood, it's play that keeps it spinning. Although play is important work for young children, there comes a time when the two tend to separate and children begin accepting a definition of work that's more in line with grown-up understandings: the things we have to do.

How can children be encouraged to become happy, helpful, and diligent workers? Probably the best opportunity comes to parents during the early years when, in a child's mind, there is no clear distinction between what is play and what is work. A single father with a five-year-old son visited a friend of ours for dinner not long ago. At the end of the meal, the host asked the boy, Tommy, if he'd like to help with the dishes. The boy nodded enthusiastically. "Can I be the one who does the washing?" he asked uncertainly. "Sure," the host replied. Together, they stood at the sink, Tommy wrapped in a large apron and standing on a stool as he scrubbed the plates in the sudsy water. As he washed, he examined the soap bubbles that stayed on his hand and then floated off in the water to pop and vanish. He held the sponge under water and then let it go, laughing as it bobbed up to the surface. The sponge and the wire-wool soap pad and the long-handled scrub brush all had different textures and did different jobs. There was water that was hot and water that was cold, things that went down the drain and things that didn't.

What kinds of "work" are fun at that age? Generally, I believe, it's activities that in some way match the inner urgencies children share at that time of life. For Tommy, the dishwashing may have been fun because, for one thing, it gave him a chance to play with water at a time when he may still have been concerned about the keeping and letting go of body fluids. It may have been only recently, too, that Tommy began to feel confident that drains were too small to slip through along with the bathwater and toilet flush.

Children of Tommy's age have many urges. A powerful one is to please the grown-ups they love and other friendly adults. Another is to feel the pride of accomplishment—particularly in tasks that are associated with being grown-up. Most preschoolers have an urgent curiosity about the world and how it works—where bubbles go when they burst, why things float, the difference between rough and smooth and what that difference means. All these urges, to one degree or another, were given expression in Tommy's washing of the dishes—those and more. Washing the dishes felt good to him, or, as he might have put it, "Boy, was that fun!"

There are many household and outdoor tasks that children may find fun because of their inner needs. Putting things in and taking things out of a dishwasher or laundry appliance can help satisfy their concerns about the inside and outside of themselves. Digging and watering the garden, or helping swab the floor with a sponge, can give outlet to young children's need to mess and smear. The setting and clearing of a table's unbreakables, or fetching and carrying brooms and buckets and wastebaskets, can make a child feel a useful helper—a useful part of the grown-up world.

Obviously not every task is a suitable one. As homes become increasingly mechanized, there can be safety hazards almost everywhere. Nowadays, parents have to be more vigilant than ever. Moreover, children can't be expected to take much real responsibility, or to accomplish tasks perfectly. "Go clean up your room" is easily said and, to us, seems a simple task to do. Giving a child the sole responsibility for carrying it out, however, may, in the early years, be more than he or she can manage. For some time, young children are likely to need adult participation and companionship.

Success is important, too, as play and work merge in children's lives. Children may not only cry over spilt milk, they can grieve when an attempt to help do a job ends up in an accident. In the beginning, at least, we need to be sure that the tasks we ask children to do are ones that they are able to carry out with the satisfaction of achievement.

As work grows out of play, an attitude toward work grows with it—an attitude that may persist all through our workaday lives. That attitude can have a lot to do with how we accept challenges, how we cope with failures, and whether we can find in the jobs we do the inner fulfillment that makes working, in and of itself, seem worthwhile.

You can see children "working" just about any time and place, and especially when there's water around: a boy in a bathtub playing with a toy sailboat . . . tipping it over and letting it spring back upright . . . holding the sail down against the water and watching it pop back up

. . . again and again. . . . What might be so compelling about that sailboat's persistent stability?

Well, it could, for instance, be a comforting feeling to see that there's something keeping that boat from capsizing no matter what happens to it. When the "keel" of our own self-control is very new, it could be reassuring to feel that there's someone around to keep us from "capsizing"—to keep us from losing control and to keep us safe. That fear of losing control is a very real and frightening one for small children.

Our consultant, Dr. Margaret McFarland, remembers how a preschooler, in the care of a very permissive teacher, awoke from a nap one afternoon in tears and alarm. When the teacher asked what was the matter, the little girl sobbed, "I was having a scary dream! Me and my friend were running all around, and you didn't know where we were and what we were doing!"

For a person, internal stability seems to come from a firm sense of being organized both emotionally and physically, and "getting ourselves organized" begins as soon as we are born. Infants' earliest caregivers provide them with the organization they need—with predictable routines of feeding and care, and with predictable reactions to smiles and cries. From these first experiences, a baby begins building his or her own sense of organization—of self and the world. It's no wonder, then, that when a baby's constant caregiver is suddenly changed, that baby, surprised with a new face, new smells, new sounds, new routines, may feel both disorganized and alarmed. A baby can go into mourning when its mother gets sick and has to give over the primary care to someone else. For the baby, losing the primary caregiver's consistent care is like losing the whole world.

Internal stability develops slowly through childhood, and children's loving caregivers can do the most to keep it growing. That's why setting limits for young children is so important; it keeps helping them learn to set limits for themselves, and that's something we all need to be able to do all life long. That's why letting children know what to expect in new circumstances is so important; it helps them to imagine and to play about it—to get themselves organized for an unfamiliar experience.

Each new stage of our development brings with it some measure of disorganization. This can be especially striking during adolescence, for instance, when physical changes combine with changing emotions to produce a sense of changing identity and of changing relationships with the people we love. This disorganization of adolescence is necessary, though. Without it, we would never grow beyond childhood.

Life events bring many times of disorganization. They may be small events that bring us feelings of "culture shock" or "jet lag." And, of course, they may be major upheavals that can come from the many losses we all suffer at one time or another. I believe that the human organism naturally seeks an even keel, but I know, too, that the course of a lifetime is never all smooth sailing. That tension between the need for stability and the inevitability of change contains both risks and opportunities. In some way that we adults can't fully recapture, that boy in the bathtub may have been doing some really important work as he practiced in his own way for weathering the inevitable storms that lie ahead.

Of course we can never know fully what is going on in our children's minds, exactly how they come to interpret individual situations, but at any given time we can be fairly certain that they are working on issues like competition, comfort and reassurance, needing times alone, family shapes, and people's leaving and coming back. But that's the way it is with children: In all they see and do, they'll find ways to express what's on their mind. Parents do know what's going on in their children's lives, and when they listen carefully, they can find plenty of opportunities for important talk—while washing the dishes or giving a bath.

Getting Things Wrong

For children to find out how people and things go together, they have to be continually learning, continually trying the new and unfamiliar. That can take courage, a courage that is best rooted in reassurance from the people a child loves. Children need to feel they are valuable, competent people . . . and that when misunderstandings, mistakes, and accidents occur, these are only healthy and natural parts of growing.

I wonder if you have the same associations with "oops!" as I have. When I hear "oops," I see a toddler heading across a room toward Mom or Dad . . . and tripping on the carpet and landing smack on his or her tummy. There's that startled look in the toddler's eye, a deep breath that could break into tears or laughter, and that's when I hear a parent saying, "Oops!" as if to say, "It's not serious, you aren't hurt, you don't need to be scared, and it isn't something to cry about."

That's a lot of meaning for one little "oops!" but the meaning seems to get across to many toddlers who soon come to say "oops!" for themselves when they trip and, without tears, pull themselves up and keep going.

Tripping like that may be one of a toddler's first "mistakes." It's not always easy to distinguish mistakes from accidents. I'm sure there are many ways to look at those two words, but accidents, to me, tend to be beyond our control, while mistakes tend to be within our control—only we don't manage to control them. Children's first mistakes are important moments because, like it or not, those first mistakes are the beginning of a lifelong series. It's generally easy to take children's early mistakes lightly, and that's the way most of them deserve to be taken, so long as we realize that they may seem important to the child who makes them. Making a mistake can make a person feel foolish, for instance, and children don't need ridicule or teasing when they get their clothes on askew, or they put a toy together backward, or their words and sentences come out higgledy-piggledy. What they do need is for someone to let them know that doing things the wrong way is sometimes the "right" way to go about learning how to do them correctly.

As children get larger, so, often, do their mistakes. When things get broken, messes get made, or feelings get hurt—by mistake—it's no longer as easy to take mistakes as light-heartedly as once we did. This is also the time by which children are usually old enough to realize that their parents and other favorite grown-ups make their share of mistakes as well: They forget things, drop and break things, and sometimes (often to children's delight) trip and stumble just like toddlers. The more parents are able to acknowledge their own mistakes, to talk about *everyone*'s need to learn to be careful and *everyone*'s need to go on learning, the more children are likely to be able to take their mistakes as an inevitable part of life . . . and to learn from them. This acknowledgment may also help the parents to be more understanding of those mistakes their children make.

Part of learning from our mistakes is learning how to put them as right as we can once we've made them. Here again, I believe it's parents' reactions to their own mistakes that determine, more than anything else, whether their children come to find it easy or difficult to say, "I'm sorry," or even to admit to a mistake once it's made. A friend remembers how she suddenly realized she'd thrown out her son's favorite teddy by mistake. "I thought about pretending that it had just gotten lost and would probably turn up sometime," she admitted, "but instead I told him what I'd done, by mistake, and that I was really sorry. For a while he was too upset and mad at me to understand what 'by mistake' meant, but at least we began talking about mistakes. For ages after that, whenever something about a mistake would come up, Sean would say to me, 'Like the time you threw out my teddy.' One day I asked him if he was still mad at me for what I'd done. He looked at me seriously and shook his head. 'No,' he said, 'because I know you didn't mean to do it.' That was important to me—to find out he did understand after all."

Understanding can take time. Another little boy was caught by his dad in the act of lopping the heads off some garden flowers with a toy shovel. When his father angrily pointed to the destruction, his son said he'd done it "by mistake." His father pointed out he certainly had *not* done it by mistake, that he'd seen him with his own eyes doing it on purpose. "That's what I mean," his son replied. "I did it on purpose by mistake."

Children who do not grow to be comfortable making mistakes can have a really difficult time later on. "A scaredy cat! That was me growing up," a friend told us the other day. "There was so much I didn't dare try! I can remember even back in first grade wanting to be able to kick a ball as well as some of the other children, but I didn't think I'd be able to, so I found something else to do instead.

"I avoided anything I thought I wouldn't do right or well, and I'd choose weird things to do because no one else would be doing them . . . and so no one would be better than I. When everyone was collecting stamps, I collected coins. When my friends got interested in riflery, I learned how to shoot a bow and fletch my own arrows. I wonder what I was so afraid of!"

Listening to our friend talk, it was clear he had plenty of curiosity, so that wasn't the problem. We wondered whether he'd been afraid of competing—afraid of losing the love of the grown-ups he loved by losing out in a competition. He didn't think so; he remembered his parents always being supportive of his efforts to do the best he could, win or lose or draw.

"No," he said, "I think it was something else. I just never learned that making mistakes was a natural part of being human and a natural part of the way human beings learn."

What an important conclusion to come to—at any time of life—but certainly the earlier the better! We all do make mistakes as we learn, and not only is there nothing wrong with that, but also there's everything right about it. But if we grow up in our early years fearing mistakes, we may really become afraid to learn or try new things.

In our earliest years, of course, just about everything is a new challenge as we learn to control all the parts of our bodies and the many things our bodies can do. During these early months and years, a child is going to pick up from his or her closest caregivers an attitude toward taking on all these new challenges.

Most of us would probably agree that by showing outright disapproval of mistakes and accidents during this busy learning time, parents could dampen a child's willingness to try. But I believe there's another pitfall, too, one that may be less obvious, and it's this: As children strive to master the tasks ahead of them, parents can easily lavish praise and approval more on successful outcomes than on the trying itself. It may be that the most important mastery a child achieves early on is not the mastery of a particular skill or particular piece of knowledge, but rather the mastery of the patience and persistence that learning requires, along with the ability to expect and accept mistakes and the feelings of disappointment they may bring. In other words, the pleasure and pride a parent shows when a child *tries* may be more helpful in the long run than parental expressions of pleasure and pride when a child *succeeds*.

Our friend's reflections about his own growing up reminded me of the story of the young apprentice who applied to a master carpenter for a job.

"Do you know your trade?" the older man asked.

"Yes, sir!" the young man replied proudly.

"Have you ever made a mistake?" the older man inquired warily.

"No, sir!" the young man answered, feeling sure he'd get the job.

"Then there's no way I'm going to hire you," said the master carpenter, turning back to his work, "because when you make one, you won't know how to fix it!"

Tasks to Work On

Nighttime and darkness. As long as there have been human beings, the fading of light and the onset of darkness have probably touched off tremors of uncertainty. Myths, superstitions, and folktales the world over reflect the rhythms of lightness and darkness. For some people, of course, night becomes familiar, even a friend, a time to hunt or go to work. Even for the "nocturnal" humans, though, I feel quite certain that there was a time in early childhood when coping with darkness and sleep time posed a challenge—the old challenge of coping with a separation from the caregivers to whom children still felt tightly bound.

So much of the world's folklore grows out of humans' earliest feelings, even those most of us grow up to forget. Those feelings sometimes emerge in young children's everyday problems.

"My children are four and two," a mother wrote, "and bedtime is a major problem in our house. Our older child, particularly, hates to go to bed, and they both wake up often at night—sometimes as many as four or five times each. When they get up, they expect me to sleep with them. I made the mistake of doing so years ago, and now I can't seem to break them of the habit. I used to think that their nighttime waking was because I wasn't home all day, but even though I spend my days home now, they still don't sleep well."

Nighttime is an event in children's lives, and it may help to realize that. As the time for darkness and for separation grow near, children can benefit from a time of calmness, reassurance and closeness. For many children, the safest and most comforting place in the world is a loving lap, and the most settling sound, the sound of a beloved voice. A time for talking, or reading, or singing? Perhaps, but one thing's for sure: Expecting children to make a sudden switch from the stimulation of roughhousing or TV to bedtime is asking more than most of them can give.

Children need to learn that their beds are safe places to be . . . and safe places to be alone. That's hard to learn if an awakening or even a scary dream leads into Mom and Dad's bed, or to Mom or Dad leaving their bed to come sleep with you. Children certainly need the reassurance that you or someone they trust will be nearby all night, but parents generally find it works out better in the long run to insist gently that a child go back to his or her bed, even if they stay in their child's room, in a chair or rocker, for a while. That can be a time to talk about a nightmare, if a child can and feels like it. Children often need a grown-up's repeated assurance that a dream is only a dream.

Why is night? That's a question children can wonder about, and it can be helpful to children to have their caregivers talk about it. They may like to know simple things about the stars and the moon. They may like to know that when night comes for us, day is coming for other people somewhere else, that when we're going to bed, other people are getting up, ready to work and play, and soon they'll need a time to rest, to stop working and playing. Then it will be our turn to wake up and get going again. It can help to hear that everyone needs rest—that it's a time for people's bodies to take care of themselves and to grow.

Children often like to know also that even when it's nighttime and dark and most people are going to bed, there are always some people awake to look after our neighborhoods while the rest of us sleep—people who work for the telephone company or police or fire departments, people who take care of buildings, and doctors and nurses who take care of sick people. You might want to make a game with your child about all the kinds of people who are working while we're resting.

I wonder if that's one reason that many children find night-lights so reassuring. They're reminders that there is still light somewhere and people around the corner who are using it for their work and play. Night-lights may also be reminders that light hasn't vanished for ever and that before long the sun will shine on us again.

Once bedtime has become a problem, as it has for the mother who wrote to us, it can be hard to change it into a peaceful time, one of special warmth and pleasure. As we're trying, we need to remember that children are trying, too—trying to understand their feelings and their place, trying to please the people they love, trying to grow.

Here's a letter we received from a young correspondent:

> Dear Mr. Rogers,
>
> My name is Mark (age 4). My brother, Brad (age 8), is writing this letter for me. I have two problems. Problem #1 is I can't eat my food as fast as the rest of the family. My dad has counted to three and tried other things to get me to eat fast enough.
>
> Problem #2 is that I wet the bed almost every night. Do you have any suggestions to help me with these problems?

When I answered Mark, I told him that I was proud of him for being able to mention two things that were important to him right now. It made me aware of how hard he was trying to grow. His willingness to trust me with his news also suggested that he had already learned a lot about trust in his own family. I hope that what I said was supportive both of his needs and the needs of his family. His problems—and the problems they were causing his parents—are certainly common ones.

According to a note Mark's father added to his son's letter, Mark's eating problem stemmed from his habit of playing at the table. I know how irritating that can be when everyone else is ready to finish up and get on with something else. For many families, pointing out the consequences of dawdling has been a helpful approach. "We can't wait for you. You'll just have to finish eating alone," is one possibility, and not many children like to be deprived of company at the table. Or there might be a family game planned for after dinner, or a special television program to watch, "and I guess we'll just have to start without you." I believe these approaches are most likely to be successful—after a while—if they aren't phrased as punishments but rather as the natural outcomes of choices the child is capable of making. Children do need to understand that what they do has consequences. More than that, they need to feel that, in important areas of their lives, they have the ability to determine the outcomes of their actions.

Confrontations between parents and children can't always be avoided, but there are times when they obscure a more important confrontation yet—in this case, a confrontation Mark needs to have with himself.

As for his wetting his bed, I wonder if something stressful has happened to him or in his family that has made him temporarily unable to maintain the control he may recently have achieved. Either way, I feel sure he needs loving encouragement rather than chastisement—the reassurance that he can and will be dry when he's ready. One family put

CHILDREN AT WORK

up a large calendar on their son's bedroom wall and placed a fancy sticker on the days when he stayed dry the night before. There weren't many stickers at first, but before long there were stickers all over. What probably helped the most, though, was that boy's sense of his parents' pleasure and pride in him when he was dry. That was very different from the fear and anxiety he might have felt had they emphasized, instead, their disapproval and displeasure when he was wet.

It can take confidence to grow, and there are times when children need to borrow that confidence from the people they love and want to please.

I couldn't help wondering whether Mark's eating and wetting problems were somehow connected, and I feel quite sure that they were. I say that because I believe that everything in a child's development is connected—what has gone before, what is happening now, and what will happen in the future. The growth tasks of childhood involve struggles, and the effects of the struggle to achieve any milestone of growth will be, to some degree, apparent in all that a child does. It may take an expert to see the exact connection between playing at the table and wetting a bed, but any loving parent can see that both involve some aspects of self-control. And self-control is one of the hardest struggles of all. While children certainly need to learn about limits and consequences, they also need the staunch support of grown-ups who help them believe in their capacity to make it through.

Mark's problem with "playing at the table" made me think of a command you hear in just about any home where there's a preschooler—the sometimes stern, sometimes despairing cry of a parent, "Stop dawdling!"

I can recall, for instance, watching a toddler busily playing with lids and pots and pans, experimenting with the meaning of big and little, open and closed, and what thing belonged with another. But all at once she was distracted by her toes and started playing with them instead.

That seemed like natural toddler behavior, so no one thought of saying, "Stop dawdling with your toes and get on with the pots and pans!" But dawdling she was, in her own way . . . or at least leading up to the serious dawdling that can so often irritate a parent.

Getting distracted is what dawdling is all about, and by the time children are four or so, toddling and then walking and running have led to the discovery of plenty of distractions in the world beyond themselves. Curiosity about everything is characteristic of that age when a child is engaged in a love affair with the world. Now there's plenty of cause for dawdling, for being distracted by the world. Dawdling becomes so common that grown-ups even come to expect it, even if they don't appreciate it.

Ted, a friend of ours who has been blind since early infancy, re-members a time in his own early childhood when he was living at a special school and still unsure of what "sight" was all about. The woman in charge had told him to pick up his clothes before going out to play. "I went in the closet, and I got distracted with something in the closet," Ted told us, "and I wasn't picking up my clothes. I was just sitting there on the floor, playing.

"The woman in charge was way down the hallway. She hollered down the hall, telling me to get to work and hang my clothes up so I could go out and play. And I recall wondering how she could see around corners into my room and around the corner into my closet!"

Many a sighted child must have wondered much the same thing—how a parent downstairs could know that there was dawdling going on upstairs!

Clothes need to be put on when it's time to get dressed. That's true. Food needs to get eaten within a reasonable amount of time. Chores have to get done when it's time to do them. Helping our children learn to accomplish these and other necessary tasks is certainly part of being a parent. But we should expect that part of helping our children will be calling their attention, firmly but gently, back to the task at hand. Having a wandering mind is a natural part of early childhood and a sign of other needs children have.

They need to be curious: Why is that dog barking outside the window? They need to wonder: What would it be like to be a pilot? They need to invent and play: If I put this sock on my hand instead, it makes a puppet! There are times, of course, when all parents have to set limits on dawdling. Those limits, though, need to be set and explained so that children don't come to feel that we're trying to restrict their limitless capacity to fall in love with life.

There are many things children may do as they work on growing that, like dawdling, can be hard for parents to tolerate. Another, certainly, is prolonged thumb-sucking. In fact, a letter arrived recently from a parent who was concerned that her preschooler still sucked his thumb. The tone of her letter, though, was one of open curiosity about thumb-sucking and a search for guidance in helping her son control that habit. How heartening it was to get such evidence of caring and understanding parenting!

By contrast, a middle-aged friend of mine remembers growing up in a family where thumb-sucking was met with threats and punishment because it was considered a nasty habit, one that only bad children acquired. In fact, he sharply recalls one of his first books graphically depicting in words and pictures what happened to little thumb-suckers:

They got their thumbs snipped off with a long pair of scissors!

The fact is that thumb-sucking can be one of the first ways infants begin learning that the outermost parts of their bodies are actually attached to them, and that they can give themselves comfort while feeling hungry and waiting to be fed. It seems likely that the comfort they find is associated with the good feelings of sucking at their mothers' breasts or at a bottle. Many a two-year-old still uses his or her thumb as a "pacifier" at times of fatigue or stress. And it's common for the habit to persist well beyond that age—though not as far as it did for a perfectly healthy woman we know who told us she occasionally sucked her thumb until she was twenty-four years old!

The mother who wrote us about her preschooler's thumb-sucking made an interesting observation. She said that the most intense thumb-sucking time for her son was while he was watching television. We do know that a lot of what young children see on television can make them anxious and even fearful, and so, for that little boy, his thumb may have been the most readily available source of comforting reassurance when something scary was happening on the screen.

As a note, one child psychologist has offered another speculation about the effects of television. She believes that when a young child sees close-ups of human faces on the screen, the experience recalls the earliest human close-up of the mother (or father) at feeding time. We all tend to try to recreate good feelings from the past, and for a child, the contentment that came with being fed meant the warmth of a body, a loving face filling our vision . . . and something good in the mouth. This speculation might even account for the compulsion that many grown-ups feel to have something to eat or drink right beside them when they turn on the television set. If so, it certainly suggests that some of our habits are deeply motivated and may come from times well before conscious memory.

Habits can be hard to change, and when our children acquire one that we'd like to discourage, it's a good idea to ask a psychologist or pediatrician for suggestions. The recommendations that parents are likely to get nowadays are very different from the ones they might have received a generation or two ago. Back then, so-called bad habits were to be broken. If thumb-sucking were the problem, a pediatrician might have recommended painting a child's thumbs with a noxious preparation called Thumb. It was made of bitter alum and tasted terrible. But what did that do about whatever was leading a child to be a thumb-sucker? And what did it do about helping a child find alternative sources for the comfort he or she must have been needing?

I hope that today's advice would be to look for causes of behavior rather than simply confronting only the behavior. Habits so often reflect unmet needs, and if we can find healthy ways to meet those needs, inappropriate behaviors tend to change.

There's still a great deal for us to learn about how children grow and how their caregivers can be constructively responsive to the unfolding sequences of a child's growth, but by and large, I believe we're getting closer than we ever have before.

As much as a child's body and body parts can be sources of self-comfort, they can also be causes of alarm.

Brian is four. He's been seeing a pediatrician regularly ever since he was born. Until the last visit, his mother tells us, he never seemed apprehensive or resisted the nurses or doctors while in the office. This time, though, Brian kicked up such a fuss that the doctor could hardly examine him at all.

"We were seeing a new doctor for the first time because the one we'd been using had left town," Brian's mother explained. "But I'd told Brian that, and I'd told him that the examination would be just about like the old one—and it was. The doctor was very nice, gentle, and patient, but Brian was totally out of control. I felt humiliated and angry, as though in some way it was my fault for not being a better mother. And I'm dreading going back again for fear the same thing will happen. I really don't know what on earth to do."

Another parent wrote, perplexed by a different problem. Her daughter is about four also and has suddenly become terrified by the sight of adults with handicaps. The first inkling her mother had of her daughter's fear was when they were out shopping together and saw a man with one arm.

"I don't want that to happen to me!" her little girl whimpered. She became tearful and clung hard to her mother until the man was out of sight. Now, it seems, even seeing someone with a handicap on television upsets her, and her mother wonders how to bring her comfort.

These parents are puzzled because they're not aware of any circumstance that might have given rise to their children's new anxieties. While it's certainly natural to look for outside causes for such behavior, it's also easy for us to overlook changes that are occurring inside our children as they grow. For example, new awarenesses of their bodies and how they work often bring children new fears of anything that might intrude upon, or interfere with, the wholeness of their bodies. They can become very protective of themselves and their privacy. A routine doctor's examination could seem quite different from one time to another if your inside feelings about yourself had changed.

As children gain increasing mastery over the workings of their arms, legs, hands, and feet, they can also become concerned about how sturdily these limbs are attached to their bodies. Experience tells them that these body parts on toy people and animals can easily break off—and sometimes can't be put back on again. Seeing a man with only one arm might lead a young child to conclude that people can come apart just like a toy. While children do need to know that accidents can happen to people, they also need to be reassured by their caregivers that the natural way for human bodies to grow is all together and all in one piece.

Worrying about their bodies is often a healthy sign that children are beginning to value their bodies. Developing that sense of value takes time. Most parents have experienced the fright that comes with catching toddlers about to set off down a flight of stairs they can't yet manage or to stand on a chair that's certain to tip over. Little by little, though, children can understand that the limits caregivers set come from their being valued by those caregivers, that they are limits intended to help keep children's bodies sound and intact. As this understanding grows, children can learn to value themselves enough to set safe limits for themselves.

Brian's mother said she didn't "know what on earth to do." But the best thing she can do is to continue being her trustworthy, reassuring self, and Brian will grow inside and out and gain confidence in the wholeness of his body and trust in the many professionals who help him keep his body working just the way it should.

Just because a child's behavior changes all of a sudden doesn't mean it's going to stay that way. There's usually an "inside" story to every "outside" behavior.

All children, like Brian, have to go to the doctor, but they may, of course, wonder why, just as they're likely to wonder about the whys of the many other ways in which their parents try to protect them, and the many other people enlisted over time in that protection. A doctor's becoming part of a young child's life marks a significant step for everyone concerned: the sharing of care. That step is hard for some children to accept, but both parents and doctors can make it easier.

One way to help a child make that step is to help him or her understand that parents and doctors are a caring *team*. There is trust between them. That trust can be a crucial bridge for children, one that leads from trust of parents to trust of other important adults in their lives—other adults their parents trust.

Another approach is to let children know that doctors can be mothers and fathers too. They may have children of their own for whom they care in a parental as well as professional way.

Of course not all doctors are parents—and if your pediatrician isn't, you could still explain that all doctors were children once and can understand how children feel—they were children who grew up wanting to help people stay healthy when they're well and get better when they're sick.

It can take time for children, in the clinical atmosphere of a doctor's office, to realize that the people looking after them have feelings just as all people do.

I once heard a story of a little girl who didn't want to go for a checkup because, as she said, "the finger-prick lady wasn't nice to me last time." Her mother suggested that maybe the technician had been having a bad day, that maybe she had wakened that morning feeling grumpy about something. When the time came for the checkup—and the finger-prick—that was the first thing the little girl asked when they walked into the technician's lab: "Are you feeling grumpy today?" When the technician laughingly reassured her that she was feeling fine, the girl held out her finger, ready to cooperate.

Children also need truth, for it's through truth that children can learn trust. Some truths are easy and reassuring for grown-ups to give. For instance, stethoscopes and otoscopes do not let doctors hear or see a person's thoughts. (That's something many children are really concerned about.) Other truths are harder: Needles do hurt a little. But it's also a truth that the hurt they cause quickly goes away. Knowing what to expect in unfamiliar situations is helpful for all of us, particularly if some of what we have to expect is going to be hard to bear. Invasions of personal privacy can be upsetting for children as well as for grown-ups. There's certainly nothing "silly" about a child's reluctance to strip naked in a doctor's office. We need to acknowledge that reluctance, but it may help overcome a child's hesitancy to let that child know he or she can be a helper in the doctor's work and that "you'll be able to put all your clothes back on just as soon as the doctor's finished."

Always, in caring for our children, part of our hope is that they will grow to take care of themselves. If that's to happen, children need to feel, from their earliest days, that they're *worth* caring for. They can learn that best at home, but a doctor's office is another important place for them to hear from grown-ups that "there's no one in this world exactly like you, and we're going to take the very best care of you as we possibly can."

Simple, honest answers from the adults they love can do so much to dispel children's fears. Sometimes, though, children ask questions to which their favorite adults have no answers.

It may be that we simply don't know what the answer is, but we can find out, and that's what we can say. It may be that neither we nor anyone else knows the answer and that everyone wonders about it, too.

It's all right for children to know that adults don't have *all* the answers and that they, too, find plenty to wonder about in this wonder-full world!

It may be that we do know the answer, but we don't know how to explain it in terms a young child would understand. We may need some time to think about our answer, and we can say that, too.

Some questions asked by children might raise issues that make us feel too sad or angry or embarrassed to talk about. There's nothing wrong with that, either, and we can be honest with our children about it. We may be able to think of someone else, someone we trust, who could answer the question instead, perhaps a relative or a friend or a doctor.

Adults often find it helpful to ask children what *they* think the answer to their questions might be. Many times it turns out that a child doesn't want a full explanation at all, but that he or she is anxious or curious because of a misperception that is easy to correct.

"How are they going to take out my tonsils?" a little girl asked before her operation.

Rather than embarking on a medical explanation, her mother replied, "How do *you* think they're going to take them out?"

In the little girl's answer it became apparent that she thought the doctors were going to cut her neck open to get at her tonsils. When her mother reassured her that no one was going to cut into her neck, and that the doctors could take her tonsils out through her mouth, she was both relieved and satisfied.

There are times when it seems that questions are just about all a child has in his or her head. Those questions can catch us off guard. They can irritate. They can amuse. They can hurt. But however we choose to respond to them, we need to try for simple honesty and for a response that, whatever else it accomplishes, at least lets the child know *there was nothing wrong in the asking*.

One of the topics parents often find hard to talk about is death, and as a child gets to the age of four or five, death is more than likely to become a matter of curiosity and concern. Often, a child's first concerns about death reflect his concerns with other kinds of separations in life. I know of one five-year-old who began tearfully insisting to his mother that he didn't want to grow up. "I don't have to grow up, do I?" he would ask again and again. His mother's matter-of-fact replies that, yes, everyone had to grow up, didn't stem his increasing anxiety. Only over a period of time did that boy begin to talk about what was worrying him.

At first, he said he didn't want to have to stop playing with his toys. "Well," said his mother, "some grown-ups still have their favorite childhood toys." Then he said he didn't want to grow up because he didn't want to live apart from his mommy and daddy. His mother told him that he could live with them as long as he wanted to. Finally, he said he didn't want to grow up because he didn't want to die and leave Mommy and Daddy forever.

What we say to children about the separation that comes with death depends on our own beliefs and traditions. That mother told her son, "Only our bodies die. Our souls will be together again with God." Her son didn't ask for any further explanations or details. As his anxiety lessened, she realized that he had heard the only word he really cared about: *together*. At that time in his growing and wondering, *together* was all he needed to hear.

If we haven't thought about it beforehand, we're very likely to be taken aback by our children's first questions about death. Many mothers and fathers have found it helpful to discuss with each other what they are going to say when the time comes. Sometimes they find surprises in what their spouses believe, and a discussion before the fact about what to say to their child gives them a chance to find something appropriate and comfortable for both of them. For many people, it's not easy to know just what they do believe about death and what comes after. Thinking about it, though, seems to be a necessary first step in finding appropriate, honest words for our children.

Another reason why thinking ahead can be useful is that children tend to interpret what we say very literally. "My husband and I have taught our three-year-old that when we die we go to Heaven," writes one mother. "However, this summer we were bike-riding and rode through a cemetery. My little boy asked what it was, and then I had the task of explaining to him why they buried dead people even though I'd said that they went to Heaven. Needless to say, there was some confusion in his little mind!"

And what if we find, even after some thought and discussion, that we really don't know what we believe? What then? Here again we need to be honest with our children, and being honest can mean saying that we don't know and wonder about it, too. We can tell our children that different people believe different things, and we may be able to tell them a little about what those different beliefs are. If a parent has a relative or friend who does have strong beliefs, it might be possible to take a wondering child to talk with that person. Grandparents, of course, can be very special resources at times like this. Just being close to them tells a child, without words, about change and continuity, about what went before and what will come after.

As we get older, we may get increasingly interested in finding answers to the riddles of the universe, but we need to keep in mind that

"What are they doing here? I thought they'd gone to Heaven."

the universe of a young child is still small. We have to be careful not to confuse their questions with the ones we may have. When we listen carefully to a child's questions, we will often find that—however they may be phrased—they have to do with fears of separation from the people they love, about being kept safe, about what's real and what isn't, about whether it's all right to be different—all common childhood concerns.

We won't always have "the answers," but when we take the time to listen and make the effort to respond as best we can, we are giving children something that every child needs: the assurance that it is a fine thing to be able to ask questions, and that the people they love and trust will always try to answer those questions as truthfully as they know how.

Tools to Work With

Children have so many tasks to work through as they grow that, from a caregiver's point of view, overseeing them all could seem to require being alert, attentive and present every waking minute. Even then there would be children's rich, nighttime dream life to worry about.

But of course that's not the way it is, even if it were possible to be so vigilant. Caregivers come to learn that "hands-off" time is as important to a child's healthy development as "hands-on" time. Care sometimes means protecting a child from outside intrusions so that the inner processes of development can unfold at their own pace.

Thoughtful caregivers also come to realize that most children bring astounding resources of their own to the process of their development. Care sometimes means allowing children to draw on these resources in their own ways.

Children don't *always* need our active help, and many times the reverse is true: It is we who can benefit from *their* help as we continue to confront our own ongoing development. The resources we all need —resources such as an openness to discovery, curiosity, creativity, playfulness, imagination, self-expression and invention—are often fresher, stronger, more immediate for children than they are for adults, and a child's example can be invigorating and inspirational. These resources are powerful tools. As children use them in the work of their own growth, they can remind us how to use them in ours.

Do you know that "Aha!" moment when something falls into place? Perhaps it's that piece in a jigsaw puzzle that enables the rest to come together. Or it might be the piece (or person!) in the puzzle of our lives that suddenly gives us a clear sense of place and purpose.

Infancy and early childhood could aptly be called the "Aha!" years. When all is new, what is there but discovery? What a moment when the infant "discovers" his or her hands—Aha! They're attached! Or when the creeper discovers locomotion—I can move! Or the crawler discovers volition—I can go get! Or the toddler discovers self-control —I can wait! Or the two-year-old discovers individual choice—I can say No! Or the three-year-old discovers the separateness of *self*—I am *me!*

Each of these steps in growth evolves in its own good time; it's only the full awareness of their meaning that may seem to come all at once. And as each "discovery" evolves, it brings with it thousands of new discoveries about the self and the world; some small, some large, but all contributing to the grand Aha! that comes with the dawning awareness: I *am* . . . I *can* . . . I *will!*

It may seem that the price of growing older and of the world's becoming familiar is that the once frequent delight of discovery is taken from us. I don't believe that's so; I believe it's only the way it seems if we stop paying attention. A hundred lifetimes wouldn't be enough to make all the discoveries that there are about ourselves and the world. It isn't so much that discovery's delight is taken from us as that we take ourselves away from opportunities to find it. Infants certainly have a lot to teach us!

As children grow familiar with their world, they find another source of Aha! moments: sudden understandings of how the things and people they know go together, how they're associated one with another. Sometimes, from our point of view, these are misunderstandings. A three-year-old boy confidently states, "When I grow up, I'm going to marry Mom." Another child, looking out at a city after a blizzard, exclaims, "Look at all that snow pollution!" A friend of mine remembers exploring tide pools with his father and excitedly discovering a "snowflake fish." "It's a *star*fish," his father corrected, but at four my friend just shook his head; stars didn't look like that at all! And I remember seeing a film where a small boy held a leaf up to the sun, and as he studied the pattern of its veins, he shifted his gaze to the shape of a nearby tree . . . and back to the leaf . . . and back to the tree . . . and in his face there was an Aha! of wonderment.

Children's openness to new associations is one of the mainstays of their play, and their play is one of their greatest sources of both discovery and delight. A shoe can be a truck. A spoon can be a person. Sand can be a waterfall. A lid can fit on a pan, or be a hat for a head.

As we learn what things are *really* for, and how they *really* go together, it once again seems that we lose those Aha! moments. But, in fact, those moments remain to be found; it is we who have lost our openness to them, lost our *playfulness*. I believe that those adults who manage to remain playful are the ones most likely to experience the delights of discovery and problem-solving, adults like Archimedes who, while playing in his bathtub, exclaimed "Eureka" upon discovering specific gravity, and Ben Franklin who realized the effects of electricity while playing with his kite. The old saying is, "Necessity is the mother of invention." For invention's father, I'd vote for the playful mind.

When we say that we can't go back to childhood, what I hear is that we can't go back to being three feet tall or back to being tucked in at night by the adults who loved us then. That's true. Regaining the Aha! years, however, is something entirely different. We can't go *back* to them either, but that's because we can't ever *leave* them in the first place. They are as real a part of us as yesterday or an hour ago. They may be deeper within, as the sapling becomes deeper each year within the maturing tree, but even if we wished to, we could never let them go. They will always be at the core of who we are and what we do.

Bringing that joy in discovery back to the surface, making those moments more immediate . . . well, that's something else. The best way I know to do that is to encourage curiosity, openness and playfulness in our children, to share as fully as we can in the delights of their early discoveries. Children have a way of recognizing one another as *children*. It needn't be surprising, then, that the children we raise are the ones most capable of bringing flashes of recognition from the child still within us. Those meetings may be the most abundant source of Aha! that we can ever hope to find.

The creativity that can lead to discovery is a strong and natural part of early childhood. It may even be inborn and something infants rely on as they try to understand the workings of this world. After all, this life has so many questions to be answered! How do things go together? How do they work? What makes things happen? What am I? Where am I?

When you're a baby and need to suck, but there's no nipple or bottle nearby, what do you do? Find your thumb and bring yourself some contentment for a while. This can be one of the earliest experiences of creativity.

I remember watching a toddler whose mother had just told her to stop sucking a pen. From the look on the toddler's face, you could see she had a problem: How to please her mother and yet satisfy her urge to stick the pen into something. She solved her problem by finding something that was mouthlike—the hole in the side of a little cart— and for several minutes she played contentedly, poking the pen through the hole, dropping it, picking it up and poking it through again. Watching that happen helped me realize how important the limits we set for our children are for the development of their creativity: When we won't let them do exactly what they want to do, they have to search out new alternatives. Throughout life, "There's got to be another way!" is an expression of the creative spirit in all of us.

Another goad to creativity for most of us is the urge to bridge the gap between how things are and how we'd like them to be. You can see that in children's play, too—particularly as they pretend about how they or the world might be different. I can recall watching a four-year-old playing with a toy airplane. Clearly, as he made the airplane swoop and dive, he was playing at being in control, a grown-up and a pilot. After a moment or two, though, he stopped his play and looked into the plane's empty open cockpit. From his expression, I felt I could hear him thinking, "I need a pilot in there, a pilot who could be me!"

That wasn't an easy problem for him to solve, because there weren't any little dolls or toy figures that would fit in the pilot's seat. So that little boy took another creative leap. He found a small wooden cylinder meant for something else and turned it into a symbol for the pilot that was also a symbol for himself. With that problem solved in his own creative way, he happily went on with his pretending.

The urge to express our feelings is still another motivation for creativity. People who feel this urge strongly enough to spend their lives trying to give their feelings form, well, they're the people we think of as creative artists. That's not a life for everyone, but I believe artistic expression to be an important kind of expression for all children. Expressing feelings in words is always difficult, and young children haven't all that many words to work with. When I see a child making an angry painting, or dancing a happy dance, or making up a sad song, I see the creativity of childhood at its healthiest.

Visiting a friend's house the other day—a rainy, chilly day when playing outside wasn't very appealing—we happened on a young artist at work and witnessed one of those intense moments that happen in the life of even a restlessly curious five-year-old.

Marc was lying on his tummy on the living room floor, working with colored felt-tip pens on a large pad of paper. His feet were up in the air over his back, sometimes rubbing together, sometimes twisting and untwisting, sometimes waving sideways apart or up and down, but always in motion. His whole body would frequently squirm from side to side, and he'd cock his head one way and then the other as he looked at his drawing. Most of the time his tongue was out, curled tensely around his lips, and even his nose seemed to itch because now and then he'd pause to rub it vigorously with the back of his hand. Part of his mind was probably monitoring the adult conversation that was going on in the background, but to look at him, he seemed totally engaged in his artwork. His hands were giving expression to something that involved his whole being, mind and body alike. There was nothing intellectual or critical about what he was doing. Feelings were flowing out, and their flow was urgent. (What he later showed us, proudly, was a sailboat without sails on a scribbly blue sea. There were stick-figure sailors on the deck and a big gray cloud in the sky. The finished piece, predictably, went up on the refrigerator door.)

Many mothers and fathers find themselves parents of a child who loves to draw with crayon and paint. What are we to make of it?

I believe Marc was showing us what early artistic efforts often mean —the attempt to express feelings that may not be able to find their way into words but have to get out somewhere. Just what those feelings are may not be clear to us when we look at a child's painting. Each child will find his or her own symbols, and whether they're different colored blobs or a sailboat, we may not understand their meaning. Some grown-ups may get bothered by the accuracy of a child's drawing, too. Marc's sailors, for instance, were huge and would surely have capsized their boat. We need to remember, though, that children are not seeking an accurate depiction of outside objects when they draw; they're producing symbols of an inside world.

Of course we need to be thoughtful about how we respond to a child's picture. Finding ways to encourage the process of turning feelings into art, for example, is much more constructive than finding reasons to criticize the product.

"Can you tell me about your picture?" we might ask, thereby showing an active interest in what a child has done and giving it value.

"That picture makes me feel a little sad," we might say, if that's really what we feel. "How does it make you feel?" That kind of talk could help reassure a child that you understand what picture-painting is all about —feelings—and that you take it seriously.

Saving children's pictures and putting them up on a wall or a door is another way to give them value, but I don't believe it's helpful always to lavish them with words like "wonderful" and "beautiful." Extravagant praise of that kind can lead children to have unrealistic expectations for themselves, expectations that, in turn, can lead to later disappointments. "I really like that," I sometimes say, "and I'm proud of you for doing it." But I only say it when I really mean it.

What our children may need most when they show us a piece of artwork is our reassurance that whatever they've done is *acceptable for what it is*. In that way we let them know that they, themselves—feelings and all—are acceptable to us, too.

Children's expressions of self come in so many forms! While one child may find a natural outlet through shapes and colors, another may incline toward three-dimensional constructions, or body movements and dance. There's dress-up and pretend; stories and plays.

There are, of course, words themselves. I don't know what a "wufftingle" is, but then I don't know, either, what "borogroves" are, or how they look when they're "mimsy." I like the words, though. They can make a person feel playful.

Wufftingle was a word made up by a three-year-old who was asked what she saw in an inkblot picture. When the grown-up with her asked if she could say more about what a wufftingle was, the girl shook her head. It was just a wufftingle. (As for mimsy borogroves, they were invented by Lewis Carroll in his well-known poem "Jabberwocky." That poem goes on delighting generations of children and adults alike.)

Playfulness with words seems universal among young children once they have mastered the rudiments of language. Playing with sounds is, after all, how children learn language, starting from that moment in early infancy when they realize that being a soundmaker is part of what they are. You can hear babies, alone in their cribs, playing with the toy of language as they try out "ma-ma-ma-ba-ba-ba-ba." Soon there will be "da-dee" as well. (It's no accident that the names of most children's earliest caregivers correspond to the earliest sounds they can make.)

The pleasure to be found in words—both sensical and nonsensical —seems to develop naturally in very young children. Silly rhymes such as milk-pilk or purple-skurple can cause gales of laughter and lead to a host of even more absurd word plays. Nursery rhymes feed that early sense of fun, offering children "Hickery-dickery" and the like.

Nonsense rhymes expand the fun, too. For a start, they introduce absurd ideas as well as absurd words—visions of a world turned upside down where an owl and a pussycat can set off together on a seagoing adventure, or where anything else you want to imagine can happen. In addition, these verse forms bring strong rhythms to the ear—"Hey, diddle diddle, the cat and the fiddle"—rhythms that are chantable, danceable, and even pranceable. So often, their catchiness and whimsicality touch off eruptions of children's own natural creativity.

Soon after comes a fascination with riddles and jokes. At first the riddles and jokes are simple ones that play with the names of everyday things—such as a door not always being a door because sometimes it's ajar. But slowly these wordplays grow in complexity, reflecting children's increasing knowledge of their world, themselves, and, to many a parent's dismay, their bodily functions. Such wonderful toys words are! They're free and versatile, and so easy to carry about on a walk or in a car! Then, why do they seem to lose their fun value as children grow older? Unfortunately, it's a rare adult who, like Lewis Carroll, goes on spinning them around joyfully into middle age.

The increasing demands of the "real" world may have something to do with it. In school, for instance, children have to learn correctness of spelling, grammar, and usage. For many children, words then become work rather than play, and sometimes hard and discouraging work at that. There may be many reasons, but whatever they are, I believe the loss of joy in language is a sad and serious one.

Some parents may be able to help keep that joy alive at home, but for most, perhaps, the loss of joy has long since occurred, and they don't feel they know where to begin. There's a good place, though, and it's right at hand—in the careful listening to our young children themselves. When it comes to rediscovering the lost delight of humor and absurdity, rhyme and rhythm, and the elation of spontaneous creativity, children can be our best guides.

Of course, not all words that children make up are as playful and pleasing as "wufftingle." For example, Marie, a four-year-old, flew into a foot-stamping rage one day, shouting, "Pee-pee kaka! Pee-pee kaka! Pee-pee kaka!" Her parents (who were able to laugh about the incident later) were appalled at the time and, like many parents, unsure about how to react.

Unsavory words are everywhere. It's a rare child who won't hear them somewhere during his or her early years—in the family, on the streets, in stores, and, of course, on television. Try as they may, parents can't expect to keep their children from hearing them—or from using them. What's more, "swearing," to some extent, comes naturally to children; even a child who has never heard swear words is likely to make up ones of his or her own the way Marie did.

Some parents punish a child for "bad" language. A friend of ours remembers having his mouth washed out with soap, in addition to getting a severe scolding. Other parents decide to ignore their child's outbursts so as not to give the words importance. That way, they hope their child will lose interest in using "bad" words. That's only one possible outcome, though; another is that a child will find and use new words until he or she hits on one that does make a parent angry; and another is that a child can interpret the parent's response as tacit approval.

Swear words, of course, are themselves usually expressions of anger. We may not like the actual words, but it's important to remember that angry words are a healthier outlet for feelings of rage and aggression than are angry acts such as hitting, kicking, or biting. Those are the outlets that come naturally to toddlers who haven't, as yet, much language to use. Learning to replace these outlets with words instead is, in fact, a sign of healthy growth.

"Bathroom" words are often a child's first "swears," and there's a natural reason for that. The age at which children are moving through toilet training is also a time when they are rapidly acquiring language. They quickly learn that, once they're clean and dry (more or less), an almost sure way to make a parent unhappy or even angry is to have an "accident." At the same time, they still want to please the people they love, and so they're usually unwilling to have accidents on purpose. The next best thing may be turning the accident into words . . . and that's growth, too.

As they move out into the world, children soon hear adults using other expressions to vent anger or hurt. Adult example is powerfully strong in a child's life, and we may find our children not only bringing these new expressions home, but also trying them out all the time, everywhere, and even for no particular reason. Here, I believe, is where parents can set useful limits. One mother, for instance, when she realized that an unacceptable word had suddenly become a staple of her daughter's vocabulary, made a deal with her. She told her little girl that she could use that word at home and only at home. That very evening, her daughter did—at the supper table in front of her father. He, naturally, was astonished and upset, but when his wife explained the limits she was trying to set, he agreed to go along with the deal. It was only a matter of days before their daughter let go of the word altogether.

Not all parents may be comfortable with the solution that particular family found. It's seldom easy to find responses to our children's actions that set limits on their outward behavior without stifling their healthy inner strivings to grow. But when parents see an older son or daughter telling someone, "Boy, that makes me really mad!" or putting that anger into the digging of a garden, the punching of a punching bag, or the painting of an "angry" picture, they can know for sure that the effort to find those responses was effort well spent.

In addition to creative swearing, the development of language can take plenty of other surprising and perplexing turns. For instance, while we'd all agree it's natural to talk a lot about those you love, any woman's *constant* chitchat about her husband and her daughter, say, could eventually get on people's nerves. Alice was like that. Sometimes it seemed to her relatives and friends that her husband and daughter were *all* Alice talked about—even though she was only three and a half years old.

Her mother told us that Alice's imaginary family doesn't stop with a husband and one daughter, either: She has imaginary grandparents and, at times, more daughters. "I don't want to interfere with whatever's going on," her mother wrote, "and maybe all children her age go through this phase. But at the same time, I have to wonder if this much pretend is normal, and often my impulse is to cut Alice short and divert her to other activities. Frankly, I find this whole business of her imaginary family tiring after a while!"

When children's play becomes obsessive, it's often a trial for their parents. A common example is the way babies of a year or so old will repeatedly throw things out of their cribs or down from their high chairs and expect their caregivers to retrieve them again and again and again. Grown-up impatience with this kind of play is the most natural thing in the world—as natural, in fact, as is the kind of play itself. Most often, children play like that because they are working on new feelings inside and new understandings about their world—feelings and understandings that have to be tried out over and over until they can find a comfortable place to rest.

Many parents sense that their children's obsessions express some kind of need, and so, even while feeling impatient and irritated, they (like Alice's mother) feel hesitant or even guilty about cutting obsessive play short. But parents need to express their feelings, too—whether they're feelings of joy, sadness, or anger. That's an important way young children come to learn that it's all right to express feelings. Something else children need to learn, though, is that there are appropriate whens, wheres, and hows to giving expression to feeling.

It can often be helpful for parents to set aside particular times for allowing and supporting obsessive play of one kind or another—whether it's throwing and retrieving, smearing and making messes, or pretending to have an imaginary family. There might be times when Alice's mother could suggest taking the whole imaginary family on an imaginary picnic, or taking them along on a visit to a real zoo, letting her daughter know, all the while, that she's happy to go along with this pretending right now. There may be other times when she feels able and willing to be part of that imaginary family in situations of Alice's own making.

That kind of cooperation can let Alice know that pretending is fine, and it can help her learn the difference between what is pretend and what is real. And by providing outlets for her daughter's pretending when it's appropriate, Alice's mother may be able to feel more comfortable setting limits on Alice's inappropriate times of pretending and more comfortable expressing her feelings of irritation when they occur.

That Alice had lots on her mind was suggested in her mother's letter. The family had moved twice in six months—the first time taking them 600 miles away from relatives and friends. After that kind of dislocation, I can imagine that a pretend family you never had to leave could have been reassuring to have around. What's more, Alice had a new baby sister. Playing pretend mother to her own imaginary daughters might have been a way for Alice to work on her uncertainties about what this new baby might mean for her real relationship with her real mother. And on top of all that, Alice was three and a half—an age when a great many children are wondering about the difference between husbands and fathers and who "belongs" to whom in what way.

Through play, Alice was finding a means to express her feelings. Through writing, Alice's mother was finding a way to express hers. Something tells me that when Alice's mother was little, she had caring grown-ups who understood the importance of feelings and play, and I like to think of that family finding many ways to go on talking and playing through the new changes their lives will bring.

Alice's mother was concerned about pretending too much about the same thing. Another mother asked us whether there was such a thing as just plain too much pretend.

Her son Jeremy had just turned three. For some time puppets had been one of his favorite forms of play. Now, he likes it best when his mother supplies their voices while he asks them questions. One of the puppets is a monkey. Jeremy often asks him to say his ABC's. Jeremy's mother lets the monkey get about halfway through before faltering... and then Jeremy gets very serious about helping the monkey remember the rest. One of the other puppets is a lion. Jeremy always wants that lion to be insecure and a little afraid of things. The bear, on the other hand, is supposed to be loving and reassuring, often telling Jeremy how well he is doing.

All this seemed both fine and fun to Jeremy's mother until she began feeling that all this pretend was getting out of hand: Jeremy even started pretending about his pretend by imagining his puppets were with him when they weren't. "I learn a lot about Jeremy through this make-believe," his mother said, "but now he pretends they're with him at the grocery store, in bed, in the car. Is it too much?"

When parents are puzzled or worried by their children's play, they can always be sure of one thing: There's a reason for the forms it takes. We may not always be able to find the reason, but when we do, it may ease our anxieties. As we found out more about Jeremy and his life, the reasons for his play seemed fairly clear.

Jeremy is an only child. His mother is able to stay with him at home full-time. There are no other children his age in the neighborhood. The one time of the week when he has playmates is at Sunday school, but all of them are in day-care during the week. Since their parents like to spend family time with them at home when the work day is over, there's no chance for socializing during the week.

It sounds like Jeremy is using his pretend in a healthy way to give himself the friends he doesn't have right now. In fact, his story reminded me a little of myself. Having to play alone a lot when I was young was what started my own interest in puppets. Soon, Jeremy will be going to nursery school two days a week. Though he may continue to use his puppets in many ways for a long time to come, the chances are that his play will change to reflect his new experiences with real children.

There are times, though, when I believe that pretending *can* be "too much." One is when a child loses sight of the difference between what is pretend and what is real. There have been children who pretended so hard about being a superhero that they jumped off dangerously high places believing they could really fly, and children who really believed they had turned into monsters when they got angry and went around smashing things.

The line between real and pretend isn't automatically clear to young children; and parents, even while encouraging their children's pretend, do need to help them understand just where that line is.

Pretend can also be too much when it gets out of hand and becomes so frightening that children scare themselves—sometimes right into tears. It could be make-believe about something terrible happening to them or to someone they love, or it could be a made-up story about a big bad wolf who snarls and bites. One of the best ways to help children pretend in positive ways is to be encouraging of their play, and attentive to its lessons. Let them know that their pretending is their own, and that they can pretend about anything they like . . . or choose not to pretend about things they don't like.

Toys as Tools

If you were an inventor and wanted to invent the perfect toy, what would you want it to be able to do? If *I* were that inventor, at the top of my list would be the toy's ability to help children learn about themselves and their world. It would have to be enjoyable to use, of course. That means it would have to appeal to children with a wide range of tastes—something *all* children could like. In the same vein, the toy should be able to be used by children of widely different ages. That means it would have to have a lot of flexibility so that it could be used in different ways at different times in a child's life.

I'd want my perfect toy to be able to tell stories, show pictures, and make music. I'd like it to be able to build things, too. I'd design the toy so that one child could play with it alone, or a child and an adult could play with it together, or two—or several—children could play with it at the same time. It would have to be easy to share.

Since we're free to think up *anything* for the perfect toy to do, let's say that it can be used with any other toy a child may have, and that it can make those other toys more interesting—rattles, blocks, dolls, trucks, cards, board games . . . whatever.

On the practical side, I wouldn't want my perfect toy to depend on a power source. No electricity, no batteries, not even a windup key to get lost. It would have to be unbreakable. It would have to be small enough to carry around easily (but there'd have to be no risk of small children swallowing it by mistake). And it would have to be inexpensive enough so that anyone could afford it . . . and afford to replace it if it got broken or lost. But while we're at it, let's say that somehow it *couldn't* get broken and it *couldn't* get lost.

Well, anyone who could invent a toy like that would certainly seem to have a bright future in the marketplace. Just imagine! Just *imagine* . . . and of course there's our perfect toy: the imagination.

A little girl showed us how her imagination worked one day as she turned a checkerboard into a whole town of people and buildings and cars and stories that went with it all. A group of children showed their creativity as four of them sat on the bottom steps of a staircase while a fifth acted as the teacher, handing out assignments and telling the rest not to speak without raising their hands. A boy showed me his imagination as he put his teddy bear through an operation in the hospital—an operation that boy was soon going to have for real.

There was the "opera" a six-year-old sent me, and there are all the drawings and paintings children have passed along showing their worlds as they imagine them to be. Children have introduced me to their imaginary friends. They've told magical stories of their own making, and they've produced fantastical puppet plays. In fact it's hard to think of anything children, at one time or another, haven't transformed, enlarged, rearranged, or imbued with life—all with that amazing toy, their imagination.

Free . . . unbreakable . . . portable . . . no batteries . . . but, the imagination *does* need loving care, as do all things capable of growth. Though it's rare, I've known of children whose imaginations have withered so that they've almost lost the capacity to pretend. These children become unable to use imaginative play to help resolve past feelings, explore present feelings, and try out future feelings—important uses of play for all healthy children.

What nourishes the imagination? Probably more than anything else, loving caregivers who encourage the imaginative play of the children in their care. They can do so by letting their children know that this kind of play *is* important for all children. They can do so by creating plenty of time for imaginative play of children's own making (in contrast to watching television or playing pre-programmed video games). They can help their children keep clear the distinction between real and pretend, and help them keep their fantasy games within comfortable boundaries of excitement and safety.

Above all, caregivers can demonstrate the importance they put on imagination by being available to their children as they play. They can be available as co-creators—*when wanted*, as willing actors or participants—*when needed*, or simply as quiet presences that offer support and reassurance. As they do this, parents and caregivers are likely to discover another marvel about the "perfect toy": By nurturing imagination in their children, they may find it unexpectedly flourishing within themselves. By contrast, looking in the marketplace for even a "good" toy, let alone the perfect one, can lead to disappointment, frustration and anger.

"Sometimes I think there's a conspiracy against parents," a father complained to us. "It's as though the people who make things for children almost set out to turn mothers and fathers into the bad guys who have to say 'no' all the time. Children's programs on television have been a source of conflict in our family, and now there are all the electronic games everywhere you go . . . and they cost too much money to boot. Our two boys are five and seven. We live in a city. There's no escaping the seductive challenge of the blips and beeps and flashing lights. And I'm always saying 'no.'

"It happened again last weekend when we were all at the shopping mall. I told Joshua, our seven-year-old, that no, I wouldn't give him a quarter to play one of those machines. You know what he said? He said, 'You never let us have any fun!' That hurt. I got mad. He sulked. The afternoon was spoiled. And I'm sick and tired of trying to sort it all out."

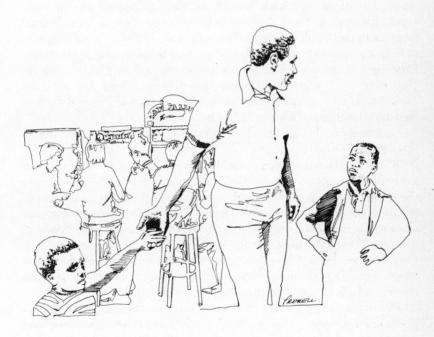

"I'm tired of being made the bad guy . . . of having to say no! *all the time."*

CHILDREN AT WORK

89

Many families—families with children of all ages—have told us that electronic games are posing a new and difficult challenge to their limit-setting. And that seems to be the underlying problem in "sorting it out"—the old, familiar problem of setting limits, whether they're limits on watching television, eating candy, or playing in safe places. That father is right: It seems there's always something to challenge parental authority.

For one mother we know, a major problem is that her children are always wanting her to buy some little toy when they go grocery shopping. She's found an answer that works for her, and it's one that applies to all limit-setting, including the rationing of electronic games. "I very seldom have problems anymore," she says, "so long as I remember to tell my kids ahead of time what we're going shopping for—what we're going to buy, and that's all we're going to buy. Usually they don't even ask for a toy. If they do, it's just sort of a suggestion—and they expect and accept the 'no' that's coming. But if I forget to let them know what's ahead, I can be almost certain that we'll have a scene about it. The key for us has been talking about it beforehand."

Rationing rather than outright forbidding is something to think about. Unless parents have very strong feelings against playing electronic games at all, they may be able to accept their use as an occasional addition to their children's play. Rationing can relieve some of the pressure that prohibition tends to build up. And the rationing of electronic games can be supported by a reason that even young children can, in their own way, understand: It takes money to play them, and it's more important to save money for the things the family really needs, such as food and clothing and a home to live in.

I'm often asked if I think there's something about electronic games that is actually bad for children. What I have come to believe is that the healthiest playthings for young children are those that a child can make conform to his or her own, unique fantasies and feelings. By and large, electronic games do just the opposite. They make a child conform to the program inside the machine. It may be true that electronic games can increase a child's eye-hand coordination and even some kinds of concentration. I'd like to think that's so. Where I do become concerned, however, is when I see electronic games becoming the mainstay of a child's play, taking over the time all children need to spend in creative play of their own making. Play of a child's own making is a must, because it's how children come to learn so many important things about being human—the meaning of self, the nature of feelings, and the need we all have for relationships with other humans.

I certainly understand the before-mentioned father's frustration and anger at being constantly cast as "the bad guy." I wish for him what I wish for all parents: the courage and patience to persist in setting limits that seem reasonable. That's the best way I know to raise children who, one day, will be able to set reasonable limits for themselves.

Sometimes it's hard to say what's a toy and what isn't. There are advertisements these days, for instance, that show happy parents introducing their toddlers to simple computers. These computers can help children learn to read and count, as well as, usually, enable them to play electronic games at home. When I see these ads, they bring to mind the old question, "What's wrong with this picture?" There's something about them that makes me uneasy.

I saw a different type of picture last summer: A caregiver and toddler in the park were digging a hole together with a toy shovel. When they had finished digging, they went over to the drinking fountain to fill a little plastic bucket, and then they returned to the hole and poured the water into it, watching as it seeped into the ground. Then back to the fountain they went . . . and again and again. Now that picture is a picture that makes me feel comfortable!

I've found it important to try to understand these two different reactions—to the ad and the park scene—and what it is that arouses the uneasiness and the pleasure. I began by thinking about my attitude toward computers. Like most people my age, I'm awed by them and somewhat baffled by their workings, but they bring me new wonderment at the ingenuity of the mind, and they've enabled us to do so much in our work that would have been impossible without them. Far from being "down" on computers, I'm very "up" about them. They are truly remarkable extensions of ourselves.

That's the phrase that gave me the clue to what I was feeling: extension of ourselves. The *development* of that self has to come before the extension of that self. How does the self grow? What feelings will that self bring to a computer? What parts of the human personality will it choose to extend—the creative or the destructive? What will the self make of the computer—a tool or a weapon?

A person's sense of self grows fastest in the earliest years. That development begins with the internal rhythms and sensations of an infant's body, grows outward and gains in depth through its relationships with its first caregivers, and then, through those relationships, moves beyond into understandings of the natural world. For a newborn, self may be little more than feelings of hunger and discomfort, fullness and pleasure. By two years of age, there's a full-blown personality, struggling to be independent and to understand the meaning of love. At three, a child might conclude that when day comes, night hides in the dark bedroom closet. At five, though, he or she can have a reasonable knowledge of how the earth turns as it circles the sun. As the foundations of self and personality are laid, so much happens in so little time!

To reach outward and grow beyond self-centeredness, very young children need other human beings, because it's through *human* relationships that a child first learns love, compassion, generosity, and creativity. These relationships bring about extensions of the spirit. By receiving nurture, a child can learn to offer it to all living things—to plants and animals and other human beings. And a child can come to approach the world with a caring curiosity.

What's in an apple? Plenty! It falls from the branch. Why? An apple smells different from other things. It's both smooth and rough ... and cold perhaps. There is sweetness and tartness in it. Its juices can overflow and dribble down the chin ... and get sticky. There are the seeds of new life inside. How do they work and what makes them grow? How can an apple help a person grow? And apples hold stories—enough myths and legends and folklore for a lifetime!

That's the kind of apple I'd like any toddler of mine to have. As far as I'm concerned, the kind with a keyboard can wait a while.

The mail tells us that concern over electronics is widespread among parents—but probably still second to the toy-related concern we hear most about: the old nemeses of gun play and pretend violence.

When Andrew was four, he picked up a piece of dry toast one morning at breakfast, took a couple of well-planned bites out of it so there was a piece left across the top and along one side—and then, holding it like a pistol, he went "Pow! Pow!" at the rest of his family around the table.

"Andrew, stop playing with your food like that!" his mother commanded. Quite cheerfully, Andrew put butter and jam on his gun and ate it.

"I was appalled," Andrew's mother told us, "and yet when my husband and I talked over what to do about our kids' gun play, we found ourselves smiling at that particular incident. It was so ludicrous. And we agreed that there just didn't seem to be any way for Andrew to understand our feelings."

Gun play is upsetting for many families—and seemingly irresistible for many children. Why should that be? As far as children are concerned, anything that seems to give them an extra measure of control over their world—even pretend control—is likely to be fascinating. Remote-control toys, for instance, extend children's feelings of power way beyond the reach of their arms and legs. The garden hose can make people at a distance run and duck and holler. A flashlight in the dark can suddenly illuminate the far corners of a room.

In children's gun play, it's often the gunslinger who "calls the shots." There seems to be an agreement among playmates that this is so, and consequently the gunslinger can give orders that will be obeyed—to march with your hands up, to fall down, to lie still, and even to "die." When you're small and young and being told what to do all the time, it can be a good feeling to be in charge for a change. In fact, it's a feeling that children need to play out.

So, should we let our children go on playing out their pretend violence? If it makes us uncomfortable, absolutely not! We need to respect our own feelings, whether our children can completely understand them or not. In doing so, we are helping our children learn to respect their own feelings as they grow.

I don't think most of us believe that children's pretend violence necessarily leads to real violence later on. All the same, our discomfort over gun play can be very painful, because it can touch the very deep feelings we may have about death, loss, love, and the value of human life. We have every right to those feelings, and every right to protect them.

Even though we try our best, there will always be times when we won't be able to explain the limits we set for our children—at least not to our children's satisfaction. This is particularly true with limits that express values our children have yet to acquire.

Andrew went along with his mother's limits on making his toast into a gun. Another child, though, might have retorted, "But Billy's family lets him play with toy guns, so why can't I?" That's a kind of question that parents often hear. The answer to it is, I believe, a simple one that children, in their own way, can understand: "But you're not growing up in Billy's family, and we feel differently about it. You are a part of our family and a very important part!"

We can't expect to control all of our children's play, and it wouldn't even be healthy to try. When our children are out of sight, they'll engage in play of their own creation, maybe gun play included. When they're with us, though, we can certainly express our values, and it's from the people they love that children learn best what is truly worth valuing.

As with pretend violence, I don't believe children will grow into violent adults because they play "violent" electronic games, or because they enter a phase when they seem obsessed by gun play. Violence that is acted out in the real world stems from sources that are deeper by far than that.

I've often puzzled over where all the real-life violence we see around us—in person, in the news—comes from in the first place. Of course there's no simple answer, but I believe that for many violent adults the start of it all lies in the earliest years of their lives. We all have angry and even violent feelings within us, but most of us learn, as we grow, how to express those feelings in ways that don't hurt either others or ourselves. Some of us never learn that, though. What is it that makes the difference?

A mother writes: "A child who is abused and battered can come to feel he or she is deserving of such treatment. A child who is not loved assumes that he is not worthy of love, and a child who is called stupid, bad, or 'no good' often can come to believe that these things are true. I don't know all the answers to these problems, but I can tell you that the effects of such situations last a lifetime."

That mother knows where violence can come from. As soon as babies are born, they start picking up cues as to whether they are considered special and valuable by the people who care for them. They learn whether they give those people pleasure or displeasure just by their being in this world. It's sad to think how many children must have heard their parents shout at them, "I wish you'd never been born!" and it doesn't surprise me that many of these children grow up thinking, "I wish I'd never been born, too!"

When children grow up feeling they are "victims of society," they may come to see the world and the people in it as enemies to be feared and hated and fought. One might think that a victimized child would grow up to be sympathetic to other victims—even grow up to join one of the helping professions. Some do. But many, many others grow up to become society's aggressors—those who victimize others. (It's now well known, for instance, that many parents who physically abuse their children were, themselves, abused when they were young.)

The love that a child can bring to his or her life comes from the love that he or she received in the beginnings of life. We are all surrounded by violence, and there doesn't seem to be much we can do to make it go away. But we do need to remind ourselves that our children will learn a lot about expressing their feelings by watching how we express ours. And we need to let them know that the violent expressions of anger that they see around them is not the way it has to be: The world is full of people who care as well as of people who hate.

Above all, we need to try to show our children that we love and value them. By doing so, we can help them learn that the world has much to be loved and valued as well, especially the people who inhabit it.

Forging Relationships

Our relationships with other people in this world are what, in large part, give our lives value and meaning. Yet while some people have little trouble making friends as they go through life, others find friendships perplexing and elusive. Those to whom friendship comes easily, though, are not necessarily the same ones who turn out capable of forming and sustaining a close, intimate relationship with one other person.

It's hard to tell about people—and hard for them to tell about us. Does that firm handshake and direct eye contact mask someone who is shy and uncertain deep down inside? One person's seeming diffidence may really be the cautiousness protecting an open and giving nature. Another's hostility so often turns out to be the anxiousness of insecurity.

From earliest childhood we've learned through trial and error that certain behaviors on our part are likely to evoke—or provoke—certain responses from others. All of us, to one degree or another, have practiced the art of manipulation. We are, it's true, inescapably who and what we are (whether we know what that is or not), but we're also who we try to be because we want to be, or because we want other people to think we are.

No wonder it can be hard for any two people to get to know one another! In fact it can seem a wonder that they ever do.

Children are trying out different roles all the time, and we can be sure that they're incorporating what they learn into their developing styles of initiating and maintaining relationships with the people around them. .We can be sure, too, that these early lessons will emerge again and again later on.

A group of children at the beach last summer, for instance, seemed to be parodying adult management styles. The children were between four and six years old, and as they sorted out their play and their games, they might have been practicing for the kind of office life so familiar to many adults.

Three of them were standing on a bench, bouncing up and down in rhythm as they chanted, "We're the captain of the ship! We're the captain of the ship!" Suddenly the oldest stopped and said disdainfully, "We can't *all* be captain of the ship. *I'm* the captain of the ship, and you're the sailors."

With that, their play fell apart. No one challenged this seizure of authority, but there was nothing to chant anymore, nothing to hold the group together. It seemed that the oldest child had identified the commonplace management problem of "too many chiefs and not enough Indians" and determined that seniority was the answer. It was as though he had issued a memo outlining a new chain of command, and no one was clear about his or her new role in the organization.

In another group, the issue became the building of a sand castle. "That's gotta be a turret!" one boy said to a girl who was scooping out a corner of the pile of sand. "Why's it gotta be a turret?" the scooper asked. "'Cause I said so," the boy replied as if to say: "And that's an order!"

But this time the command didn't work; the scooper went on sulkily scooping as though she hadn't heard a thing. So the self-appointed architect tried another approach. "Look," he said, "castles always got to have turrets." Here, clearly, he was making an appeal to company policy. That didn't work either. "I don't want to make turrets," his playmate said.

The boy went on building for a while but quickly grew frustrated that one side of the castle wasn't taking shape at all. What's more, his opponent was joined by two of her friends and they'd decided that what they were making was a cake. Now there was an undercurrent of male-female hostility in the group. The boy, outnumbered and on the defensive, tried once more. "Look," he said, brushing the sand off his hands, "are we gonna make a castle or not?" The answer was definitely "not." He didn't have any "team players" in his division.

So he issued pink slips. "Well, I'm not going to play with you anymore," he said disgustedly, getting up and giving the cake side of the castle an "accidental" kick.

"I'm gonna tell my mommy what you did!" one of the cake builders threatened. "Tattletale!" the boy sneered, but he looked uncertain about this threat to report him to a superior. Sensing this uncertainty, one of the girls launched a final barb. "Anyway," she taunted, "you're my sister's boyfriend!" and with that she stuck out her tongue. The boy glared and walked away.

She might as well have been saying, "And don't forget I know about that little dinner item on your expense account!"

Children, of course, grow up with different models of authority in their families, and it's likely to be these (at least the ones that seem to work) that they first try out in their play. But other children have other models, and so the clashes and negotiations of "office politics" begin.

Yet though it seemed at first glance that those children at the beach were parodying our adult world, a little thought made that notion unlikely. They couldn't, at that age, know our world well enough to parody it. That left another possibility—one that was much likelier but hard for some of us to accept. Far from the children parodying our world, we are the ones who parody theirs, acting out in our adult offices the management techniques and responses we've brought with us all the way from early childhood.

The same sense of previewing the future came in a conversation with a mother who reminisced about two summers in her daughter's life.

"The first was a tough summer for Amanda," that mother told us.

"She only had eyes for a boy named Josh, but would he pay any attention to her? Forget it! She'd follow him wherever he went, trying to join in his play . . . and he'd brush her off as if she didn't exist. A couple of times Amanda got really upset about it. I found it heartbreaking, too. Who needs that kind of rejection when you're three and a half?"

Josh, the object of Amanda's attentions, was not quite five that summer, yet here already was that familiar and painful scenario: the one-way summer attachment. Most of us will probably find our minds casting back to early adolescence as we remember our own summers of puppy love, but the chances are we all had intense attachments much earlier than those.

They weren't "romances" as much as early friendships, but attraction certainly played a part. Painful or pleasant, the episodes that date from the ages of three and four are seldom remembered, but their meaning and feeling stay with us nonetheless and may account for many of the feelings we bring to—and take from—romances of later years.

Most parents have had the chance to witness very personally the flowering of their children's first "early attachments." Along about three or so, a boy can become possessive and protective of his mother, often claiming with confidence, "When I grow up I'm going to marry my mom!" Girls, for their part, can become overtly flirtatious with their fathers and plan to marry them, too. At the same time, children of both sexes can show a temporary coldness or even hostility to the parent of the same sex who seems to stand in the way of these grand marriage plans.

Parents can help by being patient and understanding, and by setting realistic limitations on their children's unrealistic expectations. A

"That summer, she only had eyes for a boy named Josh."

CHILDREN AT WORK

mother needs to be able to tell her son, lovingly but firmly, "I'm already married to Dad, dear. When you grow up, you'll find someone you want to marry, too. It won't be me, but maybe it will be someone *like* me." Fathers need to be equally loving and firm with their daughters, setting appropriate limits on their flirtatiousness and letting them know that Mom has a place in the family that they can never have—just as daughters have their own special places.

Children are bound to feel tension and anger as they work on letting go of these early fantasies. But most children do let go of them, transferring their feelings as they do so to people around them. Perhaps something of that kind was happening to Amanda when she had eyes only for Josh.

But Amanda's summer of rejection was only half the story. The children met again the summer of the following year. Josh, now going on six, decided that Amanda, a vivacious four and a half, was a great playmate, and he sought out her company all the time. As though exacting a price for her misery of the year before, Amanda now cold-shouldered Josh a great deal of the time. When she did agree to play with him, it was always on her own terms and according to her own rules, and their games lasted only as long as she decided she wanted them to.

"This summer it was Josh I felt sorry for," Amanda's mother told us. "He stuck in there all month long, eager and confused, sometimes angry, but always coming back for more. I tried to talk to Amanda about the way she was behaving, tried to encourage her to be kind and friendly, but it was clear she had some deep need to be acting out the way she was."

Poor Josh! But whatever the reason for Amanda's behavior, it probably wasn't retribution or calculated unkindness. More likely, it was, as her mother surmised, some "deep need." One life event, for instance, may have been playing a part: Amanda was having trouble adjusting to the presence of her new stepfather. According to her mother, she was often sulky at home, acting willfully and going out of her way to reject her stepfather's authority. Her stepfather was holding his ground. Not getting her way with him, Amanda was perhaps taking her feelings out on Josh, who could hardly be expected to understand what was going on.

There's usually a lot going on in relationships that we don't—and probably can't—understand. Some of the mystery may come from present circumstances beyond our ken, and some may come when old feelings from days before memory float up to the surface—feelings felt and lessons learned during summers like Amanda's and Josh's. Childhood attachments in their many guises may seem innocent, charming, and even amusing, but they can be a serious part of children's work on growing, and they can bring anguish and tears that are real.

And Then Comes School

Many parents wonder when they should start their children in some kind of organized school experience. "Is preschool a necessary program for children?" one parent asks. Her daughter, almost four, is bright and happy, plays with friends, goes on daily outings with her mother to the park, the zoo, the library, or they play games together at home. "Everyone I know takes their kids to preschool," that mother writes, "and my friends tell me my daughter will be behind in kindergarten because she hasn't experienced a group environment. My feeling is that the time we will be together in life is short, and I would like to be with her as much as possible."

As that mother has learned, peer pressure isn't something only children feel. It can be very hard to trust our own judgments as parents when our feelings seem to be different from most other people's, and the best kind of friends are those who remind us that we are the ones who know most about ourselves, about our children, and about our relationship with our children.

No, I don't think preschool is necessary for a child. For most children, though, I believe preschool comes as a positive, healthy, growing experience. It offers children a chance to make new friends, learn new things, and find out what it takes to get along with other children their own age and other adults outside their families. For an only child or a lonely child, preschool can be a very helpful introduction to a wider world.

But just because something is available doesn't mean that it's necessary. What I think is necessary is a feeling of readiness both on the part of parents and on the part of children to experience what going to preschool will bring. That means feeling ready to "let go" a little, to "take on" a little, and to cope with the stresses of being separated.

That feeling of readiness comes at a different time for every child and every parent. When it comes may depend partly on circumstances we can't control. For instance, if there is illness in a family, or if a family has to move, or if a new baby has just been born, a young child might really need some extra time close to home to get used to a lot of new feelings that could make going off to school right then more difficult than usual.

One mother tells me that her five-year-old daughter doesn't seem to be adapting to preschool well at all. "She is a bright, imaginative and an independent child," the mother writes, "but her teacher is concerned about how she will get along in school because she doesn't obey and cooperate. She seems to want to be left alone and learns well when she is. She taught herself to read and now reads quite fluently." A letter like that always makes me wonder what's really important in that child's life right now—and whether it's not something that closeness rather than separation might best help resolve. One thing I feel certain about, though, is that until it is resolved, that child won't feel ready to learn in a group setting.

Here's how another parent decided about "school readiness": "I've opted to keep my children home until they are seven years old, and I feel that this has given me the extra time I wanted to establish more firmly the ideals I consider important. The children's ages are five and seven, and the older one is ready to start second grade. I am a teacher, and it always amazed me how joyfully we could learn together in so many everyday circumstances. Things that took hours to accomplish in a school setting were grasped in a fraction of the time. It seems to me that there is a valid case for extending the time that children stay in the home when this is desired by parents."

That letter doesn't tell us much about the seven-year-old's readiness, but it certainly reveals a parent who put off school until she felt her child was ready—no matter what her friends were telling her about the "necessity" for preschool! The point, I think, is this: School systems work on a fixed schedule, and human development doesn't—neither in childhood nor in adulthood. School will always be there and ready for our children, and parents are the best judges of when they and their children are ready for school.

For parents who do choose to send their children to nursery school, one family's experience seems worth sharing. Our first contact with this family came through a letter that read:

> To Mr. Rogers,
>
> Is school nice?
> Is school fun?
>
> Your friend,
> Eric

I wrote back to Eric (who was just about to start school) saying that all schools are different, but that teachers are people who care about children and who try to make things happen in ways that are best for the children in their classrooms. As for being fun, I told Eric that some fun can be silly, funny, and exciting, but that other kinds of fun are quiet and give you a good feeling about thinking, working, and learning. We heard again from Eric when he was nine years old and in the fourth grade. Here's what he found out: "When I started school it was very hard, but I went for around a year, and then it wasn't hard anymore," he said. "But," he added, "I don't really like school that much."

School wasn't all bad, though. He told us he had learned lots of new things and had made a lot of new friends.

Eric's mother confirmed that the transition to school had not been an easy one for Eric, and pointed especially to the "discipline of school and the separation from his parents." As it turned out, both Eric's parents were teachers themselves, and we asked his mother what she thought was the most important factor in helping a child adjust to school. Her answer: "A good nursery school experience."

Eric's mother explained that both her children had attended the same nursery school, one that was relatively open and unstructured. Eric's older sister had thrived there and gone on to school with excitement and success. For Eric, the lack of structure failed to help him develop his own self-discipline, and he found himself at school faced with rules and limits for which he was unprepared.

"When parents find a nursery school they like, they tend to send all their children there," said Eric's mother. "That's natural. After all, they know the people, and it's probably a lot more convenient as far as transportation goes. They may even get a price break. But I think that parents, if they can, should consider all the choices there are and make a new decision for each child. Both my husband and I are really convinced that a child's experiences in nursery school—and how a child feels about them—are going to start setting a pattern that will carry through the first years in school. We certainly wish now that we had done it differently."

That family's thoughts made me realize how easy it can be for us to overlook our children's individuality when it comes to making choices about schools, summer camps, or even everyday decisions about limits, routines, foods, clothes, activities, and the like. We know our children are different—sometimes even marvel at those differences—but what we do with those differences is another question. Do we squeeze them into a single family mold, or do we search for ways to make allowances for them, to encourage their development and expression?

Like most issues that confront parents, there's no simple answer. In this case, we probably do some of both. We may never find the perfect mixture (if there is such a thing), but parents who care enough to wrestle with the problem are likely to find a solution that serves the needs of *all* the individuals concerned.

Nursery school or no nursery school, the time for separation comes sooner or later. The work on growing that children have been doing at home will have a lot to do with how smooth or bumpy the transition is to their new surroundings and new caregivers. It seems inevitable that parents will compare the behaviors of their respective children as this transition occurs. Some will feel pleased and proud at the easy adaptability of their children, others will be concerned and disappointed, wondering, perhaps, what they did wrong as parents to have the first days of school turn out to be so traumatic.

Natural as these feelings may be, parents need to know that they're misleading. Going to school is *not* a pass/fail test of parenting, not by any means. Children's reactions are their very own, individual expressions of each child's uniqueness. Part of that uniqueness is their differing timetables for confronting common growth tasks. The visible upset that one child shows today may bring an earlier resolution to a problem than will come to a child who presents an outward calm. That calm child's turn may come tomorrow . . . or next year.

It's all part of the different ways children go about their work.

PART 3:

PARENTS AT WORK

Parental Identities

A two-foot ruler may seem like a strange size, certainly to a carpenter or a school teacher, but Steve was a carpenter and his wife, JoAnn, was a school teacher, and by the time they'd been married a year, there was nothing strange about a two-foot ruler to them.

"My realization about how our lives were going to be measured," JoAnn told us, "came on a long drive through bad weather with Jeffrey, who was six weeks old. We took a break at a family-style restaurant on the highway, and a warm, friendly, bright dining room never seemed more welcome!

"I remember feeling how pleased we were with ourselves—and with each other—as we ordered, but then Jeffrey woke up and went into one of his colicky fits of crying. That was it. The people in the restaurant lost their friendly look. The warmth chilled. The once-smiling waitress gently, but firmly, suggested we take Jeffrey out until he was feeling better. Steve and I argued briefly about who would take him back to the car—each of us insisting we weren't really hungry anyway. I won because I claimed nursing might help.

"So there I was, in a cold car with a screaming baby, watching Steve through the rainy windshield as he gulped down his dinner alone. 'Well,' I thought, looking down at Jeffrey, 'I guess I know who rules this roost!'"

Newborns do come about two feet long, and they do tend to become the measurements of their parents' lives—particularly when they're the first ones to give husbands and wives their new roles as parents. Any new role is likely to bring us a new identity; it can force us to change the ways we think about who we are and how we feel about ourselves. For husbands and wives, becoming parents can mean changing the ways they think and feel not only about themselves, but about each other as well. After all, until a baby enters their lives, husbands and wives have never known how the other will behave as a mother or father.

You can bet that Jeffrey's personality was forming as he hurt inside, as he experienced discomfort that even his loving caregivers couldn't take away, and as he found, all the same, that the hurt would go away in time. Something else he found out that evening was that someone would be with him while he hurt, trying to comfort, trying to soothe. Steve and JoAnn, of course, learned lessons of their own: that you can't always save your children from pain, that a baby's behavior can make you angry and embarrassed, but that sharing such times of anger and embarrassment with someone you love can help you grow all the closer. By any measure, everyone's new identities were growing.

Becoming a parent gives new life to old identities as well. A mother recently said to me, "I wonder how many parents feel the way I do—trying to juggle the raising of our own children while I'm still sorting out my own childhood problems!" At the time, I tried to reassure that mother that most parents probably had those feelings. After thinking about it, though, I realized that she had touched on a fundamental part of what raising children means to all of us. When people become parents, they will not only live through the experiences of their new child, but they will also relive many of the experiences of the old children that they once were. Such reliving is an inseparable part of parenting. The mother who raised this issue was having new difficulties with an old problem that many parents know well.

Some months ago, her four-year-old Robbie had spent a week with his grandparents (his mother's parents), and ever since then he'd decided that was where he wanted to live. His grandmother had a puppy. When he was with his grandparents, he didn't have to share the attention of the people he loved with his two-year-old brother. And his grandparents allowed him to do things that he wasn't allowed to do at home. The last time he was with them, Robbie had screamed and cried when he'd been brought back to his own front door.

You can imagine how his mother felt. But she also sensed the pain of her own childhood all over again. "My parents loved me very much," she said, "but they brought me up in a home full of tension and fighting, where there was little peace and quiet. Even though I'm twenty-eight, my mother can't seem to let go of me. She's critical about the way I raise my children, but she babies Robbie when he's with her. And now he prefers her home to ours. I resent that!"

Letting go is seldom easy—whether it's letting go of our children, our parents, or our old childhood feelings. But just as the root systems of plants often have to be divided for healthy growth to continue, the different generations within a family may have to pull apart for a while for each to find its own healthy identity.

Being a parent and a child at the same time can be very hard. It may mean feeling caught between two different sets of responsibilities and two different sets of affections. As we try to sort them out, we often have an inner wrestling match—between the self we were and the self we have become.

Fortunately, revisiting our childhoods isn't always painful. For some people it may be full of pleasurable associations as they recreate the family habits, pastimes, and rituals that they remember with delight from their youth. But even if our childhoods were relatively problem-free, growing always presents us with difficulties to be overcome, and the memories of these difficulties are so easily awakened as our children encounter similar difficulties in their own time.

It may make matters a little easier if we realize that some of the intensity we feel as we try to help our own children with their hard times is very likely related to what we went through when we were children. It may also be helpful to reflect that as we help our children with their struggles, we, too, are being given a new chance to grow.

Many years ago I wrote a musical story called "Josephine the Short-neck Giraffe." In it, Josephine tries everything to make her neck grow because she wants so much to be like other giraffes. Of course there's nothing she can do, but with the help of her friend Hazel, an elephant, and a shy giraffe called J.R., Josephine does some growing inside and comes to accept her shortcoming.

That story ends up:

"The best times are times when you're glad to be you!"

I thought of Josephine the other day when I received a heartfelt letter from a parent who wrote: "Mr. Rogers, how do you do it? I wish I were like you. I want to be patient and quiet and even-tempered and always speak respectfully to my children. But," she goes on, "that just isn't my personality. I often lose my patience and even scream at my children. I want to change from an impatient person into a patient person, from an angry person into a gentle one."

Believe me, I know the feeling! The "Mister Rogers" on television can be patient and quiet and respectful, but the people who work with me, not to mention my children, can tell you how angry Fred Rogers can be—just like anybody else.

From our mail, I know that some children feel that Mister Rogers would make an "ideal" father. In fact, almost every child goes through a stage of having fantasy parents who are all-loving and all-giving. These ideal parents may be kings and queens in fairy tales, heroes or movie stars. What they all have in common is that they would fulfill all of a child's wishes. Real parents, of course, can't do that—and responsible ones wouldn't even if they could. Real parents express their real love by setting and enforcing healthy limits on what their children can do and what they can have.

It takes time for children to understand what real love is. It takes time, too, for parents to understand that being always patient, quiet, even-tempered and respectful isn't what "good" parents are. Parents help children by expressing a wide range of feelings—appropriate anger included. Children need to see that adults can feel angry and not hurt themselves or anyone else.

I respect that mother who wrote about her times of impatience. She clearly cares about her children; she can express both love and anger, and she can talk about her feelings. She has also identified some admirable qualities to strive for. I hope that she, like Josephine the Short-neck Giraffe, will come to feel glad about her identity as the parent she is.

A letter from a friend brought us further thoughts on parenthood and imperfection:

A little while ago, as I was on my way home after celebrating good news with friends in a bar, my euphoria came to an abrupt end with a siren's wail and the flashing of lights in my rearview mirror. After the brief preliminaries, I was breathalyzed, pushed up against the side of the car, frisked, handcuffed, and carted off behind the heavy-duty grillwork in the back of the patrol car. At the station, I gave up my personal possessions and my identity and spent a cold bleak night in jail. There it all was: the plank bed, the bars on the window, the seatless, stainless-steel toilet ...the works. And me.

Me? Who *was* I, anyway? Certainly not the responsible, successful, joyful adult of moments before. How fast that balloon popped, turning me, as it burst, into someone I didn't recognize or even care to meet: a drunk driver in jail. The child in me protested and cried, engaged in magical thinking that maybe, just maybe, if I closed my eyes and tried really hard, I could roll time backward just a little, and I'd still be in my car on my way home. Where were my mom and dad who could always make everything right? How could they dare have left me here like this and have passed beyond the reach of any telephone call? And what would *my* children, who were twenty-two and eighteen, think about this?

As the weeks elapsed, weeks full of repeated inconveniences and mortifications, money for fines and a lawyer was spent, a stern judge looked down at me and passed sentence, and the weekly, mandatory, rehab classes for drunk drivers inched by one after the other. Ever present was that child within wondering why it had all happened and trying to cope.

There was a frequently recurring memory: I was back in the bedroom I shared with my brother when we were little, and my parents were coming in the door late at night after a party to kiss us a last goodnight. Their voices were different than usual, their gestures loving but a little clumsy, and their breath had a sweet aromatic smell that I came to associate with the coziness and warmth of a safe bed, with the reassurance of a soft pillow and a down comforter.

I came to understand that my parents were dedicated drinkers; drinking was a solid and steady part of their lives. I remember, at seventeen, how they at last welcomed me into their charmed circle at cocktail time. How grown-up I felt! More than that, what approval I felt! What *love!*

There were about thirty people in my rehab classes, and they came from a wide spectrum of ethnic backgrounds and socio-economic levels. One thing they all had in common, along with me, was that the inner child of each was right out front. There those children were, face to face with authority, rebellious or scared, aggressive or guilt-ridden, cowed or cocky. Some, almost disgracefully, played up to the instructors as though desperately seeking some sign they were still lovable. Others were clearly determined in thought, word, and deed to resist any insights the classes might have provided; to the end, they defended their "freedom" and their "independence" against all appeals of emotion or reason.

I found myself wondering again and again about what roles love and parents had played in the early lives of all these people, and of course I wondered about those roles in my own life as well. I've never doubted that I was truly loved as a child, and I believe I can see confirming signs of it even in the resolution of this sorry tale. My "inner child" has been able to come to terms with what happened, and the grown-up I am is profoundly thankful that the yellow line is all that the wheels of my car ran over that night. Whatever else my parents may have passed on, they seem to have imparted a capacity to cope with life's ups and downs, the courage we all need to accept the consequences of our actions, an openness to humility, a willingness to learn from hard lessons, and (I trust) the self-discipline to set new limits on our behaviors when recklessness suggests that new limits are needed. Those are loving gifts indeed!

There are no perfect parents, and there are no perfect children. But imperfect parents can be loving parents, and the gifts of their love can be enough to preserve "the child within" from despair when times get rough. More than that, though, those loving gifts can save the lives of others—as in the case of this driver for whom the tragedy of a needless killing on the highway remains, thank God, only a specter along a road not taken.

Arrest and jail are serious trouble, and it's natural that anything so shaking to our sense of identity would be profoundly disturbing. For some people, though, it doesn't take very much. For these people, parenting, at least with their first child, may seem rough going and full of worries.

We all know for sure that there are days when the car breaks down, or the electricity goes out, or it rains on our picnic. New parents learn quickly that infants get rashes and fevers and croup. Infants wake when we want them to sleep, cry when we need them to be quiet. Their internal schedules send our timetables awry. New parents can easily find themselves disoriented, frustrated, and feeling like failures for not being able to put things right.

Some people just seem to be able to roll with life's jabs and punches more easily than others do. Why? I've come to believe that like so many aspects of character, our attitude toward disappointments and frustrations depends a great deal on the attitudes of the grown-ups we loved when we were very young. Here's an example:

An elderly woman we know was recently flying home to New York from a visit to the West Coast. Her flight was rerouted because of weather and finally cancelled, and it was well into the next day before she reached her destination. There was no way to reach the relatives who had gone to meet her. Her baggage had gone on somewhere without her. She spent an almost sleepless night in a crowded, uncomfortable and noisy airport. And yet, when she finally arrived, she was tired but in high spirits.

"I just decided I was in for an adventure," she explained to her worried family. "I learned a lot about airports, and I met the most interesting young man from Guam, who told me all about family life on that island."

When talking with her, we naturally wondered how her parents had handled similar situations. She recalled at once a time when she was little and traveling with her younger sister and mother. The hotel where they were supposed to stay had lost their reservations and had no room—and there was no room anywhere else in town, either. The hotel manager told them they could sleep on the floor of one of the private dining rooms if they wanted to, and that's what they did.

Their mother helped them pretend they were camping out, and they made a tent out of a blanket and a couple of chairs. They pretended to cook food over a campfire (the food was actually cheese sandwiches and milk from a vending machine). They did eat a decent breakfast the next morning in the hotel's main dining room, but our friend remembers both herself and her sister begging to be able to take their plates of eggs and bacon back to their "camp."

Character, the saying goes, "is caught, not taught." Patterns of behavior are caught early, and they not only tend to endure throughout life but are also likely to form part of the legacy we leave our children. Our elderly friend had no children of her own, but she does have nephews and nieces. One of her nephews has no hesitation in pointing to his Aunt Kate as the source of his attitude when things go awry: "If there isn't anything I can do about a situation," he says, "I just try to turn off the worry switch and start looking for pleasant surprises I might not have had if everything had gone right. I guess it's the difference between seeing life's obstacles as roadblocks or as opportunities for a detour."

It's hard for most of us not to fret when even little things go awry, but fortunately our earliest attitudes aren't set in concrete; they're subject to change. It may take a good deal of motivation to make the changes we'd like, but for many parents, raising children is one of the strongest motivations of all.

One of the most helpful changes many of us might make is to learn to be less hard on ourselves for our shortcomings. Here's a lighthearted questionnaire with some serious undertones. We're looking for answers that are either "ashamed" or "guilty." You might like to see how you fare.

1. You call a serviceman to fix your refrigerator because it isn't running. The serviceman comes, moves it away from the wall and finds it unplugged. You remember you unplugged it prior to cleaning it the day before. Apart from feeling that you just wasted $30, how do you feel?

2. You inadvertently let slip something that was told to you in strictest confidence. How do you feel?

3. You're having an "off" night on the bowling team—so off, in fact, that you're clearly the reason your team loses. How do you feel?

4. You have lunch with someone of whom your spouse doesn't approve. When you're asked how your day went, you slide right over the lunch part. How do you feel?

5. You're out driving and you realize you've left your license, insurance, and registration at home. You notice in the rearview mirror that there's a police car behind you. How do you feel?

6. Your teenage daughter is about to be picked up by her date to go to the movies. She's upset because, against your advice, she's bleached her hair, and it's come out all frizzy. How do you suppose she's feeling?

7. Your nine-year-old comes back from an afternoon with his gang and he reeks of cigarette smoke. He's very quiet at dinner. Apart from possibly feeling sick, how do you suppose he feels?

8. You hear a crash in the living room and find your four-year-old sitting as far away from an overturned plant as possible. You ask her what happened. She tells you her imaginary friend did it. How do you suppose she feels?

9. You think your two-year-old is toilet-trained... but suddenly he has an "accident" and comes to you distressed and tearful. How do you suppose he feels?

10. If you take another look at your answers to questions 6 through 9, are your answers different from how you might *hope* your children were feeling?

You can't score yourself on the quiz, because there are no right or wrong answers. There are only *your* answers, though some would be widely shared. For instance, you may not feel "guilty" about calling the serviceman for the refrigerator, nor about letting down the bowling team. Your daughter may not feel guilty about her hair. You *might* feel guilty about giving away a confidence or not revealing your lunch partner, but you're unlikely to feel ashamed of not having your proper papers with you in the car. To some of the questions, many people would have to acknowledge some shame and some guilt. To some, neither. Whatever our answers turn out to be, they may have a lot to do with how we were brought up.

How did you suppose the nine-year-old who was quiet at dinner was feeling? To answer that, you probably tried to imagine how you would have felt in the same place. How would it have been in your family when you were nine years old? In a family where there are strict rules against smoking, a child is likely to feel guilt about breaking those rules. In a family where there is less outright prohibition of smoking and more emphasis on strong encouragement not to smoke for health reasons, a child might be more inclined to feel ashamed for having done something injurious to his or her body.

How the four-year-old who upended the plant was feeling will probably depend on how she has been made to feel when similar accidents have happened. If she's been repeatedly told at times like this that she's a "bad" girl, she'll probably feel guilty and possibly afraid as well. If she's come to feel that accidents are to be avoided but do happen even to careful people, her feelings may be more akin to shame about her clumsiness. She may feel more that she let herself down than that she has outraged someone else by breaking a rule. (Imaginary friends can be healthy friends for children that age. They can help share difficult feelings, and the chances are that this four-year-old's imaginary friend felt much the same way she did.)

As for the toddler and that "accident," I would hope that no toddler would have to feel guilty, much less afraid of the consequences. Most toddlers, however, seem to have a healthy sense of shame. Some, at "shameful" times, will cover their eyes with their hands as though this could make them disappear, while others may turn away from their grown-ups and say, "Don't look at me! Don't look at me!" These are moments when toddlers need support rather than chastisement so that their shame will stay within healthy limits rather than turn into something as destructive as guilt can sometimes be.

One of the differences between shame and guilt is that shame seems to come before guilt in the development of children's feelings. How early shame appears, or whether or not the capacity to feel shame is inborn, no one probably knows for sure. My own sense of it is that shame is a more *natural* feeling than guilt. It arises from within ourselves in response to our own expectations for ourselves. Guilt, on the other hand, seems more of a response to outside rules, to other people's expectations for us and demands upon us.

The whole matter is far from simple, though. Among other things, the natural expectations we have for ourselves very soon can become entwined with the sometimes unnatural expectations others may have for us. The rules of overly severe and forbidding parents, in time, can come to be rules that we learn to set for ourselves. It's as if their voices take root in our minds and continue to scold us—and make us feel guilty—all life long. When that happens, we may turn out to be unforgiving to ourselves rather than compassionate, ridden with guilt about falling short of ideals no human could reach in the first place. The outcome for some people is bitterness, disappointment, and a severely judgmental attitude that they then impose on this imperfect world and all its imperfect inhabitants.

That's sad, because one thing is for sure: Neither this world nor any of its inhabitants are going to become perfect—not in several lifetimes, let alone in ours or our children's. My own wish for children and parents alike is that they learn to find joy even amidst the world's and their own imperfections, that they grow to have a clear but forgiving interior voice to guide them, and that they come to have a reasonable sense of shame without unreasonable burdens of guilt.

Though our experience as children makes a big difference in how we feel about our identities as parents, there are certainly other powerful influences, too—such as unpredictable life events. How we feel about ourselves is likely to have a lot to do with, for instance, how we feel about the work we do. In good times, we may be able to define ourselves as successful and valued contributors to the workings of the world. At times like that, we may also feel proud of our roles as the children of our parents, our roles as husbands and wives, and our roles as competent parents capable of giving our own children the care and support they need.

But when something like unemployment strikes a household, what then? For some families that kind of reversal can be a catastrophe—not only financially, but emotionally as well. There are many thoughtful people who believe that unemployment has a significant effect on the divorce rate and even on the incidence of child abuse.

Other families, though, come through the trials of unemployment with a new sense of closeness to one another, and that's the way it sounds likely to turn out for one family we heard about.

It was the father who wrote to us. He explained that he was a laid-off miner and had been unemployed for more than a year. He was a college graduate, and it was clear he had hoped that he'd be able to give his children more material things than he'd had when he was growing up.

"I grew up in a poor home," he told us. "Dad worked steady, but never made much money. Mom and Dad loved us kids and spent quality time with us. All the same, I felt inferior. Other kids had more, not just toys, but nice houses, furniture and cars. As a boy, I used to be ashamed that our furniture was old and worn, but I guess that description fits my home now, too."

Despite the serious setback of unemployment, this father sounded vital and positive about his family's ability to cope. In fact, he expressed more concern about others than he did about himself. He mentioned several things his family had found helpful.

The first help he mentioned was his understanding and supportive wife. He evidently felt secure in his marriage and knew he had a real partner in hard times as well as good. Not all couples are so fortunate, and not all parents have spouses. All the same, just about everyone has friends. It can sometimes be difficult to ask for support when we need it, but having someone we can count on to stick with us through tough times can make those times much more bearable. Good family friends can be a great reassurance to children, too.

The second help that father mentioned was that he and his family shared a close affiliation with a church. Whether it's a church group or a group of another kind, the feeling of membership in a caring community can do a great deal to replace the loss of fellowship with co-workers.

Something else this father found helpful was learning to appreciate "one of the benefits of unemployment: being able to spend more time with my wife and two children." Here, though, he had a caution: An unemployed parent was likely to feel a lack of self-worth, as well as some resentment and anger. Taking out these feelings on other family members, he noted, "could be really destructive of young children's attitudes."

On the other hand, talking about these feelings—and about the realities of circumstance—was, in this family, another help, even though both children were under five years old. "The amazing thing I've seen in my children," that father told us, "is that they do grasp the concept of Daddy being out of work. Yet they are so optimistic and encouraging. It helps us go on."

The father identifies one of the priceless opportunities of parenthood—the ability to borrow from our children's strength even as we lend them ours. He reminds us, too, of the truly essential things that can help any of us keep our sense of identity intact through life's hard times: honest talk, a caring community, and a loving partner.

Even loving partnerships, of course, can be fraught with tension. It's not necessarily the absence of conflicts that makes a partnership a loving one, but rather the loving ways that the conflicts are resolved. Among the hardest conflicts to resolve lovingly are those where, once again, marital and parental identities seem to be at stake.

"I hate being caught in the middle!" a wife and mother told us. "My husband was a military man, and his dad before him. And that's the way he's raising our four-year-old—as though Toby was a little soldier. And when Toby gets punished by his father, he comes to me for comfort. What am I supposed to tell him? That I think his dad's discipline is wrong?"

That mother certainly isn't alone in her complaint, and it isn't only mothers, either, who find themselves seeming to face divided loyalties. No husband and wife were ever raised in exactly the same ways by their parents, and so they hear different echoes from their respective childhoods when it's their turn to raise children. And, of course, watching and learning as we grow also bring us to different conclusions about how we want to raise our children and how we want them to turn out.

"But isn't it important for mothers and fathers to be consistent with one another in setting rules and dealing with discipline?" people often ask, and they're asking an important question.

I believe that consistency is helpful and even necessary for children's healthy emotional growth, but that consistency should be within the context of each parent's consistency. Knowing what to expect from a mother or a father day by day is part of the security a young child needs as he or she strives to grow in his or her own way. But something else children need is the understanding that every person is different. With that understanding can come children's appreciation of their own differences and the courage to be who they are—each one different from everybody else.

For a baby, mothers and fathers are different from the very beginning. They look different, sound different, smell different, feel different, hold their babies differently, and react differently to their babies' cues and signals. Doesn't it seem natural that they should, as time goes by, have differences in the ways they raise their children?

Husbands and wives need to talk about rules and discipline so that each can be comfortable with the way the other behaves. Agreement won't always be possible—and that's something we have to accept— but that kind of talk can help spouses show loving respect for one another's identities while keeping parental disagreements within manageable boundaries.

And when, in the heat of the moment, there isn't time to talk, and one parent reacts in a way the other finds inappropriate, and a child like Toby goes to the other parent for comfort, what then?

I can imagine Toby's mother saying something like, "You know, Toby, what you did made Daddy really angry."

"I know," Toby might reply, "but you never make me stand in the corner or shout at me like that!"

"That's right. But I'm not Daddy, am I? Your dad and I are different people, just as you're growing to be different in your own ways. One thing's for sure, though: We both love you a whole lot, and that's one way your dad and I are the same!"

Here's a letter that says so much about being a parent, and being a human being, that I'd like to share it with you:

> I'm a twenty-eight-year-old mother, and my husband passed away very suddenly when our only child (a boy) was only seven weeks old. I thought I was handling it okay—it's been two years now—and yet I struggle with daily headaches and frequent outbursts of temper. I saw my doctor, and he gave me some pills

and said I was reacting to stress and should work to eliminate it. Well, that sounded fine, but I had no idea what was causing the stress until I realized I was angry. I feel bad about admitting it, but I'm mad at my husband for leaving me alone. It's not fair to me or to my baby. I've been spending the last two years trying to be a perfect parent, teacher, homemaker, and breadwinner and to be active in my church. I don't like to have to do it all....

Intellectually, I know my husband didn't die on purpose, but

"I know my husband didn't die on purpose, but..."

PARENTS AT WORK 117

something inside me is still mad. I guess that's okay, though, and just identifying the feeling has helped a lot. But I'm not quite sure where to go from here.

I've been feeling the responsibility of being a parent very heavily, and probably more so because I've had no partner to help me make choices. So I've bought books and books and books. I felt sure that if I didn't do exactly right as a parent, my son would suffer....By his second birthday he could count to twelve and recognize all the alphabet. I was acting as if he were a little computer instead of being a human being, and felt that if he weren't properly programmed, he would never function properly. And who would get the blame? The programmer...me! That was a frustrating thought, because I worried that I just wasn't smart enough for the job.

I've since come to realize that my son needed to be a child ...and that I needed him to be one. Now that means more to me than trying to store information in his ever-expanding brain. It means letting him enjoy life as only a child can—with no weight of responsibility, few fears, and the sheer enjoyment of the wonders of God's world, however small they may be. Did you know you can see rainbows on the wings of common houseflies?

This afternoon my son and I pretended to be different kinds of animals, making absolute fools of ourselves and laughing a lot. Then we got tired, so we sat at the table and made a pin-wheel. My son didn't learn anything about the ABC's or about numbers, but he was learning how to pretend and play for fun. And I didn't feel like I had to correct him if his cow was saying, "Baaa baaa," or if his rabbit didn't look like a rabbit at all. We were having fun, and all I wanted him to know was that I loved him exactly as he was.

I'd like my son to do well in school, but if his best is only a C+, that's okay with me... as long as he grows up to be happy and caring and gentle. At last I feel I've been given permission to be the kind of parent I want to be. I'm not a teacher, I'm a mom. An imperfect mom at that, with fears and hopes and dreams like anyone else—but with an awful lot of love inside for my little boy.

How much one letter can say! Our striving for comfortable identity is an ongoing part of life and growth, changing as we and circumstances change. In that striving we will find relics of our lives as children, pressures from our lives as parents, tensions from our lives as spouses and siblings. We have to expect some measure of strife in that striving, but we can expect to find joy and fulfillment in it, too—especially as we grow into comfortable identities as our children's closest caregivers.

Parents as Nourishers

"I felt... well, like I was being violated," a friend of ours began as he thought back to his early childhood. "I can still see that spoon coming at me, loaded with lima beans. I knew they'd taste dry and mealy. I wouldn't have wanted to touch them with my fingers, let alone take them into my mouth! Part of me felt forced to, because Mother and Dad would get angry if I didn't. But another me simply refused, so right then I didn't. But those same beans turned up again, cold, for breakfast the next morning, and I wasn't allowed to go play until I'd eaten every one. So in the end, the grown-ups won again."

That someone could remember a moment like that so vividly even after more than forty years suggests it must have been a powerful one at the time. But then, for most of us at any time, the thought of having to take something we consider repulsive into our mouths fills us with disgust. If you've had the experience of having a fly land in your mouth—or of finding something unexpected in a mouthful of food—you'll probably know how unwanted invasions of that private space can make you feel!

For most of us our first food was milk—from a breast or a bottle, from a can or a cow. As infants, we had no choice; we accepted what those who care for us provided. Our bodies, mind and all, took that nourishment and changed and grew according to what we were given. In that purely physical sense, we became what we ate.

But there was much more to it than that. In those early days, it must have seemed to us that our caregivers were what they provided—and more important still, how they provided it. The smells and tastes of their bodies were the smells and tastes of our food, the source of our first feelings of warmth and fullness and comfort. As we smelled and swallowed and felt, the face close above brought us (if we are fortunate) our first sights and sounds of love.

If we grew accepting food as an expression of love from people we loved, then it's likely we'll become parents who offer food the same way—as an expression of love to those we love. We may not consciously make the association all the time; the constant preparation of food for a family may seem not only a practical necessity, but also even a chore. But the deep despair and loss of self-esteem we've seen in parents who can't keep their family well fed suggests to me that there is something very deep involved.

I have the same feeling when I see how irritated and even angry parents can become when toddlers exercise their newfound independence by stubbornly refusing the food they're given. For a toddler, these refusals may be a natural way to try out being in control, or a way to be the center of attention. That, of course, can lead to a clash of wills. These refusals may also be honest reactions to unfamiliar smells, colors, and textures. But whatever they represent, a toddler's turning down food can bring parents a feeling of rejection that goes much deeper than the rejection of the peas . . . or lima beans.

Because of food's deeper meanings, I believe it's worth a lot of patience, understanding and self-control on the part of parents to avoid turning mealtimes into battlegrounds. I'm not even comfortable when mealtimes become bargaining sessions: "You can't watch TV unless you eat up" or "You can't have any dessert unless you eat your spinach." That's not to say that parents should be so permissive that they allow their children to eat badly, irregularly, or not at all. Far from it. Part of responsible and caring parenting is helping children develop healthy eating habits, but there's often more leeway in how we accomplish that than we may think. I believe that we should offer food unconditionally even though it won't always be received the way we'd like it to be. When it isn't, we need to be sensitive to the deep feelings that its rejection may bring us.

Judy Shepard, in addition to being a friend and a mother/stepmother to six children, is a writer and publisher of cookbooks.* In her own words, Judy has "a mania for cookbooks and recipes," a fact evidenced by her vast library. Where does that mania come from? "Perhaps," she conjectures, "there's something deep in my genetic makeup that prompts me to follow the practice of centuries. Originally a matter of survival, cooking and eating now involve much more than mere nourishment. I think of myself as a wife, mother, and hostess who likes to cook for and feed those I care about."

Because food and caring are so closely associated for Judy and her husband, Marty, they shop and cook with care, searching out freshness and quality, scrutinizing labels, being attentive to guidelines for healthy eating that others have suggested or that they have formulated over the years for themselves.

"I have no doubt," Judy says, "that what you put in your body directly affects your physical, mental, and emotional well-being. But though I follow my own intuition and common sense, I'm not a purist. I try not to use recipes that violate my principles too often, but I can make my peace with the occasional breach. I tell myself, 'Everything in moderation . . . including moderation.'"

While Judy's kitchen is a caring place, it's also one of curiosity, ad-

*Food of My Friends (1981) and More Food of My Friends (1983), by Judith Shepard, The Permanent Press, Sag Harbor, N.Y. 11963.

venture, and creativity. Visual artistry and ritual enhance the act of eating. At the Shepards' table, there is far more than meets the tongue.

"It's nice to cook for family and friends," Judy says simply, "in a way, it's a gift I am offering them, and good food not only nourishes the body, it also pleasures the soul."

There must have been something in Judy's earliest experiences with food that gave pleasure to her soul, and there were probably similar experiences in the early lives of those who cared for her. Passing on the gifts that we've been given is one way to confirm our place in the sequence of generations, and there's a recipe Judy included in *More Food of My Friends*—a recipe that originates with her grandmother, Honey, and that has now passed to a fourth generation in Judy's daughter, Liza. It's called

"Honey's 'Quilting Bees'"

2 cups raisins	2 tsp. cinnamon
2 cups water	½ tsp. cloves
1½ cups sugar	1 tsp. nutmeg
½ cup shortening	¼ tsp. salt
2 eggs	2 tsp. baking powder
2½ cups flour	1 cup walnut pieces

(1) Boil raisins in water for 10 minutes and drain. (2) Cream sugar and shortening. (3) Add eggs and stir. (4) Add all dry ingredients and mix well. (5) Stir in nuts and raisins. (6) Put in a lightly greased muffin tin and bake in a 350-degree oven until done (30 to 40 minutes, depending on the size muffin tins you are using).

"When my mother gave me that recipe and I tried it out," Judy recalls, "I felt a very warm and satisfying feeling to know that I was cooking one of my grandmother's recipes. I liked the continuity."

Of course, not everyone in this world is fortunate enough to have had the pains of hunger eased when they were little. As we know, there are many people the world over who live with the pains of hunger all their lives and even die knowing hunger as their last pain as well as their first.

The world is not always a kind place. That's something all children learn for themselves, whether we want them to or not, but it's something they really need our help to understand. Part of that understanding is that often the world is made kinder by people who choose to be helpers, and that helping is something we all can do, each in our own way.

When it comes to food and hunger, those of us who have more than enough can really make a difference. In fact, there are many who believe that if each of us did what we could, there would be no physical hunger in the world. That's a big goal. One thing is certain, though: There's hunger right around us, no matter where we live, and if we choose to be helpers, we can do something about it. There are agencies, organizations and religious groups who can help us help if we're not sure how to go about it, but the chances are that each of us knows where help is needed in our neighborhoods just because we're neighbors.

I don't believe that children, when they're very young, need to be told about all the troubles in this world. In fact, they may need our reassurance that the world isn't really as sad or dangerous or scary a place as it may seem in the pictures of it that come to them through media such as television. But I do believe that exposing children to ways of helping is very different from exposing them to ways of suffering!

Children who grow up with plenty can learn to give, just as children who grow up receiving love can learn to express love.

Parents as Comforters

When babies are hungry, they cry . . . and nourishment brings them comfort. But parents are called on to provide many kinds of comfort that are not that clear-cut, and they find that there are many, many times when they're unsure of how much of what kind to provide. A mother writes:

"My son is wonderful, and I enjoy playing with him and doing all the things a new mother does with her first child, but I already have a 'problem' and he's only four months old. The problem is that he enjoys our play too much! Lately, every time I put him down, he begins to cry. The only thing that will quiet him is being held again. I know this is a mild case of spoiling, but how do I correct the problem without hurting him psychologically? Letting him cry really tears my heart. I feel so guilty! What should I do?"

That mother is certainly experiencing a lot of old, old feelings (even though they may seem new to her): the joy of motherhood, the pain of her child's distress, the urge to soothe, uncertainty, and, of course, guilt. How much there is in the cry of a child about the nature of distress and the nature of comfort!

No matter how often that mother does pick up her child, there will be many times when she can't, times when she needs her two hands for other tasks. Her voice from the kitchen may have to suffice, and her son will come to learn that full and immediate comfort isn't always available. Perhaps he will learn to find comfort in her voice instead of her arms and even discover ways to comfort himself. There will be times when that mother will be away from her child altogether, and he will cry—but also learn that she will return after she leaves. Soon, that little boy will start teething, and both he and his mother will find themselves up against the limits of comfort. Not even holding or being held will make the pain go away. For the baby, it may be one of life's earliest lessons that there are times like that. For his mother, it will be another chance to accept the difficult truth that there are real limits on how much comfort we can bring to loved ones when they hurt.

Almost all of us who have been parents have had the feeling of wanting to give our children perfect lives, lives without pain or sorrow, but of course none of us can. When there is pain or sorrow in our children's lives, as there is bound to be, there is often no way we can make it go away. But when children can cope with hard times—drawing on whatever comfort they find from us and from within themselves—their parents can be very proud indeed. That ability to cope may be one of the greatest abilities that parents can help their children acquire.

Should the mother who wrote comfort her child whenever she can? I believe that infants and babies whose mothers give them loving comfort whenever and however they can are truly the fortunate ones. I think they're more likely to find life's times of trouble manageable, and I think they may also turn out to be the adults most able to pass along loving concern to the generations that follow them.

I doubt there's ever been a child who didn't have some fears about something while growing up—or parents who weren't often perplexed about what to do about them. One of my young television friends writes that he is scared of three things: lightning, thunder, and storm clouds. He adds: "I am also scared when the electricity goes out." Well, many of us can sympathize with those fears! It could help that child to know something about storms and electricity. His parents might want to ask him what he thinks they are and how they work. They might even learn that he's afraid that someone up in the sky is really angry.

Straight information isn't always the answer, though. A teacher told me of a time when there were hurricane warnings in her area, and the young children in her care seemed to want to know all about what hurricanes were. So she found out as much as she could and put what she learned in terms they could understand. But the more she told them, the more their curiosity—and anxiety—grew. Then she told them that if ever there was a hurricane in their town, there were grown-ups who knew how to take care of children so that they wouldn't get hurt. That, it turned out, was what the children were really wanting to know, and as she assured them about their safety, their fearfulness and intense curiosity subsided.

Another parent writes about her son's fear of the vacuum sweeper—how he got to the point that if he even saw it, he would run and hide. I know that many children share this fear, and it isn't just because of the loud noise the sweeper makes. As it roars along, the sweeper seems to gobble everything up, and a small child might wonder, "Can it gobble me up, too?" For that boy, comfort might come through knowing that a person makes the sweeper work—turns it on and off and decides what it's going to suck into the hose. A sweeper can't go around sucking things up by itself!

Sometimes children may be afraid of things that do what they, themselves, are trying to learn not to do. Most children pass through a stage when they have an urge to bite, for instance, and when they're trying to master that urge, they can be very frightened of things that can or do bite. One parent tells us her child wants her to throw away their *Little Red Riding Hood* book. Another says her son is terribly afraid of the Big Bad Wolf—not just in the story, but every night at bedtime.

I wonder if what these children are really afraid of is losing their growing self-control and hurting someone they love.

Parents can often get clues about what's bothering their children by unobtrusively watching their play, their drawing or pretending, or by listening to the stories they make up. But whether or not we understand what's at the root of a fear, it's important that we encourage our children to go on playing about their feelings. The more they can handle scary things in their play, the less scary such things need to seem everywhere else.

Among the most perplexing of children's fears are those seemingly unaccountable ones of things that aren't real—at least not real in the way adults have come to think of "reality." A recent letter contained a typical anecdote.

"I have read about nighttime fears," wrote this mother, "but I don't know how to handle daytime fears. I love my daughter very much and have taken her to the zoo and a farm because she likes animals. But now she is afraid of tigers. She comes running up to me, holds on tight, hides her face, and says that tigers are hiding out there and she is afraid of them. I don't know if it is normal for a two-year-old to develop a fear like that, or if it is something that I did to cause it. I can't think of anything new that has happened in our house to cause it."

For another little girl, a three-year-old, there is a "big, bad mommy" who stands in the hall and watches her during the day. The only thing that seems to help is being held by her real mommy. Telling her that the other mommy is just in her imagination doesn't seem to make any difference. Not surprisingly, the girl can't put into words whatever it is that lies at the root of her fear, and so her mother is left feeling inadequate because she can't find a way to provide the comfort she'd like to.

The truth is that there are many times in early childhood and beyond when parents can't solve their children's problems. Perhaps all they can do is to provide a safe and loving place, and a caring willingness to listen and to talk while children work through whatever is bothering them. That's what I call "being there," and, far from being a passive, helpless role, this is often the most active and helpful kind of comfort parents can give their growing children.

It certainly is normal for children to have all sorts of fears as they grow. It's also normal for these fears to take the shape of imaginary creatures or imaginary people. That may be the best way children have available to express them. But whenever we find ourselves alarmed by our children's behavior, it's a good idea to consult someone who may have deeper insights than our own. Reaching out to professionals at times like that can be both helpful for our children and reassuring for ourselves.

I've heard parents say, "You don't need to be afraid. There aren't any tigers out there." (Some parents may even say something like, "Don't be silly!") But in fact, for a reason we may not understand, that child does to be afraid, and it could be more helpful to say, "There aren't any real tigers out there, but I understand you're scared, and I'll be here to keep you safe." With reassurance like that, a child may feel strong enough to think about the "tiger" and, eventually, tame it.

And a "big, bad mommy?" Where would that scary image come from? I can easily imagine a loving mother being upset when her child creates an imaginary monster version of herself. "What have I done to deserve that?" she might wonder. Well, there might be lots of different reasons for a child to have such a fear—ones that a professional could find, but it's likely that the mother hasn't done anything but try to be a loving mother. The people who love us do get angry at us, and that's because they do love us. It can be hard for a child to understand that a parent can be both loving and angry. It can be harder still for a child to understand that he or she, too, can have both loving and angry feelings toward a parent.

Even when a child's fear seems tied to something concrete and specific, it may be unclear *why* that fear has arisen or what kind of comfort can best help.

Jimmy's mother came in to say goodnight to him before going out to a fancy-dress party. She was dressed as a fortune-teller. Jimmy was four, and even though he knew this figure was his mother, his lip started quivering, and he almost started to cry. "It's only me," his mom said. "I thought you'd like to see my costume." Jimmy nodded, but he wasn't completely reassured.

At five, Bobby wanted to go trick-or-treating dressed as a mummy. His parents helped wrap him up in bandages, face and all, and he seemed to feel fine about it—until he looked at himself in the mirror. "I don't like it," he said nervously. "I want to take it off." He kept insisting until his parents gave in. He went out in his cowboy suit instead.

Both these boys seem to be having difficulty with dress-up and disguise. There could be many reasons, but costumes frequently play right into common childhood fears.

One fear that we probably all had in the first years of our lives was that the person we felt most a part of would suddenly leave us or suddenly change into someone different. Infants do feel a part of their closest caregivers at the beginning of life. Such caregivers give an infant's world organization and meaning and provide what security and comfort an infant first comes to know. More than that, these close and constant caregivers are most responsible for babies coming to feel lovable and capable of loving. Because so many of our earliest feelings about ourselves and our world come to us through these caregivers, it's hardly surprising that losing sight of them can, during the first years, be deeply upsetting.

Jimmy was certainly old enough to "know" his mother was under that gypsy costume. All the same, her dramatically changed appearance may have touched off some fears that had been very real to him only a year or two before. Just seeing Mommy with a different hairdo or dark glasses has made some toddlers break into tears.

Bobby's concerns were probably quite different. As children get to be his age, they're often working hard to understand their bodies—to understand that body parts all hold together, that broken bones mend, that cuts won't let all the blood leak out from under the skin. Five-year-olds can be very sensitive about their appearances and proud of what their bodies are learning to do. In short, they're working on their sense of independent security, on their sense of who and what they are.

Bobby probably didn't count on seeing such a scary change in the body he was coming to value. Just as Jimmy "knew" that the gypsy was really his familiar mommy, Bobby knew that his familiar body was somewhere under those bandages. I can certainly understand his compulsion to get rid of them and make certain, though, and his mother provided just the right kind of comfort by taking his feelings seriously —whether she understood what was going on or not.

Parents as Limit Setters

The role of comforter is a pleasing one for most parents. Sometimes it is frustrating, to be sure, when we can't provide all the comfort we'd like, but all the same it's a loving role. Being cast as the limit-setter can feel quite different. There parents often find themselves feeling that they're the "bad guys."

Parents begin trying to set limits as soon as they start encouraging their newborns to develop a regular schedule for eating and sleeping. It's a useful time to remember, since there is a real mutuality in the limit-setting. Parents have no choice but to find compromises between their desires and the unique, inborn characteristics of their babies. At this time, "discipline" doesn't have any meaning, and later on it might take on a more positive meaning if that early mutuality still persists as parents continue in their limit-setting roles.

The limit we hear most complaints about from frustrated parents is "Bedtime!" We've already tried to suggest some of the reasons night can be a time of anxiety for children (see p. 4) and mentioned the importance of "winding-down" time. What emerges most strongly, though, as we hear from parents who are working on the bedtime problem is the importance of recapturing some of the mutuality of infancy instead of making bedtime a time of discipline and conflict.

That may be why many families include in the wind-down time particular rituals such as singing, storytelling, reading, or prayers. It's very common for adults, looking back on their childhoods, to recall bedtime rituals with special vividness and pleasure, and they may find themselves passing on the ones they remember to their children. A friend told me how her father always made up a story for her and her brothers at bedtime, a story about three little ducks who, night after night, had a series of different adventures. "You know," she said, "no matter how bad we had been, he never threatened not to tell us that story. He never used that time with us as a punishment. I certainly didn't think about it then, but now I believe that his continuing stories reassured us that there would be another day coming after the night, and his presence somehow told us that just as life would continue from day to day, so, too, would love."

In another family, a little boy seemed to have a lot of trouble staying in bed once he had gotten there. Again and again he would appear on the stairs holding his special little blanket. His parents let him know firmly that while having to go to the bathroom was fine, just plain "getting up" wasn't. They reassured him each evening that they would always come to him if he really needed them, and then they put a wall calendar in his bedroom. Each time he was able to go to bed and stay in bed, they put a star or favorite sticker on the calendar the next morning. The choice of the sticker was his . . . and soon the calendar was full of them.

One mother found it helped her three-year-old son get over his nightmares if they talked about them the next day. Often, she realized, her boy didn't even remember the scary dreams he had told her about during the night, but talking about them in the morning seemed to help him come to realize that dreams were things of sleep and the imagination, not of the real world.

Lots of children, of course, want to stay up later than their parents want them to just because they want to be a part of whatever is going on. Some parents seem to prefer to negotiate the hour for bedtime anew each evening—something that I don't think my wife or I would have had the patience to do, and that I believe would have been confusing for our children. Both my wife and I grew up in families with limits, and perhaps that's part of why we set limits for our children—limits that I hope reflected the mutuality of our diverse needs and personalities.

Here's another common complaint: "I feel like I'm living with a teenager!" complains a mother whose little boy is only two and a half.

Charlie, the two-and-a-half-year-old, is making life truly hard for his mother. He's testing limits—just to provoke her, she feels—and won't stop even when she reprimands him. Over and over again, it comes to punishment.

She's tried spanking him, but that's a losing battle because she doesn't believe in spanking and feels bad about it. She's made him sit on a chair in the corner, but when she tells him that he can get down now, he won't.

She's tried sending him to his room, and he ends up playing there contentedly, refusing to come out when it's time for supper.

Why has Charlie become so stubborn and willful? What can his mother do about it?

It seems to me that Charlie, like most children his age, has come to feel that he isn't, after all, just a part of the grown-ups around him; he's a separate individual. What that means isn't yet clear to him, but refusing to go along with old ways and familiar limits is the best thing he can find to try out his new feeling of separateness. It's also a way he can experiment with his growing realization that he has some control in his life. Charlie's feelings are perfectly normal and even necessary for his healthy emotional growth. Even though they may be tough for his parents, Charlie's stubborn feelings can be positive and can be used in positive ways.

One of the best ways to use them is for choice-making. When we give a young child choices, we acknowledge that child's individuality. And when a child's urge to be an individual gets channeled into choice-making, it's less likely to go into contrariness. Offering choices is another way that parents can bring a healthy mutuality to their limit-setting.

Charlie's mother may be accustomed to bundling him up and taking him shopping whenever it's a good time for her to go. The time may have come to let Charlie decide if he wants to go shopping before or after his nap, and which sweater he'd like to wear.

Where once Charlie may have readily complied with the order, "Go clean up your toys," he may now respond more positively to something like: "Do you want to clean up your toys before bed or first thing in the morning?"

Of course there are some options we can't give our children, and that's particularly true when it comes to limits we set for their safety. But if other parents' experience is any indication, Charlie's mother will find it easier to maintain that kind of limit in a firm but loving way if she can let her son make reasonable decisions about other parts of his life.

Living with a two-year-old child can be a lot like living with a teenager, because the old, important issue of identity comes up again in the teenage years. I believe it may turn out that the more we can encourage our child's expressions of individuality during the "terrible twos," and the more we can keep a spirit of reasonable compromise and mutuality during that time, the less likely we are to find ourselves suffering from a case of the "terrible teens."

One sensible piece of advice I've heard about limit-setting is this: Try to make sure that the limits we set (1) match what we're trying to accomplish, and (2) are limits we're going to be comfortable enforcing. That sounds like simple advice, but it's not always easy to follow.

When five-year-old Kathy came back from playing with her friend, Nan, she was grumpy and sullen. It wasn't the first time this had happened, and her mother didn't like finding herself with a cranky child on her hands.

"Look," she said to her daughter, "if that's how you're going to be when you come home from Nan's, I'm not going to let you play with her anymore."

One morning recently, Kathy and her older sister began quarreling about who was the skinnier of the two. Their mother was trying to get them ready for school, and when one accused the other of holding in her stomach so as to look skinnier, their mother said, "Hey, you two! If you don't stop this nonsense about being skinny, I'm not going to let you watch any TV, because I know that's where it's all coming from. Now hurry up and get ready!"

Those probably sound like scenes that are common to many households, and in fact they did to Kathy's mother who told us about them. "But I don't feel good about it," she added. "I'm not really going to stop Kathy playing with Nan, because I want Kathy to have friends. And I'm not really going to unplug the TV, either. So why do I make idle threats like that? They don't even seem to do any good!"

As Kathy's mother has found out, idle threats usually don't have much effect, and yet almost all parents find themselves, at times of exasperation, responding with them. The only useful threats, though, are ones that we fully mean to carry out—and that suggests that, when we find ourselves in confrontations with our children, we'd best be careful about what we say we're going to do.

One way to begin is to ask ourselves, calmly, what it is we're trying to accomplish.

From Kathy's point of view, it may have seemed that her mother was threatening to punish her for feeling grumpy. But, surely, that wasn't the case at all. Kathy's mother, like most parents, would agree that children need to be allowed to have their feelings and that it's only in the acting out of them that parents may need to set limits. What Kathy's mother wanted to limit was her daughter's behavior at home, not her playtime with Nan. If she wanted that playtime to be more peaceable, then she'd have to find out what was causing the trouble and talk with the two girls and with Nan's mother about it. This would be much more likely to be constructive than any idle threat.

It's important that we mean, and that we fully intend to follow through with, what we say. Our threats not only need to be real ones, but they also need to be closely associated with whatever situation has caused us to make them. As her two daughters wrangled over who was the skinnier, their mother most likely wanted to limit their dawdling, or their competitiveness, or their overconcern with being thin . . . or all three at once. It must have seemed strange to the girls to have their television time suddenly become the focus of their mother's concern. She might, instead, have said something like, "Now stop all this arguing. It makes me uncomfortable. It's time for school now, but I want to talk about it when you both get home." That way, she'd have avoided making an idle threat, and she'd also have had the time to think through what really was bothering her, and how she might appropriately go about limiting or altering her daughters' behavior. In addition, she'd have announced a future action—talking about it—that she was prepared to carry through.

It can be hard, on the spur of the moment, to know what to say, and it can be all too easy to make a quick retort rather than a thoughtful response. Many parents, though, have found it useful to get into the habit of simply stopping what needs to be stopped right at the moment, and then following up, when tempers have cooled, with some talk about what happened and why, and what limits will have to be set if it happens again.

None of us is superman or superwoman, and we adults have our feelings, too. But just as we may have to set limits on our children's behavior, we may also have to keep on setting limits on our own. When we make the effort to do so, we are showing our children that one day they'll be able to do the same thing for themselves.

Parents as Transition Makers

From oneness with the mother to a new, separate, unique, independent, feeling, decision-making...person! That's quite a journey, and most of it is taken in the first three years or so of life. In one sense that transition happens quickly; three years, after all, is a short span in most lifetimes. Yet it happens slowly, too. When three years is the whole of your lifetime so far, it can seem like forever (which, in a way, it is), while for parents who are eager for their babies to talk and walk, the course of their children's development can seem full of delays and dawdlings.

A child's closest caregivers are, of course, the most important elements in this transitional process. It is through them that a child first encounters the world. These caregivers determine what goes into a baby's mouth or hands. To a large degree they determine what consistent sights and sounds a baby first sees and hears. They choose the materials that babies feel against their skin. They regulate the first sensations of wet and dry, warm and cold, that "ouch!" of hungry and the "ahh!" of full. They help the infant, baby, and child learn what all these things mean.

More important even than the transition to the world of things, though, is a child's transition from oneness with the mother to relationships with a world full of people—first other people in the family, and then all those people beyond. Even when relationships have grown smoothly and strongly within the family, bridging to the outside can be difficult—and not just for the child. Some parents find it takes harder work on their parts than they expected.

One mother writes: "I have never left my daughter in the care of anyone other than my husband, sister, mother, or father. If she is playing outside, I am out there watching. I have been accused of being overprotective. I like to think that I am being loving and caring. The thought of entrusting my daughter to veritable strangers is disconcerting."

That mother certainly is loving and caring, and I hope that she can resist pressures from others who chose to express their lovingness and caringness in different ways. For a child to begin making nonfamily relationships, it's not only the child who needs to feel ready but the parent as well—perhaps particularly the parent, because in the earliest years, it's solely a parental choice. Sometimes parents may give their children more protection than their children need, but we do well to keep in mind that parents have needs, too.

As soon as our children are old enough to move about with some independence, most of us worry about their encounters with strangers. Parents have asked me many times how to raise loving and trusting children while, at the same time, giving them a sense of healthy wariness of strangers. The problem often arises early. For instance, a parent wrote: "I have a 4½-year-old daughter who will be walking to school. In spite of the fact that we live in a reasonably safe neighborhood and are having practice walks, I am still anxious. Although the walk is only two and a half blocks, I fear strangers. I'm willing to walk my daughter to school, but there is peer pressure on myself, as well as on my daughter, not to do so."

It's hard to know what to tell a small child about strangers, to find an explanation that is simple enough to understand and yet not frightening. It can be helpful to tell children something like: "There are some people who care about children and who know how to take care of them, and there are some who don't. If someone you don't know ever wants to give you something or wants you to go somewhere with them, always ask a person you know if it's okay first. The best way to meet new people is through the grown-ups who already care about you."

That's a message we may need to repeat many times. It can be helpful, too, to find books in the library about meeting strangers and read them with our children, or to make up stories about meeting strangers, or to play about meeting someone new. The more we can talk with our children about our concerns, the more likely we are to find our children talking with us about them.

As for the peer pressure the mother was feeling, I hope that she can stand her ground. A few telephone calls and a little organization among other concerned mothers may make it possible for there always to be someone to accompany her daughter and her friends to and from school. If that doesn't work, then I believe that mother belongs with her daughter along the way as long as she feels the need to be. And when her daughter says, "But Emily's mother doesn't walk her to school!" perhaps she'll be able to tell her little girl, "That's because every family does things differently, and this is the way we do it in our family, because we love you and need to know that you're safe."

Here's another example of a parent and child in transition: When the phone rang at 5:30 in the afternoon, Laura's mother didn't expect to hear her five-year-old daughter on the other end. "Hi, honey," she said. "Been having a good time?"

"Yup," said Laura. "Hey, Mom, Karen's mother says it's okay for me to stay for supper and spend the night. Can I, Mom?"

Laura's mother didn't know what to say. To begin with, she was surprised, because it would mean her daughter's first overnight at someone's house other than her own and her grandmother's. Part of her thought, "Why not, so long as she wants to?" But another part of her wanted to say, "No," and she knew that part was the stronger of the two. She wasn't sure right then what was making her so reluctant; it was just a mother's feeling.

"Honey," she said, "not this time. You get your things together and I'll be over to pick you up in about fifteen minutes. But why don't you ask Karen's mom if you could do it another night? That way we can make plans for it."

"Oh, Mom . . . please? Can't I?" Laura pleaded.

"No, hon," her mother said. "But I promise you can do it another time."

On the way over to fetch her daughter, Laura's mother thought about her reaction. Something told her that a five-year-old's first overnight with a strange family was an important step, and she didn't want it to go badly. Maybe Laura was ready for it, and maybe she wasn't. She couldn't be sure. Above all, though, she knew inside that she herself wasn't ready for it. She needed a chance to talk it over with her daughter.

During the week that followed, they did talk about it. They played about it, too, pretending that someone was sleeping in a strange place for the first time and imagining the new sounds that person might hear. Laura's mother explained to her daughter that different families did different things with their children at bedtime. Laura always said a little prayer just before getting into bed, but that might not be something that Karen's family did. There might be new things to eat, and new rules. Each family does things differently, she explained, and that can be part of the fun of visiting. At the same time, it can mean surprises. "But there's one thing I want you to know, hon, and that's that if for any reason you really want to come home and not stay there all night, your dad or I will come right over and get you."

Before leaving for Karen's the next Friday, Laura and her mom packed a little suitcase together. They put in washing things, pajamas and a change of clothes. They also put in a small pillow from Laura's bed, a teddy and a couple of favorite toys. Without her daughter knowing it, Laura's mom slipped in a card that said, "Have fun. I love you." And off Laura went.

The overnight was a complete success. "It might have been just fine the first time, too, if I'd said yes," Laura's mother admitted. "But I know I'd have worried. And I'd have felt . . . well, sort of cheated. I needed time to get ready just as much as I thought Laura did. As it worked out, I was excited for her, pleased for her, relaxed, and confident. To me, at least, it was worth the short disappointment Laura had to go through."

That mother's story says something very important about being a parent. Whenever we're anxious or uncomfortable about something our children want to do, we need to be honest with ourselves and with them and say so. Talking about it may help, and sometimes we may want more time just to think about it. I've often said that children need an "inner readiness" before they can try to master something new, whether it's potty training or sleeping away from home. I know that's true for children, but that mother reminded me that as we parents continue to grow with our children, it's true for us as well.

When a child's first experience with something new goes wrong, how hard that can be on a parent and child alike! It can take a long time to get over, too.

One little girl went to the dentist for the first time when she was almost three. It was for only a checkup, and her mother had made an appointment with a children's specialist recommended by her own dentist. Her daughter, Jenifer, was a cooperative child. She was already comfortable with her visits to her pediatrician, and her mother didn't expect any trouble, either, as she took her daughter to see a new kind of health-care provider. There was trouble, though . . . and much of it seems to have stemmed from the fact that neither mother nor child really knew what to expect at all.

Jenifer and her mother first met the specialist in the waiting room the very day of the examination. That certainly didn't give them much time to get to know one another, or for Jenifer to understand where she was and why. Some parents take their children for a preliminary visit just to meet the dentist and look around. These children have the chance to see that funny-looking chair and learn how it works; what the bright light is for; how the paper bib goes on around their neck and comes off at the end; how those little hoses work that squirt air and water, or act like tiny vacuum cleaners. And they have the chance to meet the person who is going to be caring for them and poking things in their mouth—something that still causes many of us anxiety even when we're a lot older than three.

Why those "getting acquainted" visits are so important, however, has most to do with what happens at home later on, when there's time to think and talk about it, to play and read about going to a dentist, and, of course, to ask questions.

As it turned out, Jenifer's mother felt uncomfortable with the specialist from the start. You can be sure that Jenifer picked up on her mother's uneasiness. "Jenifer's dentist confused me with his psychological jargon," her mother told us. "He did say that Jenifer wouldn't be physically restrained, but I didn't understand what he meant when he said that she'd be 'subject to his voice control.' And then he asked me to stay in the waiting room while he took Jenifer away. That surprised me because my husband and I have always accompanied her for her medical examinations. Moreover, I'd told Jenifer I wouldn't leave her alone."

Jenifer showed her own unease by starting to cry, and she kept on crying until her mother insisted on coming into the examination room. By that time, the situation was out of hand and Jenifer was, according to her mother, "totally uncooperative." "What's more," she added, "the dentist blamed me for being a 'typical mother' and berated me for my ignorance and for not trusting him. In the end, I left with a feeling of complete failure."

Something positive did come out of that experience, though—at least for Jenifer's mother. From now on, she's going to listen to her instincts as a mother, no matter what professionals or well-meaning friends tell her. Whenever she feels that her proper place is at her daughter's side, for instance, then that's exactly where she's going to be. Looking back at that unhappy visit to the dentist, she now realizes that her sense of failure had less to do with failing to make the visit a success than with the feeling that she had let her daughter down when she needed her.

Health-care providers and others who help us take care of our children do have their own ways of working. Their ways may not be "right" or "wrong" any more than our ways of raising our children may be so. In most cases, we each act as we believe best for the children in our care. But what is important is that professionals and parents agree beforehand and feel comfortable about one another's styles of caring. And whenever a parent doesn't feel comfortable giving his or her child over into a particular person's care, especially when that feeling is a rare one for that parent, well, then it's probably time to go looking for someone else.

Parents have every right and every reason to be as careful and choosy as they like about who else cares for their children. No one needs the kind of experience we heard about from one set of parents who went away on a weekend vacation and had a truly disturbing experience with a babysitter.

This mother and father had hired the sitter through a well-known agency, and the agency had been recommended to them by a friend. The sitter was a young woman in her twenties. She had preschool teaching experience, and when the parents interviewed her, they liked her and thought she would get along well with their children who were ten, eight, and four.

When the parents called home the first evening, they became suspicious. The sitter said she couldn't put the children on the telephone to say hello because they were outside playing. The wife then called her mother and asked her to go to the house and see how things were going. The grandmother found that the sitter had been drinking, had verbally abused the children, had hit the ten-year-old and locked the four-year-old out of the house while the two older ones were away at school. The house was in a terrible condition. The sitter was dismissed, and the parents came home at once.

"We are a very upset family," the mother wrote. "As parents, we feel just terrible that we exposed our children to such a miserable and dangerous situation."

It's seldom easy for loving parents to leave their children in someone else's care. I suspect we feel a little guilty about doing it at all, even though we know it's natural for us to have to be away at times or just to need some time together with our spouses or even by ourselves. How best can we choose other caregivers when we need them?

There are three things I'd look for in a babysitter: caring, confidence, and common sense. An initial interview may not tell you whether a person really has these attributes, but it's surprising how often even a brief meeting can give you the feeling that a person doesn't. We can always be wrong, of course, but in deciding to whom we're willing to entrust our children, we have to go by our feelings.

If I felt positive about someone, I'd want to try that person out—for a couple of hours during an afternoon or for a short evening. After a tryout like that, I'd listen very carefully to what she or he could tell me about my child. Does the account of their time together suggest alert-ness, interest, and those all-important three C's: caring, confidence, and common sense? And of course I'd listen just as carefully to what my child had to say—bearing in mind that babysitters who can set and enforce sensible limits may, to begin with, get some bad marks from a child. I'd certainly try to let my child know how important it was to me for him or her to feel comfortable with any substitute caregiver—and that it was always all right to talk with me about anything that was not comfortable. Any relationship takes time to grow, and I know I'd want to feel that a healthy relationship had grown between my child and a babysitter before I'd leave my child in that person's care overnight.

Life is always going to have unpleasant and unexpected surprises, but we need to remember that the reverse is true as well. A friend of mine who has moved many times all around the country spoke warmly of several babysitters his children had had as they were growing up. Four, in particular, were still "part of the family"—even one who was now married and had children of her own. As he talked about them, I found myself thinking of one of life's grandest surprises of all: The mo-ment we realize that someone who had once been a stranger had now become a friend.

Parents as Problem-Solvers

As parents and their children move out and about more and more in the world, they're bound to encounter the unexpected—and have to cope and make do on the spot. Sometimes it's children themselves who seem ingenious in devising dilemmas to test their caregivers' resource-fulness.

It was a classic summer scene—families and children around a swimming pool, sounds of splashing and laughter—but for one of the parents, it became a classic confrontation of wills and limits.

Ali, who was almost two, wanted to go back in the water. She'd already been "swimming" for more than a year and was confident and capable so long as she wore her floaters—inflatable armbands that kept her head and shoulders above water. But right then, Ali didn't want to wear her floaters. The only alternative was for her mother to go back in the pool with her, but her mother wanted to dry off in the sun and talk with friends.

"I'll go in with you in a little while," she told her daughter. "If you want to go in now, you'll have to put on your floaters."

"Don't want floaters," Ali protested, starting to cry.

"No floaters, no pool," her mother insisted, and Ali started a tantrum, setting up a howl that was sure to annoy the other swimmers and embarrass her mother.

There's a lot at stake in these kinds of confrontations. For a start, there's the risk of being branded a public nuisance. Then there's the threat to a parent's self-esteem as everyone's disapproving eyes seem to be saying, "What an inadequate parent!" or "What a spoiled child!" Between parent and child there is always the challenge of who's in charge—who gets his or her way. And for a child, there's the urgency of growing autonomy and the need to say, through actions, "I am an individual and can have some effect on the people and the world around me."

That last one—a child's autonomy—may really be the most important issue of all, and yet it's so often the issue that gets lost in the turmoil. Even as we have to curb our children's inappropriate expressions of individuality, we also need to nurture in them the belief that it's all right to try to make out of the world what they will and to assert themselves according to their own needs and desires. It can be one of parents' most difficult jobs to walk the fine line between giving in to their children's whims and punishing them for what are basically healthy attempts to discover who they are.

Ali's mother tried to reason with her daughter. "All your noise is disturbing everyone, Ali," she said. "We'll have to go do something else until you can calm down. How about reading a book for a while? Or going for a walk?" This reasonable approach had no effect whatsoever on Ali's tantrum, and, as her mother said afterward, she didn't expect it to have. "It made me feel better, though," she said. "I felt I was giving Ali choices, even if she couldn't use them or even understand them right then. And I wasn't loosing my cool."

When Ali kept on howling, her mother just took her away on a walk down the road and sat with her under a tree. Getting out of sight of the pool, in itself, probably helped, but in any event, Ali's tantrum shortly subsided. When her mother felt the moment was right, she gave her daughter another choice. "Are you ready to go back to the pool now, honey?" she asked. Ali nodded. When they got back, her mother had no trouble getting her into her floaters.

Not all confrontations resolve so peaceably. A child's tantrum in a crowded restaurant, or perhaps in an airplane, has pushed many a parent beyond his or her limits of self-control to the point where both parent and child lose their tempers. In fact, it's hard to imagine a family where seriously angry flare-ups don't happen from time to time. Even these situations, though, can have positive outcomes. Once the incident has passed, a parent might say, for instance, "We were really angry with each other, weren't we?"

That may seem like a small thing to say, but the saying of it can be a way to help a child understand something important: That anger, on the part of adults and children alike, is a natural and permissible human emotion; that it can be expressed and talked about; and that even when people who love each other get mad at each other, love does not diminish but sometimes even strengthens as the good feeling of harmony returns.

Speaking of airplanes . . . another confrontation we watched unfolding under circumstances that had all the makings of a disaster involved an active twelve-month toddler, an anxious young mother and father— all three sandwiched into the middle aisle of a jam-packed, stuffy jumbo jet that was delayed on the runway prior to a three-hour flight.

The toddler's parents had given him a lollipop—their first attempt to keep him quiet and happy. The boy seized the sticky end with his free hand, then, standing on his father's lap, reached into the hair of the woman in the seat ahead. His parents yanked him sharply back, and when his father took the lollipop away and ate it himself, the boy set up a howl. From there it was downhill all the way.

"It's going to be one of those flights . . ."

PARENTS AT WORK

His parents gave the boy the in-flight magazine, but he tore it and got scolded. They enticed him with the snap-out tray table, but when he repeatedly banged on it, his mother slapped his hand—gently but firmly. He screamed and squirmed down to get off the seat. They jangled a set of plastic keys in front of him. He snatched them and flung them into the aisle, wriggling and sobbing.

By this time, the passengers all around were shaking their heads and rolling their eyes as if to say, "We can see what kind of flight this is going to be!"

The mother tried the bottle. The boy, crying hard, struck out at it and hit his mother instead. The mother struck back, not hard, but with anger enough to provoke a real scream of temper from her son. And so it went—for the half-hour delay before takeoff and all during the first hour of the trip until finally the boy, exhausted, fell asleep in his mother's lap.

There's no pretending that there's an easy solution to such dilemmas, but the real-life scene above made me realize once again how sensitive young children are to their parents' feelings—how easily they "catch" the feelings of the grown-ups close to them. In this instance, the boy was "catching" both anxiety and anger, and he certainly became anxiously angry himself. Who knows what his parents were going through? This trip may have been difficult for them from the moment it was booked.

Unfortunately, their son's reaction was making the whole thing all the more difficult for them.

There may have been an alternative, though. If the parents could have kept their own tensions under more control, their son might have caught some calm instead of catching mostly stress. I found myself wondering what they did with their son at nap time or bedtime. Could they have tried some rocking or stroking or singing? Of course, if they needed a lot of comfort themselves, it would have been hard to comfort someone else—but that's often what's required from parents, isn't it? I wondered, too, whether their son had some familiar comforting object at home—a teddy bear or blanket he associated with quiet times—that they could have let him bring on board. Instead of trying constant distraction, those parents might have had more luck lessening their son's level of stimulation by making their laps safe, quiet places in the confusing new environment of the airplane.

Certainly this kind of parental calmness can be very difficult and hard to maintain, but so often it's just this kind of self-control that young children need to borrow from us before they have self-control of their own. Of this we can be fairly sure: When our young children find themselves in new and confusing situations, they'll look to us for clues and cues... and that makes what we're going to offer worth thinking carefully about.

Situations that require lengthy waiting almost always pose a challenge to caregivers with young children. How do you make the time pass without restlessness, whines, scoldings, or frayed tempers?

Well, you might have brought a favorite book along, but maybe you didn't. Or a favorite toy, but maybe that got left at home, too. There are hand games and finger games that you may remember from your own childhood, but often these diversions don't seem to work for very long.

Story-telling can be one of the best ways to keep a child's mind busy. You may be able to remember a story you and your child have read together, or you may be able to make up one, but there's another alternative a young mother demonstrated recently: remembering a real-life story together. You may relive an event you know your child can remember. In that remembering may be the greatest source of diversion of all.

This mother and her "almost two" were waiting on a bench for a bus that was to bring the child's father back home. The bus was late, the noon hour was hot, the little boy made it clear he was hungry. The scene had all the elements for trouble, and fifteen minutes into the wait, trouble seemed just moments away. The boy grew tired of counting trucks that passed (and, of course, he couldn't count very high), and "I want something to eat!" became a more and more insistent and whiny refrain.

"Do you remember when we had to wait for Daddy at Kennedy Airport?" the mother asked, and with that the magic began. The boy nodded a little uncertainly—an uncertainty that suggested his mind was suddenly divided among the lateness of the bus, his hungry tummy, and the remembering of the time at the airport.

"What did we see while we were waiting?" his mother asked.

"Airplanes," the boy said.

"How many airplanes?" his mother asked, taking her son onto her lap.

"Lots of airplanes!" the boy exclaimed, making a gesture with his arms that took in the whole sky. "One, two, three, four, five, six, nine, ten, thirteen, fifteen, eighteen...."

"And do you remember how we had to wait... and wait... and wait...." Bouncing her knees up and down, she began a swaying body rhythm on each "wait" that made her son smile.

"And then we went inside with all those people, and we had to wait... and wait... and wait...." Now, as the boy bounced and swayed on his mother's knees, his mouth formed "wait... wait... wait...."

"And then the big doors opened, and people started coming out, and we looked for Daddy, but we had to wait . . . wait . . . wait. . . ." By this time the boy had a sly, expectant smile, and his eyes were locked to his mother's as he anticipated what was coming.

"And then who did we see?"

"Daddy!" the boy shouted, and both mother and child clapped their hands.

The trouble was, the bus still wasn't in sight. "Honey," the mother said, "I know you're hungry, and we'll get something to eat just as soon as. . . ." Her son interrupted her: "Tell me the part about Kennedy Airport again!" he commanded.

So the mother began again from the beginning, spinning out a much more elaborate story, adding as many opportunities for the bouncing and swaying and the "wait . . . wait . . . wait . . ." parts as she could. Before she was halfway through, the bus *did* arrive, Daddy *did* appear, and together they *did* go off to get something to eat.

"You're a really good waiter, Alex," his mother said as they walked away.

Watching and helping children like Alex grow is inherently fascinating, and that partially accounts for all the talk that goes on about it. It's easy to laugh, for instance, about mothers who, when they get together, seem to talk about nothing but their children. Have you listened, though, to fathers who've remained intimately involved in their children's daily upbringing when they get together?

Whenever parents get together it's a chance for them to find reassurance for their natural uncertainties and to tap a source of new solutions for commonly shared problems—two irresistible inducements to "talk children." There's so much that parents can learn from one another!

A good example of shared problem-solving was highlighted recently by a group of friends (all parents) who wondered why it is that play among three children so often ends in a fracas, even though in twos the same children play together just fine.

The question arose because one mother described how her five-year-old, Roberta, preferred to play with friends her own age than to play alone. In fact, her mother said, Roberta seemed bored when she was by herself.

Fortunately, this mother continued, Roberta has a best friend, Marlene, who lives nearby. The two of them make up stories and adventures together, cooperate, share, and have no problems taking turns when their play calls for it.

Unfortunately, Marlene has another friend she likes to play with as well—Judy. When the three of them get together, here's what happens: Marlene and Judy gang up, exclude Roberta, make her jealous and angry ... and then send her home. It seems to happen every time. Naturally, Roberta's mother is upset about having her daughter come home over and over again in tears. What might be done about it?

"The mothers should talk, all three of them," one friend suggested. "But," she cautioned, "they should try not to blame one another's children. We all tend to take that personally. At least they could try to arrange their children's playtimes so that for a while the three girls seldom play together at all."

Another friend came up with this suggestion: "I'd try to create some playtime for Roberta and Judy—without Marlene. Then, if they develop some interests together, they might develop a friendship as well. That could change the whole thing around."

Both suggestions sounded helpful, so long as no one expected instant results. Friendships at any age take time, and at five they often seem mysterious in their day-to-day workings.

The group came up with two other suggestions. One was that the mothers take turns accompanying the three children on outings—to the zoo, on a picnic, to a museum, or just to an airport to watch airplanes. That way, the girls would not be solely responsible for organizing their play, and the mothers would each have a chance to see, firsthand, how the children behaved together.

The other suggestion was that the fathers take a hand in the matter. In fact, it was a father who made the suggestion. "You don't have to be a psychologist to know that girls at that age act very differently around their fathers than around their mothers," he said. "If Judy's father took the girls somewhere and made sure to pay some special attention to Roberta's ideas and interests ... well, I'll bet that his daughter and Marlene would take a different view of their friend." It's true: So often fathers and their particular importance to young children's development still get forgotten.

Something that Roberta's mother had said made me think of another idea. She mentioned that Roberta seemed bored when there was no one around to play with. That's worth the effort to try to change—not by finding more friends, but rather by finding projects that Roberta can enjoy when she's by herself. To begin with, it's likely to mean some supportive and cooperative help from both her mother and her father. But there are times all during life when we need the inner resources to keep ourselves busy and productive all by ourselves.

That kind of self-sufficiency doesn't always come automatically. It comes from the people closest to us giving us, when we're little, that feeling we all need—that we're worth something just for being who we are. And that's a feeling parents have a special way of giving one another—that they're worth something *just for being parents*.

PART 4:

WORKING AND GROWING TOGETHER

Making Contact

As children and their caregivers work and grow together, they develop deep and subtle ways of communicating with one another. Usually, neither the adults nor the children are really aware of what is going on; they haven't made a conscious effort to learn each other's language, and the common language of words, gestures and facial expressions they come to "speak" just seems to grow all by itself. Then, too, adults and children are generally more concerned with the outcome of particular messages than they are with the nature of the messages themselves. Here's a typical example:

A four-year-old boy was clearly frightened. The X-ray table was hard and cold to lie on, and the huge X-ray machine itself hung above his small body as though ready to crush him. The technician prepared to fasten the strap that would hold him down.

"I can do that," the boy's mother said. "It's okay, honey. We need you to hold real still when they take the picture, and the strap is just to help you not to move."

"Is it going to hurt?" the boy asked, not for the first time.

"No, hon. It won't hurt at all. Nothing will even touch you. It's just like a camera taking your picture. Having your picture taken doesn't hurt, does it?"

The boy shook his head. "How long is it going to take?" he asked.

"Just a couple of seconds," his mother answered. "You'll hear the camera buzz."

"You going to stay here with me?"

His mother stroked the side of his head. "I'll be right by the door," she said. "You'll be able to hear my voice."

"Ready?" the technician asked.

"Ready?" the mother asked. The boy hesitated for a moment. Then he braced himself and nodded.

"I'm right here, hon," his mother said from the doorway.

"Deep breath..." said the technician. "Hold it..." There was a buzz and it was over. The boy's mother gave him a kiss and undid the strap. "I'm proud of you," she said. The boy sat up and gave his mother a hug. "It didn't hurt at all! All it did was buzz!"

That's a simple scene, and it—or another like it—may be familiar to many parents. But when you look at it closely and think about it carefully, these kinds of scenes are examples of the remarkably complex communications that children and their caregivers develop very early in their lives together.

It's hard to say just what the very first communication between a parent and child might be, because so much is happening at once, right from the beginning. For a mother and a just-born infant, there's certainly face-to-face communication and eye contact as the baby's vision comes into focus. Many infants seem to come into this world with a wail, so there's likely to be immediate voice-to-ear contact as well. Most mothers will respond to their baby's cries with soothing sounds of some kind, so this voice-to-ear communication takes place both ways. While all this is going on, mothers and babies are getting messages from each other through smell, too.

And of course there's touching—the kind that comes from being held, stroked, patted, nursed, washed, dried, and changed. All these touchings feel slightly different from one another, just as the same face can have different facial expressions, or the same voice can take on different inflexions, or the same body can give off different smells.

Words come along relatively late in the communications game, and useful though they are, a great deal of their meaning comes from all the months of more "primitive" forms of communication that have gone before. A word lying on a page has meaning, but that meaning may change somewhat when the word is spoken—even by an unfamiliar voice. If that voice happens to be a familiar one, the meaning may change again. There will be a difference depending on whether or not you can see the familiar speaker's facial expressions, and it will make a big difference whether the speaker is calling to you across a room or holding you close and whispering in your ear.

Somehow, almost miraculously, young children and their caregivers sort out all these nuances until, after only three years, they are capable of sending and receiving complicated and subtle and fragile messages —and weighty ones, too, such as the trust that that mother was able to convey to her son on the X-ray table.

I don't believe there's any such thing as a meaningless communication between caregiver and child, not from the very first touch or coo. Each, no matter how seemingly insignificant, adds to the stored experience of all messages that have gone before. All this stored experience affects how each new communication is understood.

I'm sure that boy had already repeatedly experienced his mother's truthfulness, because he was able to believe what she was saying. Now, after the X-ray, they would find it even easier to trust one another the next time something difficult came their way.

A great deal of what parents communicate to their children is information about how the world works. Some of that information is hard to give because it's hard to put in words a young child can understand. Other topics, though, pose a different kind of communications problem. Some are likely to be so emotionally charged *for adults* that parents find themselves tongue-tied and often would rather not talk about them at all. Two such topics are death and sex. Being the way it is, however, the world has a way of raising these issues without warning. Then come the questions.

A piece of advice that I've found helpful is this: Find the simplest truthful answers.

When the family cat was run over, one mother counted herself fortunate that her three-year-old son was away visiting relatives. Upon his return he naturally wanted to know where the cat was. "Tabby just wandered away and didn't come back," that mother chose to say, protecting, as she thought, both her feelings and her son's. Instead, the boy began showing signs of increased anxiety about being separated from the people he loved and about situations in which he thought *he* might get lost. Perhaps he feared that if his beloved Tabby could just wander away from him, so could his caregivers. Worse still, he might wander away without meaning to because certainly Tabby hadn't meant to. After all, she loved him.

In another family, the parents chose to tell their son that "God took Tabby to Heaven." To their surprise, he persisted in repeating his question, "Where's Tabby?" again and again as the days went by. They kept giving him the same answer until finally he came up with a different question that made his insistent curiosity clearer. "What does God want with a dead cat?" he asked. What he really wanted to know was what had happened to Tabby's body.

The simplest truth is that all living things die, and in the long run it's not helpful to pretend with children that this is not so. However we choose to phrase it, something like, "Tabby's dead, honey, she was hit by a car, and we buried her body in the garden," is probably as close to the simple truth as we can get. If that answer leads to other questions about the facts of death and what happens when animals or people die, then we can go on trying to find the simplest truthful answers. The chances are, though, especially with very young children, that these further questions will come only little by little, over a long period of time.

I've come to feel that the difficulties adults have in talking with young children about death lie not in the fact that death is too difficult for young children to understand, or that it might produce strong feelings from which children need to be protected, but rather that those of us who find such talk difficult still have the need to protect ourselves from our own feelings—feelings with which we may never have come to terms.

Parents often write us of stories from their own experience that bring sharp focus to the concerns we care about. Here is one such example:

> I was sheltered from death when I was little. I never wanted to go to funerals—out of fear, I guess. I had loving folks who let me stay away. I was twenty-two and married when my father-in-law died. I was scared brainless at the funeral and had to sleep with a light on for three months until my husband nearly went crazy. All because of my not having come to understand about death when I was little.
>
> My father was the closest person to me all of my life. He had cancer and died two years ago. I was thirty-two. When that day came, I stood strong and tall for the first time and understood real true death—the stillness, the coldness of the body, the feelings of loss. My son was almost two and named for my father, but my father made me promise not to bring him to the funeral. I broke that promise. Why? Because he loved "Pop-Pop," and I didn't want him to be as sheltered and scared for years and years as I had been. At the funeral, my son pointed to the casket and said, "Pop-Pop." He knew in his way, I guess.
>
> He has asked me many questions. I find it hard at times to answer. I choke down the lump and answer frank and true. My son is almost four now. At Christmas he asked, "Where's a present for 'Pop-Pop'?" I said, "We'll bring it to his grave, okay?" He made clay ornaments, which he took there.
>
> He wants to go to the grave with me when I go and is mad if I don't bring him. He waves to Pop-Pop when he leaves. Many times he has asked, "Is Pop-Pop coming back?" I say, "No, Pop-Pop is dead, honey. But he loved you and would be so proud of you now."
>
> Death is hard to deal with, and I wish I could have had it dealt with differently in my childhood. I am growing by my own experience with my son.

Though that letter is about a mother's and her son's experiences with death, it says so much else that I believe can be both a help and a comfort to us all. It's true that we take a great deal of our own upbringing into our adult lives and our lives as parents, but it's true, too, that we can change some of the things that we would like to change. It can be hard, but it can be done. All of us, when we were little and exploring the many chambers of our feelings, locked certain doors to places we found it scary to go. To enjoy the fullness of being human, we may need to unlock some of those doors later on but we don't know how. Sometimes it is our own children who bring us the keys.

Sex, on the other hand, may be less painful to talk about than death yet no easier. A mother recently wrote to tell us that her three-year-old had asked when their cat was going to have kittens. "She's never going to have kittens," the mother truthfully replied, knowing that the cat had been spayed. But her son wanted to know why. "I couldn't imagine what to tell a young child about spaying a cat," that mother said, "so I changed the subject." All the same, she knew that changing the subject hadn't changed her little boy's curiosity. What she may not have considered is that while her son's curiosity about kittens might not have changed, his feelings about curiosity itself could have. If you ask about things and your parents won't give you answers, you may start wondering, Is it all right to ask in the first place?

What she might have said was something like, "When Tabby was small, we asked the vet to give her a little operation so that she couldn't have kittens. Mother cats can have so many babies that there aren't enough homes for them, so sometimes it's better for them not to have babies at all." That, it seems to me, is at least close to the simple truth.

Any question that bears on sexuality can make us unsure and uncomfortable about what to reply. Adults' inventiveness under fire can be astounding, as the following explanations that have accompanied the sight of two mating dogs can reveal. "They're just scratching each other's backs," is one explanation of the scene that I've heard. And I've been told of another quick-thinking grown-up who told a child, "The dog in front is sick, and her friend is pushing her to the hospital." That's inventiveness, to be sure, but is it helpful? Probably not. "That's the way dogs make puppies," might be quite enough for the moment. It could well be some time before a child feels the need to ask more, and more time still before a child feels the need to know how mothers and fathers make babies.

One mother, while driving her preschooler home one day, was asked, "Mommy, where did I come from?" "I almost drove off the road," that mother said. "I knew the time had come, and I realized my son needed an answer, but I had no idea where to begin."

Sooner or later, in almost all families, the question of where babies come from does turn out to be a real one. When a child first asks, the chances are that all he or she needs is a very simple answer. A father, for instance, might reply, "You grew inside your mommy." It can also be a good idea to find out what answers our children have already imagined for themselves by asking, "Where do you think you came from?" Gently bringing their fantasies more in line with reality may be all we need to do . . . for a while. As they become comfortable with whatever new information we've given them, they'll let us know they're ready for more by asking again.

Long before children wonder about the mysteries of reproduction, they naturally want to know why boys and girls are made differently and what those different parts are called. For most families, that's likely to be where "sex education" begins. That time may be the most important time of all, because the way we respond to our children then can set the tone for all our later conversations about sexuality. Our earliest responses may even determine whether or not there are further conversations about sex. As we grapple with these first questions and answers, it may be helpful to remember something that has nothing to do with sexuality: Children's curiosity always needs to be encouraged and supported. More important than what we say is letting our children know that we welcome their asking us about anything they don't understand.

Families tend to find their own names for the parts and functions of the human body, names they find comfortable to use. Some like to use the "proper" names for body parts right from the beginning, while others prefer using simpler, childlike words they may have used when they, themselves, were little. Many children, when their mothers are pregnant, will say that their mommy has a baby in her tummy. Though not strictly accurate, "tummy," for a small child, probably means anywhere inside that general area of the body . . . and that may be all a child is ready to understand at an early age. One three-year-old, though, surprised us by announcing: "My mommy has a baby in her u-ter-us." Her parents clearly did believe in accuracy from the start, but I doubt that little girl had any more "accurate" sense of just where the baby was!

The mother who was driving her son home from preschool, however, hadn't thought much about these things. Her story continues: "I bravely began answering his question the way I remembered my mother beginning with me. 'Well, honey, when a man and a woman love each other very much . . .' But three or four minutes into the explanation, I realized I wasn't doing very well. I was getting tongue-tied about what to call things. What's more, I was way over my head and, I felt sure, way over my four-year-old's. 'Does what I'm saying make any sense to you?' I asked rather lamely. My little boy shook his head. 'Uh-uh,' he said. 'What I mean is Timmy came from Boston and Ellen came from Pittsburgh. Where did I come from?'"

Children's ability to understand their bodies and their world develops slowly. As their curiosity prompts them to ask questions, the best answers we can give are ones that meet their needs at the time. The awareness of sexuality, too, grows only little by little, and providing simple information that same way, from the beginning, can be one of the best ways to keep sex mentionable and manageable, and a healthy part of the continuing trusting relationship that fortunate children find with their parents all life long.

I don't believe it's helpful to pretend that such things as death and sex don't exist, or to make it seem that such things just aren't to be talked about, or, on the other hand, to jump the gun and tell our children much more than they're ready to understand or even want to know. No matter what our children ask us, we can always say, "I'm not quite sure how to explain that right now, honey, but we'll talk about it later."

"My mommy has a baby in her u—ter—us."

That's a promise that needs to be kept, but as a response to questions about touchy subjects, it's often the simplest truth of all.

Fortunately, not all common life events and common human feelings assume the emotional proportions of sex and death! Even the more ordinary occurrences, though, can test adults' and children's capacities to get through to one another with needed knowledge, reassurance, or comfort. Take moving, for example.

"I know it will be all right once we settle in," said the woman in the next seat on the airplane, "but I dread the next couple of weeks. All the confusion and the goodbyes. And Alan doesn't want to leave at all, do you, Alan?"

She looked down at her four-year-old, who was curled up against her. He was staring at the back of the seat in front of him and shook his head with determination.

Another family on the move. This mother and son had just been to visit their new home in the Southwest. The father was already working there, living in a temporary apartment. He'd be back to help with the final drive from Maryland, but before this family would be reunited, there was going to be plenty of stress.

Parents often worry about how their young children are going to weather a move like this. From some experiences I've heard come these ideas that could help make the experience a positive one—difficult as it may seem at the time.

One important suggestion is to acknowledge the feelings of loss that everyone is likely to feel. It's rare for a family to move without suffering at least some pangs over leaving people and places that have grown familiar. For many families, these feelings are very deep and very painful.

The more we can talk about them, though, the more we're likely to be able to manage them. It can be comforting for children to hear that their favorite grown-ups feel sad, too, and at times even angry, about having to leave friends. They need to know there's nothing wrong with having feelings like that. Parents are often surprised to find how readily their young children offer them comfort at times of honest talk. Children need to feel needed just as much as the rest of us do!

Many parents have discovered the importance of play. For instance, two boxes can represent the two houses, old and new, and anything like a shoe box can become a moving truck. These are simple props, but they can let a child practice moving little toys from one place to another. They can help a child understand that what goes into the truck at one place will come out again at another. The place, of course, is different, but many of the old familiar furnishings will be the same.

(Children sometimes become upset, though, when the movers don't take the old stove and refrigerator. These appliances are so closely associated in children's minds with nurturance, love, and care that they may need reassurance that there will be new ones with new good food in the new house.)

A friend of mine remembers moving across the country with his two small sons, and how important it was for each son to have his own small suitcase that never left his side. In the suitcases were things of the boys' own choosing—a bottle, a teddy bear, toy trucks, a little pillow, a favorite T-shirt. The older boy, who was five, always wanted some "emergency rations" in his suitcase: a sandwich, an apple, and a granola bar. "No sooner had he finished one set of rations," that father recalls, "than he insisted on having a new batch in his suitcase ready for another time. And he never let that suitcase out of his sight!"

Alan's mother mentioned the value she had found in taking time out from the constant sorting and packing. "I let it become more than full-time at the beginning," she explained, "and then I realized that every couple of days both Alan and I needed two or three hours together, by ourselves, away from all the mess. It didn't seem to matter what it was we did, whether it was going to a movie or taking a picnic to the park. I found that giving him these times of undivided attention stopped my mind spinning for a while. And Alan generally calmed down, too. He'd be less clinging and whiny—more like his old self. I think these times helped him feel reassured that he hadn't been forgotten and wasn't going to get lost in the rush."

Who knows what fantasies Alan may have been having about that move to a new home—about who and what was going to go and who and what wasn't . . . and who would still be with whom when it was all over? I wonder whether his mother had been through moves of her own when she was young, and what lingering feelings she had about those experiences. It's the unknown answers to questions such as these that can turn even seemingly simple communications between adults and children into such conundrums.

A mother told us about a time she and her little boy were watching television. The program was a children's series they often watched. That particular episode included a visit from a child in a wheelchair. Jason became upset.

Later, they were walking in the neighborhood and passed someone in a wheelchair. Jason turned away and burst out crying. "Please, Mommy," he sobbed, "don't let anything like that happen to me!" Though his mother tried to reassure him—then and on other occasions —Jason remains afraid.

Being a concerned parent, his mother has tried to talk to him from time to time about handicaps. She's explained that there's nothing to be afraid of, and that often people with handicaps are brave people we can admire. Although Jason seems to understand, he just shakes his head and says, "Mommy, I could never have that kind of courage. I'd rather die!"

His mother considered two things to help Jason overcome his fear. One was to rent movies that have characters with handicaps (the family has a VCR). She feared, though, that she might increase his anxiety. Another was to encourage Jason to play out his feelings. "But how," she wonders, "do you encourage a child to 'act out' handicaps?"

Moreover, Jason's mother had strong feelings of her own about that kind of pretend. "I grew up in a superstitious family," she explained, "and although I know it's not true, I still have the feeling that if you pretend to be unfortunate, you will soon become that way as a punishment."

I'm always heartened when I hear of families who talk about their feelings—among themselves and with outsiders they believe might be helpful. Whether we're old or young, childhood feelings come back again and again . . . and Jason and his mother are working on at least three important ones.

The first is their feelings about individual differences. Our attitudes toward the world's diversity of people take shape when we're very young. I believe Jason's mother is wise not to confront him with more examples of handicaps right now. She might find it helpful to read books and play games with him that suggest the endless ways that things, animals, and people are different—that suggest diversity is part of what makes this world a rich and interesting place in which to be. In time, Jason may be able to realize that each of us is like and unlike everyone else, has limitations and abilities, has a wholeness of our own, and has value as a unique human being.

The second thing that Jason and his mother are working on is their feelings about punishment. Many children believe that people with disabilities have been punished for something they did—that if you're blind, you saw something you shouldn't have looked at, or if you're deaf, you listened to something you shouldn't have heard. When children believe this, they may be seriously afraid that something similar could happen to them. If these feelings are not understood and resolved, they can stay with us.

And the third area for work is Jason's and his mother's feelings about pretending. At different ages, we'll pretend about things in different ways, but at any age we need to feel secure in the knowledge that pretend is only pretend. Our pretending can't make anything real happen.

At the foundation of healthy communications is truth. Speaking the truth, though, is not always easy to do, nor is it always easy to know just where truth lies. Come to think of it, lies are no simple matter either.

There's little chance we can remember our first lie, but most likely we told it for self-protection. Before that time, we'd probably been caught crayoning on walls, or been nabbed in the act of knocking a dish off a table, and so we knew something about "crime" and "punishment." But then there would have come a moment when no one was around to witness our heedlessly committed deeds . . . so who was to know who did them—unless we told the truth? So we tried a lie.

"For as long as I can remember, I was truthful with my parents," a friend recalls, "but I know I came to truthfulness through fear. It was a big thing in my family to 'fess up and take your medicine like a man. Not doing so meant the 'medicine' would be far worse. I saw my older brother get in lots of trouble for trying to lie his way out of things. It seldom worked for him, so I chose the lesser of two evils and told the truth."

Afraid to tell the truth . . . but more afraid not to. What a dilemma for a child! It also seems like an improbable way for a child to grow into an appreciation of truth as a cornerstone of human communications.

Another friend remembered her early life differently and offered another dimension on lying. "I often lied to my parents when I was little, and I still do now," she admitted. "It's not that I've been doing anything awful that I'm ashamed of. It's just that from early on in my life I felt I was very different from my parents and that they wouldn't understand some of the things I did, the books I was reading, and even the friends I wanted to spend time with. Lying has come to seem the simplest way to avoid confrontations and protect my parents' feelings—and mine."

As I thought about that, I realized the close relationship between *truth* and *trust*. If that friend had been able to trust her parents to love her for the unique person she was, if she had felt that being herself would bring her parents joy rather than anxiety or disapproval, how differently their lives might have turned out based on truth! As for my other friend who came to truth through fear: If he had been able to trust that his parents' feelings and responses would have stayed within the boundaries of love, if he and his parents had trusted one another enough to talk about those feelings and responses, then his parents' "discipline" might have come to seem less like punishment and more like the keeping of loving limits. Truth would have looked different.

Crayoning on the wall, or breaking a dish or a rule, is bound to make someone angry. When we can talk about that anger and express it in appropriate ways, it doesn't have to be such a threatening thing. So long as children can feel that the love of their loved ones is secure, they can begin to understand how it is that truth *can* set all of us free—free from, among other things, fear and deceit.

Telling the truth and telling lies, of course, flows both ways in a family. As much as our early caregivers insisted on our telling the truth, we probably came to a time when we had to face the fact that our parents sometimes lied to us. We learned who the Tooth Fairy really was, and that Santa Claus didn't come sliding down the chimney. Our dog didn't run away after all; she was run over. Uncle Bill didn't go away on a long trip; he and Aunt Mary got divorced. Fortunate parents have found what freedom truth can bring them when they can trust their children enough to talk honestly with them about important and difficult things.

Just what is a "lie," anyway? Is it in some degree different from an untruth, a falsehood, or a fib? How about a "white" lie or a "half-truth"? (There's a even a "tarradiddle"—a *truly* insignificant untruth.) And do we have to hurt someone's feelings by telling the truth when we know that's exactly what the truth will do?

As children meet truth in all its complexity, they need to know our feelings about these things—our *honest* feelings, even if that means telling them we wonder about the answers as well. As with so much in life, it's what children first are given that they grow up most able to give, and if we've done our best to trust our children with truthful communications from the beginning, it's likely that we'll find them doing their best to trust us with the truth, too.

Ready? Get Set . . . Grow!

We're always interested in the letters we get from parents telling us about how their firstborn children adapted to the arrival of a baby brother or sister. That's not only because it's a really big event in a young child's life, an event that challenges any child's capacity for growth, but it's usually also an event that provides a kind of "stress test" of the communications systems parents and an "only child" have worked out together. When a new baby comes, many firstborns aren't old enough to talk about their feelings yet—at least not with the verbal clarity that an older child might. What they do say in their own ways, though, gives us wonderful examples of how even very young children can use the words and thoughts and understandings about their world that they have to try to let us know what's on their minds. Of course, the arrival of a second child provides abundant opportunity for *mis*understandings, too.

I feel quite sure that virtually all children have times of uncertainty and jealousy about the newcomer in the family. Almost every child must wonder now and then whether a mother can have only one baby, and if so, whether there's going to have to be another mother somewhere to take over. There's no mistaking that kind of wondering when a child says, "When the baby comes, who's going to be its mother?" Or, "Who's going to be my mother when the baby comes?"

It can be very scary for a child to think about losing his or her mother or his or her place in the family. Young children do tend to take what we say very literally. When they hear a "new" baby is coming, they may well wonder whether the "old" one will be sent away—like an old pair of shoes.

Two mothers wrote recently about their children's reactions to a new baby. One firstborn was a girl, the other one a boy. Both mothers prepared their children for the events as well as they knew how, talking openly about pregnancy and the need to be in the hospital for a few days. The children were even prepared for what the hospital would be like when they visited. In one family, the four-year-old daughter actually visited the hospital before her mother's confinement, and the mother in the other family took pictures of the room where her three-year-old son would be coming to visit. The little girl was going to have to share a room with the baby when it came home, and her parents let her help decide how the room that had been hers alone should now be rearranged.

"All the same," wrote the little girl's mother, "nothing prepared Martha or me for life at home with the new baby. Martha, always a loving, bright, talkative child, turned overnight into a sullen, volatile one. She resented the baby, and when he cried, she requested we 'put him in a drawer.' I wasn't ready for my own conflicting feelings, either. On the one hand, I felt such great love and devotion to our new baby, and on the other, I felt I had destroyed a beautiful relationship with my daughter."

As for the boy, Toby, the day after his baby brother came home, he made a frowning face out of clay and said, "This guy's sad." "Why is he sad?" his mother asked. "He's sad because he doesn't like the baby," Toby replied. To which his mother said, "Tell him that's okay. Big brothers feel like that sometimes." So Toby held the frowning clay face right up to his mouth and quietly said, "That's okay. Big brothers feel like that sometimes."

When the two-week-old baby went along on the ride to Toby's nursery school, his mother warned Toby that some of the children in nursery school might act very interested in the new baby. "Great!" Toby replied. "Maybe one of them will take him home!"

Well, as those mothers found out, caring talk and preparation do pay off, even though they can't eliminate all the rough spots. "In time things came around," Martha's mother told us. "My Martha came back to me and has become my right hand in caring for the baby. I would never have dreamed it could have turned out so well." A year after the birth of his baby brother, Toby and the other children in nursery school were asked to tell the teacher what made them happiest. Toby: "When my brother plays with me." The next question was what made them saddest. Toby: "When my baby brother cries." Adds Toby's mother, "Most of the time we have a loving older brother who has never needed to display his anger physically. I feel pretty good about the preparation we did and also about our willingness to allow Toby's angry feelings to emerge when they had to. I was so proud of the way he could talk and play about those feelings."

There's lots to be proud of in those two families. Parents, certainly, can feel proud of themselves when they find ways to allow their children natural feelings and care enough to listen and talk as those two mothers did. I hope that one day they will feel proud all over again as they watch their daughter and son talking with and listening to children of the next generation.

If there's any consistent lesson that anecdotes from parents seem to teach, it's how unforeseeable are the outcomes, and the routes to those outcomes, as we go about raising our children. Martha had to "act out" before she could "come 'round." Toby had to feel the anger and sadness of displacement before he could feel the security and love inherent in his new place in his family.

Naturally, all the stress and strain doesn't come between the parents and the children. There can be plenty between the children themselves.

"It hasn't worked out right at all," a mother complained. "I mean, one of the main reasons we had a second child was so that Mark would have someone to play with and be close to while growing up. Now they're seven and four. Little Jimmy's old enough to play, but Mark says he hates playing with him because he won't follow the rules—no matter what they're playing. So he goes off playing with friends his own age, and, of course, he never wants Jimmy along. I really feel very sad about it, sad for Jimmy, and I wonder if we did the right thing after all."

When I read that mother's lament, I thought, "Yes, that's the way it so often is!" Then I thought, "But why does it have to be so?" The child in me replied, "Because!"

Mark doesn't understand Jimmy—who he is, what he's about. Only three years between them, but Mark has forgotten what it was like to be four. Perhaps that's the way early memory works. Perhaps it doesn't seem important to Mark to remember. Perhaps what's important to him is what it's like to be seven . . . and wishing and dreaming about being ten.

Part of being seven is the excitement of learning and mastering new things—difficult and complicated and mysterious things like secret codes, and why polar bears don't eat penguins, and, yes, rules to games. Knowing the rules, like knowing a magic spell, can bring the power to control what happens and what other people do . . . so long as people will follow your rules. When they won't, your power is gone.

Jimmy, for his part, hasn't the slightest idea what his brother is all about. Oh, Jimmy's excited about learning and mastering, too. He's mastered how to walk, to run, to climb. He may still be working on how to stay dry and clean all the time; or trying hard to understand that when people you love leave, they haven't left you forever; or that something like a toy can come to pieces, but the parts of your own body stay together. For him, a checkerboard is a place of shapes he's learned and colors he knows, a place full of paths of his own making. It's an arena for stories he can make up—about cars that zoom here and there on the way to "wherever," bumping into one another if he feels like making them crash . . . or stories of little checker-people who go away from one another for a while . . . and then come back.

Rules? What's all this stuff Mark's coming up with about "You have to do it this way or that"? Jimmy's learned he can do it whichever way he feels like doing it, and that's power!

Meanwhile, Mark and Jimmy's mother feels powerless and unhappy because her hopes and expectations for her children aren't working out the way she wanted. Her feelings made me think of seeing a father playing with his new daughter one day when she was only a few months old. He wanted her to hold on to his finger, really hold on, and when she did, he'd pull and say, "Turn over . . . come on, turn over. . . ." When she wouldn't because she couldn't, he looked disappointed. He didn't understand his baby was busy trying to learn other things: that her hand wasn't just something that floated around out there, that she could make it stop sometimes and sometimes even make those things that wiggled on the end open and shut. What, she must have wondered in her own way, is all this stuff about "turn over"?

As children develop, in their own ways as individuals and as sons and daughters, and as brothers or sisters or playmates, there's a dance going on. To borrow a phrase from the author Anthony Powell, it's a "dance to the music of time." That dance has its own rhythms. The steps to that dance can be made more comfortable and easier to learn, but they can't be hurried. Mark's mother can help this older son of hers learn to be understanding and patient, learn that it's safe to give up some of his power some of the time, and learn that there are new kinds of power in being a caring teacher. Together, they can help younger son Jimmy learn little by little (when he's ready) what rules are and that games' rules can be fun—win or lose. They can all learn the dance from one another. What none of them can do is speed up the music.

In their "dance" with their children, parents are sometimes surprised, and even dismayed, to find their children insisting on dancing *backward* for a while.

We first heard from the Finley family about three years ago when Mrs. Finley wrote to tell us about the relationship between her two sons. John, she told us, was five and a half, and her youngest, Keith, two and a half. The story was one that will be familiar to many parents.

"Ever since Keith was born," Mrs. Finley wrote, "there has been nothing but jealousy, competition, and fighting between the two of them. . . . I've tried everything I possibly could to stop this jealousy, but nothing seems to help."

What's more, Mrs. Finley was expecting another baby, and she was worried about what that child's birth would mean to her two sons. Specifically, she said, "I wonder if I'm going to go through the same problems with Keith as I did with John."

Recently we had a chance to catch up with the Finleys. John was now seven, Keith four, and little Erick nine months old. "The love John has for Erick is overwhelming," Mrs. Finley told us. "He constantly protects him like a mother hen." John, it seemed, had come to feel that his place in his family was secure and that he could welcome the newcomer, perhaps even with pride at being the firstborn and eldest.

And Keith? It seems that everything started out fine, with Keith acting "very lovable" toward his new brother. At the time of writing, though, the situation had changed. "Keith seems very jealous of the baby," Mrs. Finley wrote. "He will do things to Erick and not share any toys with him. He is also forgetting his toilet training—every day, sometimes twice a day, and yesterday he did it for the first time in school. . . ."

Keith seemed to have more on his mind than he could comfortably handle! Not only did he have a new baby in the house, but he also had just started preschool. In addition, Mrs. Finley mentioned that the family had gone through a major move shortly after Erick had been born. Now that adds up to a lot of separations and uncertainties for anyone, and Keith seemed to be saying that he just wasn't quite ready to deal with it all, so he thought he'd go back to being a baby for a while—toilet training included.

One measure of how deep and essential is a young child's need for a consistent, loved, and loving caregiver is the frequency with which separation from such a caregiver figures in children's developmental upsets and bouts of "dancing backwards."

When Bobby was almost six, his mom and dad planned to go off on a week's cruise. Bobby knew and liked the person who was going to be staying with him and his two-year-old brother, but as the day of his parents' departure neared, he became anxious and wanted to know why he couldn't go, too.

"What if the boat driver can't find his way back?" was one of the many questions he asked.

His parents tried to reassure him, but as his worry mounted, he began sucking on his baby brother's pacifier—a source of comfort he hadn't used since he was a toddler. His mom and dad ignored this new habit, figuring he would give up the pacifier once they returned.

According to the boys' babysitter, they all had a good time while the parents were away—a good "vacation," she called it. Even after his parents returned, however, Bobby went on sucking the pacifier. They tried to distract him, to bargain with him, and they even scolded him. When nothing had any effect, they talked to Bobby's pediatrician. "Don't worry about it," was that doctor's advice, and he went on to explain that being a sensitive child, Bobby had probably found it diffi-cult to cope with his parents' absence. It could, he said, take three to six months for him to stop his sucking. But even eight months after he'd begun, Bobby was still at it, taking the pacifier to bed with him. That's when we heard from his mother.

It sounded to us as if Bobby was using one of children's most natural and healthiest ways to cope with any kind of stress: to take a step or two backward in their development for a while. How long this retreat lasts depends on a child's inner feelings and the reactions of his closest care-givers. What form it takes varies, too. It might be turning back to baby talk, becoming whiny and clingy, giving up the ability to dress or bathe alone, and, frequently, losing control again of bowel and bladder. Bobby may have found it particularly hard to have his parents go away at a time when he may still have been wrestling with the idea that he'd like to be a baby again and get that special care and attention that babies get.

There's an alternative, though, to the remedies Bobby's parents tried—distraction, bargaining, and scolding. This other choice is ac-cepting the step backward and treating it as normal, which it is. Scolding, certainly, is likely to suggest to a child that what he or she is doing is not normal, that it's wrong and even "bad." Having your loved ones tell you that could be an added source of stress and could make a child cling still more fiercely to habits from some earlier time.

Moving forward through the early stages of development for either a first or second time takes both a push and a pull. The push comes from inside feelings of readiness and confidence. It's a push from within to go on growing. The pull, on the other hand, comes from the pleasure a child's caregivers show at signs of growth, and it tugs on every small child's desire to please the people he or she loves.

Finding the right words to talk to a child about this push and pull can be difficult, and it's important for each family to find its own way. In Bobby's case, though, I can imagine his parents are trying many ways, as time goes by, to tell him, "I know you feel like sucking a lot right now. That's something you used to do when you were little. But you know something? I'll be glad when you feel you don't need your pacifier anymore!"

It can be very worrying for parents to see their children losing ground like that, seeming to go backward in their patterns of growth. It may be reassuring to know that most people who work with young children believe that these times of "regression" are often necessary for growth—that under stress, children sometimes need to let go of the struggles of their actual age and go back to an earlier time to gather their strength and inner resources. Many parents have noted that these "backward" times are followed by a sudden surge of forward growth that takes their children even beyond where they were to begin with.

We adults have times like that, too, times when we don't feel up to doing the everyday things that we can do, times when we need a little "extra looking after" until we feel strong enough to go on coping for ourselves and growing beyond where we've been. Thinking about how we want to be treated at times of our own regression can give us a clue about how we might best treat our children when they need to feel little again. I don't think we want to be scolded or made to feel guilty or "bad." I think we want the people we love to understand, to let us know that it's all right to let down our guard now and then, and to lend us a bit of their strength until we feel strong enough to go on once more on our own.

Children need that sense of inner readiness before they can master many common childhood tasks. We heard the other day of a boy who was really afraid of having his hair washed. He lived with his grandparents, and it was his grandmother who told us: "From the time he was a baby, Mickey has always been laid down to have his hair washed. This winter, before he was four, I said he had to learn to stand up and put his head in the sink. He gets hysterical, no matter how we explain it."

We heard also about a little girl, Julia, who is two. Her mother has decided that it's time her daughter was potty-trained. A couple of times a day she's been putting her daughter on a special seat that fits on the big toilet and hoping for the best. Each time, though, Julia has become scared, even though her mother stayed right with her, and the experiment has ended with a frustrated mother and a tearful child. "Now I'm trying a potty-chair on the floor," her mother says, "but Julia just says 'no' and won't go near it."

Julie's mother, just like Mickey's grandmother, is stumped. It may seem to these caregivers that if only Mickey and Julia would just do what they're being asked to do, they'd find out how easy it is and that would be that. Why can't they?

When you're little, little things can seem scary. Take Mickey's anxiousness about hairwashing. Many children share Mickey's feelings, and that's because when you're just beginning to feel how your body works, anything that interferes with its workings can be frightening. Having water go into your mouth or up your nose so that you can't breathe would be hard for any of us, and most likely we've long since forgotten how long it took us to feel comfortable holding our breath or to learn to breathe through our mouths without breathing through our noses. Having water go in our eyes so that we can't see, even if there isn't soap that stings, can make us feel panicky, too . . . and it probably wasn't easy for us to learn to hold our eyes tight shut until someone told us it was all right to open them again. It all seems simple to us now, but that's because we've grown.

As for Julia, that seat on the toilet may have seemed awfully high, as well as awfully hard and cold, especially after being used to soft, warm diapers. An on-the-floor potty-chair can be hard and cold, too. But more than that, learning to let go of parts of yourself and have them swirled away in a rush of water is something that many children find difficult to deal with. If I let part of me go, they may wonder, can all of me go, too? That may seem strange to us adults, but it can be a very real worry at two!

There are times when explanations, no matter how reasonable, just don't seem convincing, particularly when you're only three or so. Even grown-ups, though, can probably think of something that would be scary to do—climbing a precipitous mountain, for instance, or parachuting out of an airplane. It might be something more ordinary, too, such as going for an interview or having an operation. For most of us who have faced situations like these, explanations ahead of time probably weren't enough to reassure us fully, but if someone we trusted gave us the explanation, at least we knew what to expect. Knowing that, we'd have a chance to think about what was really going to happen and, perhaps even more important, a chance to let go of some of our scary fantasies about what we imagined *might* be going to happen. Explanations can certainly help, even if they can't do the whole job.

We may have to rehearse the event in our minds many, many times before our feelings settle down into readiness to do what we have to do. It may be most helpful of all if we're given the chance to practice doing it—to pretend about it before we have to do it for real.

There's another part to these puzzles, and that's the unrealistic expectations caregivers may have as they try to help their children grow. It's not just that they may expect too much too soon, like that father who wanted his baby daughter to turn over before she possibly could, but it's also that parents may expect to make decisions that only their children can make. For instance, it's realistic for caregivers to expect to decide the time is right to suggest doing something, or to encourage doing something, but it's probably unrealistic to expect to decide that the day has come for a child actually to do it. That's a decision for each child to make in his or her own good time.

We can talk with our children about what we'd like them to do. We can find books to read together about those tasks and about the feelings that go along with trying to master them. Perhaps most important of all, we can be supportive of our children's play about those tasks. I wonder, for example, if Mickey and Julia have little toy people and toy sinks and toilets to play with. Does Mickey have a washable doll to play with in the tub or at the sink? Does Julia have a stuffed animal she can put on and take off the potty-chair? That's not to say we should structure our children's play for them, but by offering them appropriate toys to play with, we let them know we understand that play is an essential part of their work toward mastery and growth.

Is the time right for doing something new? Books may say so, but we need to remember that many, many "normal" children depart from the so-called norms, and that all children develop the different parts of their minds and bodies on unique schedules. It may be that caregivers can only find ways to ask children about their feelings of inner readiness, and that they'll find fewer "problems" by letting their children give the answer for themselves.

Growing Character

If even experts can't be specific about when a particular child will develop a particular skill, we certainly can't expect to predict when character traits will (or won't) emerge in the children under our care.

Whereas skills can usually be taught, character is more likely to be "caught" from the feelings and actions of the people children love, and children's sensitivity to these acts and emotions is acute.

Some character traits, however, come close to being skills; the line between the two isn't always clear. How much easier life would be for parents if children were born with the ability to think ahead! But they aren't, and in fact as most adults find out, that particular "skill" stays a difficult one to master all through their lives. One reason is that fore-thought takes many different understandings. It's like juggling several balls in the air at once, and, where children are concerned, we need to remember that even the best juggler first had to learn to toss and catch one ball at a time.

Josh, who was four, was zooming his toy truck around the table top. Veering around a sharp bend, the truck caromed off an antique glass vase of flowers and sent it crashing to the floor. His mother ran in from the kitchen and surveyed the broken vase, the scattered flowers, the wet carpet. "Oh, Josh," she sighed with a weariness beyond anger, "now you've broken Grandma's vase. When on earth are you going to learn to watch what you're doing?"

But for Josh to "watch what he's doing" the way his mother would like him to, he's going to need (at the very least) a little more control over his body, better eye-hand coordination, a better understanding of appropriate places for different kinds of play, the awareness of "break-ableness" in objects, and a sense of what breakable objects have partic-ular meaning to his mother.

While her mother and a friend were talking, Sarah, a three-year-old, worked her way right through a box of candied popcorn and was headed for a box of fig bars when her mother saw what was going on. "No, Sarah!" her mother said. "That's enough!" Sarah tried to get a fig bar into her mouth all the same, but her mother snatched it out of her hand. "Listen," she said, "you can have the fig bar if you put it in the empty popcorn box and save it for after your nap." Sarah took the fig bar and thought about it for a moment, and then put it in the box... along with two more.

Sarah's willingness to wait suggests that she'd already learned to jug-gle some important elements involved in thinking ahead. To think ahead, you have to have at least some understanding that there is a real time ahead to think about. It was helpful that her mother mentioned such a time in a way Sarah could understand—after her nap. That kind of future time is so much easier for a child to understand than "later" or even "in a few minutes"—just the way "when you wake up in the morn-ing" is likely to mean a lot more to a child than "tomorrow."

On top of the matter of time, Sarah had grown to know that even if she couldn't see the fig bars in the box, they were still really there. She'd evidently come to trust her mother to make good on her promise to let her eat them when her mother said she would. Sarah may also have done a quick and surprisingly complex analysis of possible futures: The certainty of a fig bar after my nap is better than the probability of no fig bar at all, and if I go along with Mom now, I may even end up with three!

Some lessons are more difficult for children to learn—and equally hard for their parents to teach. A father told us once that the only time he spanked his son was when the boy was two and couldn't seem to learn to keep quiet in the early morning when his father and mother wanted to sleep. "It was the umpteenth time he'd woken us up. He just couldn't seem to understand a simple thing like playing quietly, and finally I lost my temper." A mother remembers getting spanked once when she was little because, despite repeated warnings, she opened the garden gate and went out to make friends with a stray dog.

One of the hardest things for very young children to understand is that their actions have real consequences for others. That's because, for a time, a child's own world seems like the whole world: That's all there is. We can't expect a two-year-old to think ahead beyond the joy of early-morning play to what that play may mean for other people—particularly people you can't even see. (Can you remember thinking that if you shut your eyes you became invisible?) At that stage, the idea of immediate consequences isn't likely to have much meaning, and it may take a long time for a child to think clearly about *possible* consequences—those that might follow, for instance, from letting yourself out a garden gate.

Forethought, of course, is a two-way street. It's as important for parents as it is for children. In the case of Josh, the little boy who broke his grandmother's vase, his mother *could* have had him play within her sight, and she *could* have kept her valuable, breakable possessions beyond his reach. The mother who spanked her daughter for leaving the yard *could* have had a more secure latch on the gate. It's true that sometimes our children's apparent lack of forethought in fact exposes our own, but that's the way it will always be. No one can ever think of all the possible consequences of any particular act—least of all, the act of having children!

We hear from many parents who are worried about another characteristic that seems somewhat akin to forethought, and that's concentration. "How can I help increase my child's attention span?" they may ask. Or, "Why can some children concentrate while others can't? What makes the difference?"

There's no doubt in my mind that learning to look and listen carefully is a really important part of a child's learning to learn. I certainly understand parents' concerns when they don't see their children developing the ability for sustained attention. I've come to believe, though, that almost all children are born with the ability to concentrate. Something seems to happen later on that interrupts the development of that ability. You've probably seen infants "concentrating" with their eyes on people's faces, or on patterns, or on things around them that move slowly—even their own little fists that wave around in front of them. Most of us can remember watching toddlers "concentrate" for minute after minute as they poke a crayon through a hole in a toy again and again, or fill up a little box with odds and ends, dump it out, fill it up, dump it out.... And who hasn't watched an older child lost in reverie, daydreaming?

Yes, daydreaming can be a form of concentration, too! These early forms of concentration may not seem important to us. In fact, we may interrupt them because we'd prefer our children to start concentrating on shapes, or on the names of animals, or even on letters and numbers.

We've forgotten what a lot of time we needed just to figure out how our bodies worked, let alone to begin to understand how all the separate pieces of the world around us fitted together. So often, that's just what babies and toddlers are concentrating on most: the relationship between their bodies and the world. Breasts and bottles go into the mouth, so maybe a crayon should, too. "No," says a parent. "Not in your mouth!" So maybe the crayon should go into something else that looks like a mouth—like a hole in a toy. A child may need a lot of time and concentration to understand that relationship, and it will only be much, much later that a child can come to understand that a crayon "belongs" with a piece of paper.

A friend of mine, whose child was already well along in school, was worried and frustrated because his son didn't seem able to pay attention to any problem long enough to work his way through to the answer. His mind just seemed to skip. That boy did seem interested in how the world worked, though, and so that father bought some simple models of airplanes and cars, and every evening that he could, he spent time with his son in the basement putting them together, following the directions step-by-step, one at a time, until the model was built. The father was surprised to find that his son could concentrate after all—for an hour or two at a time.

Perhaps their evenings together gave that boy the time he'd missed earlier, the time to figure out how his mind and hands went together, how separate pieces of the world went together, how patience and trying could produce results, how some things took time to happen—like glue to dry and models to be built. As time went by, the boy became less interested in models, but his ability to concentrate spread to the other activities in his life. Without realizing it, that father had stopped asking, "Why can't my boy concentrate?" and had asked, instead, "Where can my boy concentrate?" By finding the answer to that question, he had found a missing link in his son's natural development.

I feel sure that something else happened, too, during those hours in the basement: In working together the boy had felt his father's interest, love, and pleasure. We all have a natural desire to produce such feelings in the people we love, and that's another way character gets "taught."

While some character traits seem close cousins to skills, others appear to be far more abstract, harder to define, more puzzling in their origins, less easy than forethought and concentration, for instance, to learn and practice. Take *empathy*. Where might that come from?

In one family where the husband had to spend the weekdays away from home, the wife often felt sad and lonely. Her two young children kept her busy, and, for the most part, she was able to look after them cheerfully. One evening, though, her three-year-old son leaned up against the chair where she was sitting, and asked, "Are you sad, Mom?"

"Yes," she said, realizing her loneliness must have been showing. "I miss your dad when he's away."

"I miss my dad, too," said the boy. "We miss him together."

In another family, the mother was sad because a friend had died in an accident—a friend her four-year-old had never met. When her little girl asked her one day why she was sad, she explained what had happened. Her daughter nodded thoughtfully. "I'll be sad with you," she said.

Children's sensitivity to the moods of their caregivers begins very early. Even babies tend to react differently to the sight of a solemn face or a smiling one. But though children may seem to pick up particularly quickly on moods of anxiety or sadness, they're usually just as alert to moods of joy and excitement. What many parents find remarkable, though, is the extent to which their young children seem both eager and able to share the feelings of the people they love—and the natural way children will often take on the role of the comforter.

Toddlers may become very concerned at a baby's crying, whether or not it's a baby they know. They may want to go over to the baby and pat it, talk to it, make the crying stop. Their reaction may partly be anxiety, but I believe it also shows the beginnings of kindness and demonstrates a tendency almost all children share as they grow: the natural inclination to become the doers, by themselves, of the things that were earlier done for them.

You can see this inclination working in many ways. For instance, there comes a time even in the first year of life when most babies will try to feed the people who have been feeding them. This usually happens long before babies can feed themselves. What they offer their caregivers to eat may not be very appetizing—the nipple on a bottle, or a soggy piece of cookie. Parents certainly don't need to feel obliged to eat what's offered, but it's important that the offer itself be appreciated. It is, after all, an act of giving, and a parent's reaction of disgust may seem to a child to be a reaction to the act rather than to the gift itself.

You can also see the urge to become the doer as children begin finding ways to bring themselves pleasure. They may seek out a chair where they have often been held on a lap and clamber up to sit on it by themselves. They may rock back and forth there, as they have been rocked, or sing to themselves as they have been sung to. Many children will hold their dolls or teddies almost exactly as they, themselves, were held, and most parents at one time or another have overheard a child talking to such toys in the same loving or scolding words that they themselves have used.

The way those two children with sad mothers behaved makes me think that it's not only simple skills that grow out of the early inclination to become the doer. When you combine that natural inclination with a sensitivity to other people's feelings and moods, you may be close to the origins of valuable human attributes such as generosity, altruism, and compassion. Those are big words, but it's my belief that they grow from small acts early in life—the acts of our first caregivers that set the patterns for the kinds of care that we, in our turn, will become capable of giving.

People who are particularly sensitive to the feelings of others run the risk of not being considered strong, and most of us, I believe, admire strength. It's something we tend to respect in others, desire for ourselves, and wish for our children. Sometimes, though, I wonder if we confuse strength with aggression, or even violence. One of the signs of this confusion is the way many people seem to consider strength an appropriate attribute of men, and gentleness a quality that women should possess. That, to me, seems very far from the truth. We all need the capacity for both strength and gentleness. The opposite of strength isn't gentleness but weakness, and the opposite of gentleness isn't strength but violence.

One parent writes: "My four-year-old son has hemophilia complicated by an inhibitor that renders today's treatment ineffective. When he watches television, the boys and men are stereotyped as very aggressive and physical. Our son needs to know that he can be masculine and gentle at the same time." It was this thoughtful letter that started me thinking about gentleness and strength. Not only does that boy need to know that men can be gentle and still be men, but also that he and his family will need strength of many kinds as they cope with his disability. Strength is neither male or female; but it is, quite simply, one of the finest characteristics that any human being can possess.

Just as many people seem to think that there is something especially female about gentleness, so they seem to think that only girls and women should cry. There are just as many who disagree, however, and I'm certainly one who shares the viewpoint expressed by this mother:

"Being the mother of a boy I have always been concerned about the fact that if he cries, people will call him a sissy. I feel that my son has as much right to cry if he is hurt or if one of his toys gets broken, as a girl does. It has always annoyed me that people have such a double standard."

Confronting our feelings and giving them appropriate expression always takes strength, not weakness. It takes strength to acknowledge our anger, and sometimes more strength yet to curb the aggressive urges anger may bring and to channel them into non-violent outlets. It takes strength to face our sadness and to grieve and to let our grief and our anger flow in tears when they need to. It takes strength to talk about our feelings and to reach out for help and comfort when we need it. There is no "masculine" or "feminine" when it comes to anger or sorrow, and certainly no weakness in expressing feelings that are human and common to us all. Yes, it takes strength to cry.

I am heartened by the way double standards are giving way in many arenas where there were stereotypical ideas of what men "should" do and what women "should" do. As I look around these days, I can see that we, as a society, are growing in some really important ways. Not long ago a young child wrote to say: "We watch your show a lot. We watched your show about manholes. You only said men can go in manholes. My sister and I think that women can go in manholes, too."

You bet they can—just as women can be strong and men can be gentle, and both can cry.

The capacity to forgive is another character trait that can run afoul of widespread misinterpretations of strength—interpretations that seem to value the harboring of grudges and the wreaking of revenge.

Forgiveness is a strange thing. It can sometimes be easier to forgive our enemies than it is our friends. It can be hardest of all to forgive people we love. Like all of life's important coping skills, the ability to forgive and the capacity to let go of resentments most likely take root very early in our lives. I believe forgiveness is as important to our emotional well-being as being able to wait for what we want, or to cope with stress.

A father told us of an experience he had with his four-year-old son. Something the boy wanted to happen didn't happen, and in a fit of angry disappointment, he ran off sobbing to his bedroom and slammed

"I guess life isn't fair, is it, Dad?"

WORKING AND GROWING TOGETHER

the door. His father followed to comfort him. "It just isn't fair!" the boy complained through his tears. "It isn't fair!" Then, even before his father could begin finding words of consolation, the boy wiped away his tears with the back of his hand, took in a long, uneven breath, and said, "But then I guess *life* isn't fair, is it, Dad?"

"Now, that's a big philosophical question," that father remarked as he recalled the incident. "I was taken aback to hear it from a four-year-old, and I was somewhat at a loss for what to reply. I think I said that the things that happen to us in life don't always seem fair; that there are hard times as well as easy, fun times; and that's the way life goes for all of us. I remember my wife and myself worrying that our son was turning into a very young cynic. But he's growing up now with a sunny, optimistic disposition, so perhaps our fears were groundless. He might just have been expressing a sort of forgiveness toward life, beginning to accept it the way it is, without harboring a grudge or thinking the world was out to deceive and disappoint him. I really don't know *what* was going on in his mind right then, and naturally he's forgotten the incident altogether."

Forgiving and forgetting are often paired together, but the one certainly doesn't necessarily follow the other. Some injuries, real or imagined, we may never be able to forget, even though we say we've forgiven them. Other injuries we may never even be able to say that we forgive. Those are the ones, it seems to me, most likely to involve people we've loved, and so I'm inclined to look at what our experiences of forgiveness may have been like from the first people who loved *us*.

The first time we required forgiveness, we probably did something we shouldn't have when our closest grown-ups thought we should have known better—and we made someone angry. We were to blame. What did the first brush with blame begin to teach us?

If we were fortunate, we began to learn that "to err is human": Even good people sometimes do bad things. Errors might mean corrections, apologies, repairs, but they didn't mean that we, as a person, were a bad person in the sight of those we loved. The second thing we learned (if we were fortunate) was that having someone we loved get mad at us did not mean that person had stopped loving us; we had their *unconditional* love, and that meant we would have their forgiveness, too.

Not all children are so fortunate. Some hear, again and again, that *they* are bad, not just what they've done. They're told they're "always breaking things," or "always spoiling things," and that's how they come to think of themselves: as spoilers and breakers. They grow with little sense of forgiveness, and they grow fearful of their parents' displeasure and unsure of their parents' love—unsure deep down that they, themselves, are even lovable to begin with.

Sad to say, there are even less fortunate children still, and statistics tell us they are many. These are children born to parents who are unable or unwilling to care for them. Already from the time they are nursing or sucking from a bottle, they can see in their reluctant care-givers' eyes that they are one too many a mouth to feed, one too many a body to look after. Children like that don't have to do anything "bad" to get blamed; they get no forgiveness simply for having been born. For these children, an early sense of love and forgiveness has to come from someone else, and happily it often does—as it does for many children who grow through otherwise unforgiving childhoods.

When it comes to forgiveness, there are fortunate and unfortunate parents, too. The fortunate ones are those who find they have forgiving children. There are times when all parents need their children's for-giveness. We can never meet all our children's hopes and expectations, and so we are bound to disappoint them. We will always make some hasty promises that we can't keep. Many of us will find that our chil-dren have a way of making us feel guilty about our shortcomings, and some of us will find ourselves angry at our children for doing so—and find ourselves behaving as if it were our children who were to blame. All of us, almost without exception, will be judged by our children once they realize we're not the infallible, omnipotent creatures they once thought we were, but are, instead, mere mortals doing the best we can.

Life *isn't* always fair, as that four-year-old was coming to realize, and he, like most children, sooner or later probably came to realize that parents aren't always fair either. There's nothing unnatural about chil-dren feeling resentments of many kinds toward their parents. Coming to terms in our own ways with resentments and disappointments of many kinds is a universal and important part of growing up. There are, after all, lots of dreams we have as we grow that we'll never see come true.

Sometimes we have to give up our dreams because they were unre-alistic and beyond our capabilities. A young friend of mine began danc-ing when she was six and dreamed of being a prima ballerina. She had unusual talent and worked hard at it, with success, for fourteen years. Just recently, she decided to give up dance as a career. It was a tearful and painful decision, but she and her family talked it over and con-cluded that reaching the top ranks wasn't within her grasp. Her dis-apointment and grief were real.

A grown-up friend dreamed of going to medical school when he was young. He worked in his father's small auto repair shop all the time he was growing up, but he knew that one day he was going to be a doctor. That dream never came true. When he was finishing high school, his father had a heart attack, and my friend took over the auto repair business to support the family. That's still what he does today.

"Sure, I'd like to have been a doctor," he says, "but what's a person to do? It was tough to let go of that dream, but I've found a lot of satisfaction in my work, even though I didn't think life would work out this way."

A mother with a disabling illness writes: "I have a beautiful six-year-old daughter and a wonderful husband. But for four years, my little girl has been a victim of my illness. Although she is used to my being ill, I'm not, and I'm filled with guilt and sorrow over how I have messed up her life. There are so many things I had planned for when I had a child, so many things that I wanted to show her and do with her. Now all that has changed, and it is so hard for the whole family. My husband has to carry twice his share of the load and give up so much."

Disappointment, sorrow, guilt, and, I'm sure, times of anger are things that that dancer, that mechanic, and that mother know a lot about. So does each of us, each in our own way, and how we deal with the big disappointments in life depends a great deal on how the people who loved us helped us deal with smaller disappointments when we were little. Perhaps we couldn't go to the circus because we were sick. Perhaps we didn't get the present we wanted for our birthday. Perhaps we lost a race we had tried so hard to win. If we were fortunate, the people close to us let us know they understood our feelings, let us know we were still loved and helped us through our disappointment into better times beyond.

It sounds like the six-year-old daughter of the mother who wrote is growing up in a loving family. Her mother certainly cares deeply about her, and her father seems to be accepting the extra burdens that have come his way, as well as his own disappointments. Through the hard years ahead, that child may grow up with some of the reassurances we all need when life seems unfair.

How great it is when we come to know that times of disappointment can be followed by times of fulfillment; that sorrow can be followed by joy; that guilt over falling short of our ideals can be replaced by pride in doing all that we can; and that anger can be channeled into creative outlets that may lead to unexpected achievements . . . and other dreams that we can make come true!

For parents, one of life's bitterest disappointments can be not having the wherewithal to give their children what they'd like to be able to give them, and even, sometimes, what their children *need*.

"Can I have another helping?" "No, there isn't enough food."

"Can I have a toy like Jimmy's?" "No, there isn't enough money."

"Can I have a room of my own?" "No, there isn't enough space."

To have to tell a child, "No, there isn't enough," can be a painful necessity for parents. It can lead to feelings of failure and guilt and wonderings if we are worthy parents at all. Those can be hard feelings to live with, no matter how we tell ourselves that our having to say "no" to our children is part of their real world—and ours.

Truly deprived children soon become aware of their deprivation, but how they feel about it is quite another matter. They may feel sad . . . or hopeful . . . or, like one five-year-old in a family day-care center, clearly fearful. This little girl came from a home where there was seldom enough to eat, and on her first day at the center the mid-morning snack was a plate of buttered toast squares. She was given the plateful first, and when the woman in charge asked her to take a square and pass the rest along, the girl burst out crying and hung on to the plate with both hands. For once in her life she had enough, and yet she was to be deprived again!

Children's attitudes toward not having enough (as toward almost everything!) emerge from the attitudes of their first and closest care-givers. If those caregivers are bitter and resentful, a child may come to see the world and the people in it as hostile. If they blame the child for their deprivation—"You're just one more mouth to feed!"—that child may grow with guilt and a sense of being a burden to everyone. On the other hand if these caregivers can—through the emotional, spiritual, and physical nourishment of others—begin to understand their own worth, they will be able to pass on to their children a sense of well-being and the belief that good things are possible even when times are hard. It takes a certain amount of hope in order to be able to believe that life is worth the effort of living.

Empathy . . . forgiveness . . . The character traits we define as desirable for our children to develop say so much about our own value systems. People tend to develop passionate commitments to the values they inherit or acquire, and judging from our mail, many parents feel they are waging a losing battle to keep the values they care about central in their children's lives. The influence of the larger world of friends and television and society seems too strong to combat.

One mother writes: "In our neighborhood there are eleven children who play together. They often play 'Hulk,' 'Charlie's Angels,' or 'Dukes of Hazzard'—which means the boys play like monsters and crash up their cars, while the little girls prance around in a sensuous fashion capturing them. I still want to see my little girls playing with dolls and dishes.

"One day our four-year-old was drinking a glass of water and said, 'Should I pretend this is beer, whiskey, wine, or champagne?' We're not drinkers and were amazed by her worldly knowledge. Some of the children my ten-year-old plays with have a vocabulary of sex words that almost exceeds mine, even though they come from nice homes and good parents, and we've known them since they were babies.

"How do I explain my concern without coming off as a prude or as self-righteous?"

Several things come to mind as I think about that mother's question: We're never going to look "perfect" to the people we know—not to our parents, not to our friends, and not to our children. The more we can accept that, the more we're likely to feel comfortable and confident with our own values and beliefs. No two people will ever have the same values, and even two people with very similar values may express them quite differently. Comparing ourselves to others is one way of finding out who we are and what we want to be. It's also a way of appreciating other people's differences.

Certainly, the desire to be like the people they love shapes children's values in their earliest years. They want to be loved in return by those people, so they try to please them. They find that some of the things they do produce this pleasure, and others don't. Those that do begin to give rise to a child's set of values. During the first years of life, the fear of losing love can be a very powerful influence.

A little later, children long to be liked and admired by their friends: to be accepted. They may find that what it takes to be accepted by their friends is at odds with what it takes to be loved by their family. The conflict can bring hard choices for a child. We are seldom able to "throw away" values we held when we were young, even if we consciously reject them for a time in favor of new ones. Early values have a way of persisting. Sometimes they cause us sadness, anger, and guilt. Often, though, they give us the strength, courage, and compassion we all need during life's harder moments.

Our children will go their own ways and be their own selves. They will find values of their own in addition to the ones they take from us. It may be painful for us to see them modifying or even rejecting ideas that were important to us and adopting others that could never be comfortable for us. Such times may produce conflict, but out of that conflict can come the reinforcement of other important values.

One is belief in the value of standing up for who we are. When our children are small, we can set those limits on their behavior that we feel are appropriate. Later, as our children move away from us and set their own limits, we lose this control. Nonetheless, we can, in our own lives, go on trying to be true to who we are, what we believe, and how we feel. Seeing us do this, our children, particularly at times when they are in value conflict with us, can learn the courage to stand up for who they have become.

Another is a belief in the value of tolerance and the awareness that people who disagree over even the things they hold dear can live together in love and respect for one another.

Yet another is tolerance of a different kind—tolerance for people at times when they fail to live up to their values. We all have such times. Such times are commonplace in early childhood, and how parents react to them is probably critical in determining how their children will feel about such lapses in themselves and others later on.

In early childhood, a child's values are still unformed and often seemingly inconsistent. It can be hard to believe that the child who says "I hate you!" is the same child who says "I love you!" How can the child who bit his baby sister yesterday be the same one who holds her so tenderly today? And this child who is usually so willing to share . . . suddenly she's become fiercely possessive. How can it be?

Such apparent changes in character can be perplexing for parents— perplexing and sometimes upsetting when the "darker" side of a child seems to be eclipsing an otherwise bright and sunny disposition. These shifts often trouble children themselves. "Sometimes I clean up my room when I'm told to," a young boy wrote us, "but other times I just don't want to clean up my room and I cry a lot." Another boy told us about mornings when he was happy to get up and other mornings when he didn't want to get up at all. "What can I do so that I'll feel like getting up every morning?" he wondered.

As grown-ups, most of us have come to take for granted that we're going to have "moods." There are times when we need to be with people, and there are other times when we need to be by ourselves. Some mornings we feel full of energy, and the world seems full of promise; other mornings we're lethargic, and the world seems hardly worth getting up for. Some days we're glad to be who we are . . . and some days we're not.

Accounting for our moods and learning to control them are ongoing tasks. As we grow and change, our life's events and circumstances change, too—and so do our moods. The ups and downs we were subject to five years ago are not necessarily the same ones we feel today. These changing patterns are particularly true for young children for whom internal and external changes occur dramatically and frequently. When you think of all the new experiences that a child is likely to have between birth and the first day in school . . . well, it's little wonder that children can sometimes be found wondering, "Who am I, anyhow?"— just as parents may scratch their heads and wonder where this "new" child came from all of a sudden, and what became of the "old" one they were used to.

Amidst all this change, there are at least two kinds of stability that parents often strive for—for themselves as well as for their children.

The first is the stability of even temperedness. As soon as dark moods surface somewhere within the family group, they're chased away, cut short, or denied altogether; when you're angry, the thing to do is to swallow your anger. When you're sad, hold back your tears and keep a stiff upper lip. When you're discouraged or depressed, take a deep breath and keep slogging ahead . . . with a smile.

To stifle our emotions in this way is a tough road, and one of the reasons it's so tough is that it leads in a direction that's contrary to the natural tendencies of human nature. Though it may work for some people and some families, I believe the risks are certainly at least equal to the possible benefits.

A friend of ours remembers the times in summer he spent with his grandmother—good times, but in some ways difficult times, too:

"Gran was loving, no doubt about that," our friend told us, "but she was tough. She'd been widowed twice and in later life came to be independent and proud of it. She had no time for what she called 'idle regrets' and certainly no time for tears. She had no use for sulky moods or angry outbursts, either, and whenever my dark side would get the best of me for one reason or another, she'd look at me sternly and say, 'There's that bad little boy again. You know I don't like him. I want him to go away right now!'

"After spending a couple of weeks with Gran, I'd actually start to see myself as two people—one good and happy, the other bad and moody. The bad one got to be scary because I couldn't always control him, and he was sure to make Gran displeased. But I worked hard at staying the good, happy child Gran liked, and she and I were close until she died. But you know, there were whole parts of myself and my life I never felt I could share with her. When I wanted to talk about feelings, it had to be with someone else."

There's the risk: Important feelings may go untalked about. That's especially true for young children whose closest caregivers see even-temperedness as stability. When you have to stifle your feelings for fear of getting upset and upsetting the people you love, who *can* you talk to, and what *does* become of those emotions?

A different kind of stability comes from allowing ourselves and our children to express the full range of human feelings. It comes from believing—and encouraging our children to believe—that having dark sides as well as bright sides is part of anyone's being a whole person, and it comes from trusting the people we love to accept our dark sides while helping us manage them.

That can be a tough road, too; such trust and acceptance is often not only elusive but sometimes the source of deceptions and disappointments as well. But I believe this road is a road toward growth in addition to stability. For children, it can be an avenue to finding out so much they need to know about who they are and what they can become. What's more, that road can lead us, when we're young, to one of the most important discoveries of all: that people can like us just the way we are—our dark sides, our bright sides, and all our other sides as well.

Help!

We've most likely all heard someone say (and we've probably heard ourselves saying as well): "The world is divided into two kinds of people . . . " To hear tell, the world can sure be divided a lot of different ways!

I heard a new one the other day. Someone said, "The world is divided into two kinds of people: those who lean on other people, and people upon whom other people lean." I wondered, Which am I? Neither and both, I decided, because, like most people I know, I have my times for leaning and my times for being leaned upon. As I thought about it, it seemed to me that being able to do both is an important part of anyone's ability to keep in balance. If the world really were divided into the dependent and the independent, the helpers and the helped, the leaners and the leaned upon . . . well, we'd probably *all* fall down.

It's easy for humans to learn to accept help—in the beginning at least. It's been said that human young are dependent on their caregivers longer than are the young of any other species. Certainly for the first year or two of life, help for babies and toddlers would seem to be close to a necessity for their survival. The natural urge toward *in*dependence soon grows, though, and parents can usually see it clearly at work as soon as their babies begin creeping and crawling. You've probably watched a crawler testing out his or her independence by setting off to explore across the room. You've probably noticed, too, how important it is for that crawler to stay in touch with Mom (or with whomever is right there at the time). First, it's off to explore a little, time for a little independence. Then, it's back to Mom for some reassuring dependence, for a hug or some lap time . . . then, off again to explore some more.

As children get older, their times of independent exploration tend to get longer. So long as they can see or hear their caregivers, they may not need as much touching and hugging as they once did; their eyes and ears can bring them some of the reassuring support they need. But one thing seems certain: Knowing that dependence is both available and encouraged when it's needed makes it easier for young children to learn to be healthily *in*dependent.

Learning to "stand on our own two feet" takes a particular kind of balance. It's easier for us to find that balance—and to risk losing it now and then—when we know there's someone we can lean on when we need to.

If you watch a three-year-old for any length of time, the chances are you'll see needs for both dependence and independence struggling side by side. The other day we saw a mother and her little daughter walking back to their car from the grocery store. The mother had a bag of groceries in each hand, but all the same her daughter was whining to be carried because, she said, she was tired.

"I can't carry you, honey," her mother explained, "but we don't have far to go." Just then they came to the curb of the sidewalk. "Hang on to my little finger as we cross," the mother said, holding out her pinkie, but her daughter stopped still and shook her head. "I want to cross alone," she said. It was such a typical standoff for any mother and her three-year-old! The little girl's longing for the dependence of being carried was matched by her wanting to be independent crossing the street. No doubt there was some measure of retribution in her behavior as well: You wouldn't carry me, so I won't hang on to your finger!

That mother solved the problem in a very practical fashion. "Hang on to my finger!" she ordered, and when her daughter still refused, she shifted both grocery bags into one hand, grabbed her daughter's wrist with the other, and pulled her kicking and howling across the street. Lots of parents, in exasperation, would probably have done much the same thing. The situation might have been an opportunity, though, for that three-year-old to move a little beyond both dependence and independence. She might have learned something about letting people depend on *her*.

The same opportunity often comes up in doctors' offices when a child has to have a shot, or a throat culture, or something else that's unpleasant. "Hold still!" is seldom as effective as letting a child know that you *need* to depend on him or her for help in getting the procedure done. Many doctors have told me that saying "I need you to help me by holding still right now" can result in a surprising level of cooperation. My guess is that that's particularly true for children from families where the acknowledgment of *mutual* dependence has already become a regular fact of family life.

We can't know what the outcome would have been for that mother and her three-year-old stalled at the curbside had she said something like, "Look, honey, my hands are full, and I need you to hang on so we can get across safely." The situation might have ended up exactly the way it did . . . but maybe it wouldn't have. Children who have learned to be comfortably dependent can become not only comfortably independent but also comfortable with having people depend on them. They can lean, stand, and be leaned upon, because they know what a good feeling it can be to feel needed.

Help and love are tightly intertwined all our lives. Whether it's parents and infants, brothers and sisters, a friend and a friend, the help that one person gives another often carries with it the opportunity for love of different kinds to grow. Husbands and wives are sometimes referred to as "helpmates." Certainly in their loving commitment to one another there is the intention to help one another through hard times as well as good times.

The relationship between help and love, though, isn't a simple one. An example of its complexity came to us in a letter from a mother. Her tone was one of puzzlement mixed with a little hurt as she talked about her four-year-old son. There are times, she explained, when her little boy clearly needs help to do something, but he will refuse her offers. "It's not that he wants to do whatever it is by himself," she explained. "I could understand a need to feel independent. What he does sometimes, though, is refuse my offer only to turn to his aunt instead! Why?"

Not knowing that family firsthand, there's no way to answer that mother's "Why?" for sure, but the rejection she feels is such a natural response to the way help and love grow in most families. In the total dependence of a newborn on a parent, help and love are almost one and the same thing. The feelings that grow around them are deep and strong. In the giving of help, a parent experiences one of the best feelings that any of us can have: the feeling that life has a meaning because we are needed by someone else. Watching a baby grow with our help tells us something else we like to feel about ourselves: that we are competent and loving. As for the baby who receives our regular, predictable and caring help, well, that's how babies first come to feel that they are both lovable and loved.

Most parents find it easy to encourage their toddlers toward some kinds of independence—for instance, doing what they can for themselves. "Mommy do!" a toddler may demand, holding out a baby bottle in one hand and its twist-on cap in the other. "You can do it. Kathy do!" the toddler's mother may insist. A toddler can become upset at these refusals of help. On some level they may suggest that love is being refused as well. With loving encouragement, that shadow usually passes. When Kathy succeeds in putting the top on the bottle for herself, she can feel proud. She'll also feel the pleasure she has brought her mother, and her mother will have feelings of pride and pleasure of her own. That's one way love grows.

Then, one day, the tables will turn. Seeing our imaginary Kathy struggling with something else, her mother will offer help, and her daughter will be the one to refuse. Kathy's mother will probably appreciate her daughter's new striving for mastery and independence; but she, too, may fleetingly wonder whether her daughter's rejection signals a lessening of love.

And what if our children turn to someone other than us for help, just as the little boy who was turning toward his aunt for help?

That brings two thoughts to my mind. One is that the relationship between help and love changes, and needs to change, as the relationship between children and their parents changes. Whereas help once meant a one-sided dependence, it grows healthily to become a mutual and loving supportiveness. The other thought is that there is much more independence than learning to master new skills. One of the most important parts of independence is learning to form new relationships with other people, and that may be exactly what that little boy was trying to do. Moving confidently toward independence, though, depends to a great extent on there being a sure foundation of early love to build on, and a fundamental trust that help will be there when we need it. Love and trust are what most enable children to risk trying to be themselves.

Independence means some letting go on both sides. That can bring some difficult feelings, but it can also bring a new understanding that in the withholding and refusal of certain kinds of help, there can be just as much love as in its offering and acceptance.

Special needs and special circumstances, of course, can bring demands for special kinds of dependence and help. How best to meet those unusual demands is a common parental quandary.

One day during the holiday season, a mother and father both overheard their daughter sing the first two lines of "Deck the Halls" in a clear, true voice, right on key and in rhythm. Jessie was only three and a half, but even so, her parents weren't too surprised; they had already noticed that Jessie had an unusual capacity to catch the tunes she heard.

But they were quite unprepared for what their daughter did next. She sang the same two lines again, but this time in the minor mode— something she was unlikely ever to have heard and a feat that would baffle most adults. "That," said her father, "was when we suspected Jessie was musically 'gifted.' Then the question was, What to do about it?"

It's true that occasionally children will do something that seems well beyond the so-called normal capabilities for their age. And their parents, like Jessie's, are often perplexed, even while feeling proud. The letters we receive tell us of children who seem exceptional at working with their hands, calculating with numbers, using words, or working with pencil, crayon or paint. Sometimes these exceptionalities seem to be parts of normal development that are growing faster than others, but in these parents' descriptions, there is almost always a spoken or unspoken question of how far they should push these talents to their fullest—to even, possibly, toward greatness. What kind of help should they give?

I believe that the best use of a child's early talents, even unusual ones, is in the service of that child's whole development, particularly in the early years. Children have so much they need to learn about themselves and their world—not just the facts, but the feelings that go with being human. There is love, anger, joy and sadness, hope and disappointment, and all the shades of feeling in between. Children need to learn to ask their trusted caregivers about these feelings, to learn what such feelings are made of and what to do with them. Perhaps the most important work of early childhood is the development of healthy self-esteem, the sense of being valuable.

An unusual talent can present an unusual opportunity to get on with this important work, but it doesn't always turn out that way. It can happen that parents lose sight of the difference between wanting their children to be all they can be and wanting their children to be who they, the parents, want their children to be.

I was fortunate that when I started showing an early talent at the piano, my parents encouraged me to use the keyboard as a means of self-expression in any way I chose. At the same time, they helped me learn about excellence and accomplishment, about the need for diligence and persistence and patience, about the giving of pleasure and the receiving of praise. Through all that, I came to feel the joys of creativity, and over the years I've also learned that all children have gifts.

Some early talents seem to go unrealized. Jessie's parents were much like mine—supportive but in no way pushy or overbearing. Whereas for me the piano remained central to my life and work, Jessie grew up to be a wife and mother with a career in medicine. If her parents had pushed her harder, would she have made more of her unusual early musical awareness? Was something lost? Does it matter?

That's hard to say, and whatever our opinion is, it probably says a lot about how our own early talents were treated by our parents. All I know is that Jessie claims to have no regrets and says she *does* feel that she's a worthy person with a life worth living in a world worth living in. That, I believe, is what ends up mattering most of all.

Special demands for help, naturally, often stem from unfortunate circumstances and adversity. These are times that can really highlight the ability parents and children have to work and grow together.

"In a period of four hours," a mother writes, "my son went from a three-year-old who laughed and ran and played to one who cried in pain and couldn't walk. The diagnosis: Perthes' disease—a hip disorder that will mean his wearing a brace for a long time to come. Where once he was a helpful little boy, now he expects to be waited on hand and foot. It's hard for my husband and me to understand how to handle these changes. We don't want to spoil our son, but we don't want to force him, either. What's more, we have a newborn, who deserves a lot of our attention. We really have our hands full and need all the guidance we can get!"

The sudden onset of a disability in a young child is bound to be a traumatic time in a family. Our children are a part of us as no one else can be. Any damage to their emotional or physical well-being comes as an assault on our feelings and material resources. Many parents feel in some way responsible for what has happened to their child. They often feel guilty about it. Some parents feel punished for something they may have done. They often feel resentful and angry. Others, on the other hand, see in their child's misfortune new meaning for themselves: a special calling to be caregivers to a child with extra needs. Most, perhaps, fall somewhere in between. Taking a deep breath, they leave the whys unanswered and do the best they can, with what they have, day by day.

However we feel, it's important to acknowledge those feelings and let ourselves have them. There's no "should" or "should not" when it comes to having feelings. They're part of who we are, and their origins are beyond our control. When we can believe that, we may find it easier to make constructive choices about what to do with those feelings.

Perthes' disease, nowadays, is generally correctable. That doesn't mean, though, that one day the little boy whose mother wrote will be getting on with life as though nothing had happened. Something *has* happened, and it will have consequences in who he becomes—as Perthes' disease had for another young man we know.

John was diagnosed at two years old. This was some twenty years ago, and the first doctor's prescription was a full year of bed rest. When John was three, his family moved to another city, and there a second doctor recommended a walking brace. For John, this brace meant a new and unexpected freedom rather than a sudden restriction; he'd already spent eight months in bed. When we first knew him, he was four, active, joyful, dependent in some ways, to be sure, but often he was told to slow down by his parents as he strove to keep up with his three older brothers. He couldn't always keep up with them. That made him sad and angry at times, just as his brothers had days when they resented the extra attention John got from his parents, or the extra care his parents expected them to provide as well.

John had time to listen to lots of stories... and soon turned into a mimic and storyteller on his own. He made up for much of what he couldn't do by becoming the family entertainer, and during the year or so he spent in his brace his imagination flourished. Though he eventually left his brace behind, he took his imagination with him as he grew, acting in school plays and then becoming a serious student of theater in New York.

"If he'd been able to go out and play ball with the rest of the kids," his father tells us, "I doubt all that would have happened. Certainly not the way it did. John's not acting now; he's writing plays. One was produced last year off-off-Broadway and has just finished a long run in Los Angeles. He's settled in Los Angeles now, working on others. It's hard to call a handicap positive, but handicaps are bound to be formative and can have some positive outcomes."

John's parents don't talk much about their role in John's recovery and his becoming who he is. They don't talk about their years of anxiety, sadness, and expense, about all the extra time and energy and emotion John's condition demanded of them. They don't talk about their constant quandary of trying to balance helping with not helping, dependence with independence, optimism with discouragement, encouragement with realistic acceptance of limitations... nor about keeping their four sons all aware of their equal love for them.

In short, they don't talk about all the work they put into John's (and their own) continued growth. It's my hope for the mother whose letter we mentioned earlier that she and her family will find, in the extra burdens they have to shoulder, the unexpected opportunity to work and grow together, too.

The Family Kaleidoscope

Some of us would rather spend time with our family... and some of us would rather spend time with our friends. How do *you* feel about your kin and kith?

The usual phrase is "kith and kin." "Kith" are friends and acquaintances. "Kin" are our relatives, close and distant. Most playbills list the cast of characters in order of appearance, though, and as the dramas of our lives unfold, kin are almost always the earliest actresses and actors upon our stage.

If we were to list the cast "in order of *importance*," that might be somewhat different, but for most children kin would still come first. Our first kin are our parents—whether natural parents, adoptive parents, or foster parents—and as the uniqueness of our "selves" takes shape in our earliest days, weeks, months, and years, our parents have a formative influence on us that will be with us all our lives. Theirs is certainly not the only influence, and the influence they have will be modified in many ways by other kin and kith we meet and by all the experiences we have as we grow. Although those later encounters may have less intensity than our first relationships with our parents, they are certainly essential contributions to whom we become. Part of their importance is precisely in their being different.

I know a family in which there are two children, and when those children were young, they still had a great-grandmother. She lived far away but visited about twice a year, and her visits were eagerly awaited by everyone in the family. "We all called her 'Babie,'" the children's father told me. "She was my wife's grandmother, and my wife and Babie had always been very close growing up. I came to love her deeply, too. Our children adored her. By the time the kids were three and five, though, we had a problem."

That father explained that Babie, like many older people, didn't sleep much during the night, and she slept with her light on and with the door a little bit open. Every morning, when the parents would get up, the two children would be in Babie's bed, surrounded by books. Sometimes they'd be sound asleep, cuddled up against her. Little by little the parents realized, with some concern, that the children might have been there much of the night, and that Babie would never dream of sending them back to their beds no matter what time it was when they found their way through her open door.

Then, one day, when the mother was tidying Babie's room, she found dozens of candy wrappers. She told her husband she feared that the children not only weren't getting a full night's sleep, but also that Babie was letting them eat candy all night long. Together they agreed that something had to be done to head off this disintegration of family schedules and limits.

So, gently but firmly, they confronted Babie with the evidence and asked her, please, to cooperate with the family routines they were trying to establish with the children. They got nowhere. Babie drew herself up to her full five-foot-three, fixed them with a steely glare, and said, "I am the children's *great*-grandmother . . . and I shall do with them what I please!"

"Well," the father told me, "neither my wife nor I could find an easy response to that. We talked it over and came to the conclusion that it was all too complicated to unravel in the course of Babie's short visits.

We took what seemed the easy way out. We made sure there was time for naps in the afternoon and insisted on more toothbrushing. Now that Babie's dead, I'm thankful we didn't spoil that special relationship. But what still strikes me as odd is that once Babie would leave for home

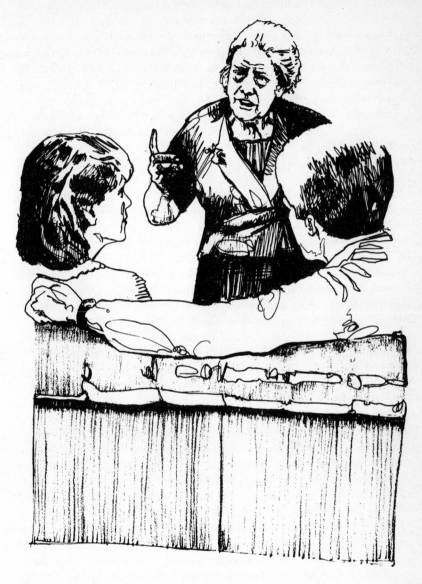

"I am the children's great-grandmother, and I shall do with them what I please!"

WORKING AND GROWING TOGETHER

after each visit, the children never tried to continue her pattern with us. They simply went back to sleeping in their own beds and accepting our limits on eating sweets. Our relationship with them was one thing; their relationship with Babie was quite another."

What a train of thought that story started for me! One of my grandfathers was deeply important to me when I was growing up. My relationship with him was quite different from my relationship with my parents. He allowed me to do things my parents would never have, and his limits, though firm, were different from theirs as well. I can't remember confusing the two, either. As I thought about Babie, I wondered whether perhaps that mother had been able to accept her grandmother's actions more easily than if it had been her *mother* who was keeping the children up and feeding them candy. That primary, root relationship between mother and child might have been too intense for someone who found herself cast in the dual role of parent and child.

As for those two children, their memories of Babie are strong and loving. Now that they're older, they admit to residual feelings of delight that someone could override "parental discipline" and get away with it. Babie was a special haven amidst the necessary tug-of-wars of family life.

Not many children can remember having great-grandparents, but lots, like me, found havens with grandparents. Children can find the same sense of safety and acceptance from certain aunts and uncles. Being a generation younger than a grandparent, an aunt or uncle may be more active, able to take a child on more strenuous adventures. Many people I know can remember a favorite "Auntie Mame" or "black-sheep uncle" of whom the parents didn't altogether seem to approve! That guarded disapproval often comes from an aunt's or uncle's different sense of what's allowable and what's not . . . but in that generation the mothers and fathers and aunts and uncles are brothers and sisters; old rivalries have a way of surfacing later on as new jealousies.

Children can find strong support in relationships with cousins. Cousins are often about the same age, but even though they may be almost like brothers and sisters, cousins never have to vie for the affection of the same set of parents. What's more, cousins frequently find themselves comparing grievances against their respective parents and profiting from one another's experiences. It's common for children to find an earlier ally in a cousin than in a brother or sister; brothers and sisters, by definition, have a lot more feelings to work out day by day!

Children with strong relationships with different kinfolk may be the ones who find it easier later on to form strong relationships with people beyond the family—with "kithfolk." On the edges of a family there are often "courtesy aunts and uncles" and "kissing cousins"—close family friends who are not blood-related. Removed from family concerns, these not-quite-relatives can become safe repositories for a child's confidences, available ears for a child's woes, and sources of support for a child's strivings to grow. It's these early kith who may set the pattern for later bonds with friends of our own choosing, bonds of friendship that sustain us all life long.

There's another way to list the cast of characters in our lives, and that's "in order of preference." Once we're out in the world on our own, that list may look very different from our earlier lists ordered by appearance or by importance. We may find that there's still a "Babie" on that list, or a brother or a mother, and then again we may find that list made up mainly of friends. For many people, the top person on the list becomes a spouse, followed by a new generation of children who begin their own ordering of the cast of characters in *their* lives.

Even the closest family members cannot always be all things to one another—not parents to children nor brothers to sisters. We all need many different people to help us develop a full and confident sense of who we are. Though kin may come first, we all need kith as well, and that's something loving parents can help their children learn.

What is this thing called "a family," anyway? What does it take to be a "mother" or a "father"?

It was a letter from an adoptive mother that raised these questions. As she told us about her experiences and the experiences of friends, it became clear that there is still a lot of traditional thinking that the only "normal family" is one where children are being raised by their biological mother and father, and that you can't be a real father unless you sired a child or a real mother unless you've given birth to one. The same thinking would also have us believe that children who don't grow up in families like this are bound to be disadvantaged and even at risk.

This is a kind of thinking that needs to be challenged again and again, and that's why we'd like to give you a brief glimpse into this mother's family.

"Parents who seek to adopt," she wrote, "are often frustrated because they've been unable to fulfill their desire for children. It's good to let children know that people who adopt children wanted those children very much and had to work hard to get them. Like pregnancy, the adoption process is often long and exasperating, and can be a source of anguish.

"We don't dwell on the adoption process with our two adopted children any more than natural parents dwell on the pregnancies that preceded their children's births. But we do talk about how long we waited for them and how much we wanted

them. Kathy, our oldest, is now four and a half, and I think waiting for our next child is helpful to her in understanding how we
felt when we waited for her.

"She knows that if our next child is a girl, her name will be
Margot. The other day she said to me, 'I feel so lonely for Margot
today I feel like crying. Do you ever feel like crying about it too?'
I acknowledged that I do, and then she asked, 'Did you cry
when you were waiting for me?' I assured her that I did.

"Kathy loves to hear the story of how we went to the agency
to get her, and she remembers our trip to get her brother, Daniel.
She's eagerly looking forward to going again to get her next
brother or sister.

"Without meaning to, people can be so insensitive! It's particularly troubling when someone asks about our children's 'real'
mother, when they mean birth or biological mother. I am their
real mother. As one of my friends put it, 'Motherhood is
achieved, grown into, worked at. There should really be two different words for giving birth and mothering. I like the way another friend described the adoption process. She called it 'a
natural process of giving life to a family.'

"I wish people could understand that families are really families, whether the children come into the family through birth or
adoption. Adoption neither assures success nor invites calamity
in a family. In our case, our children know they're our children,
and we know we're their parents. No matter what anyone else
thinks or says, we know we're a family."

What that mother says has meaning for all children, whether they
grow up with single parents, grandparents, or foster parents, or in an
orphanage. It's a fact of life that bloodlines and love lines don't always
coincide. Children may need the right bloodlines to grow into kings
and queens, but when it comes to growing into healthy, whole, and
fulfilled human beings, it will always be the love lines that count the
most.

Another kind of worry about families turns up frequently in our mail:
Is it all right to have an "only child"? One reason for its recurrence, I
believe, is that it's really a whole lot of questions—different questions
for different people.

A thirty-four-year-old mother asked us that question again just recently. As she did, she expressed many of her feelings. At the start of
their marriage, that husband and wife agreed they wanted only one
child, and they had a daughter. By the time their child was two,
though, the mother had changed her mind. She thought she'd enjoy
having a second child, and she thought a baby brother or sister would

be good for her daughter. (Both the mother and father had brothers and sisters, but they weren't close because of large differences in age.)

The family was on the move at the time, and so the decision about a second child was delayed for the two years it took for them to settle down in their new city. By then there were other concerns: whether they had the financial resources to raise another child; whether the mother's age would increase the likelihood of birth defects; whether, if they adopted a child instead, they'd be able to love both children equally; and whether the age difference there would be between the children would mean they'd lost the chance for close childhood companionship.

But there were new pressures to have a second child, too. Their daughter said she was sometimes lonely and would like a brother or sister; there were no close friends or relatives nearby who had children their daughter's age; and some people in the neighborhood were expressing both pity and criticism about any family with an only child.

"Is it bad to be an only child?" the mother asked us. "Is it bad for children in a family to have an age difference of five or six years?"

No, there's nothing bad about either one, as many, many people who grew up either one way or the other can tell you! I was an "only child" myself until I was eleven. That certainly affected my growing up by directing me toward things I could do by myself, by encouraging me to invent the companionship I didn't have. Playing the piano became important to me, and playing with puppets. Today I'm still doing those same things and finding fulfillment because of them.

Everything about our childhoods has some influence on who we become—where we grow up and how, and, of course, with whom. But it's not "better" to grow up in a small, medium-sized or large family, any more than it's "better" to grow up in Arizona, Iowa, or Maine. Usually what's best is what's best for the whole family, and that means, first and foremost, what enables parents to raise their child or children most comfortably and with most confidence.

I believe it's a fact of life that what we have is less important than what we make out of what we have. The same holds true for families. It's not how many people there are in a family that counts, but rather the feelings among the people who are there. The deprived child is the child who lacks caring and love, and the fortunate child is the one whose family, no matter how large or small, provides the inner resources to make the most out of life in his or her own way.

There's lots to be learned about what "family" means when a family's standard shape is forcibly altered by choice or circumstance. Two children, living far apart but both just old enough to write, painstakingly shaping unfamiliar letters to tell us of the important events in their lives...and both concluding with exactly the same words: "I live with my mommy. We are divorced from my father."

There is so much yet to be done in those young lives, and already so much to be *un*done!

In our work with children and families, divorce is a constantly painful reality. Just the other night at dinner, a young mother confided that she and her husband were heading toward divorce. Her eyes filled with tears as she said, "I'm so afraid our divorce will wreck our three-year-old daughter's life!"

There was much I'd have liked to have said to that wife and mother, and most of it would have expressed concern and compassion for anyone entering divorce's fierce trials. But I felt frustration and anger, too. Part of me wanted to shout, "Listen! Divorces don't wreck children's lives. *People* do!"

I didn't say that, though, but I certainly thought it, and the thought persisted as that mother went on to tell me about the custody battle that was sure to come. It all seemed such a sad, familiar, and seemingly hopeless story.

Yet I know the story is *not* hopeless, even though the road to a positive outcome will be a hard one for that mother and father to take. The key lies, of course, precisely in that couple's reminding themselves over and over again that they *are* a mother and father as well as a husband and wife, and in their finding the self-discipline to conduct certain aspects of their divorce from the perspective that they are *still* a family. Motherly love and fatherly love do not cease when the love between husband and wife ends and turns to anger. It's up to mothers and fathers to let their children know that, but in order to do so, they have to know it themselves—know it so fully and deeply that their parental love is expressed in acts and not just words.

Although there can be no such things as divorce between parent and child, that is not at all clear to many children, as it obviously wasn't to the two who wrote. I know one girl who is trying hard to "divorce" her father right now. Her parents separated two years ago and are now divorcing. When the separation occurred, this girl wrote her father, whom I know she loved a great deal, telling him she would never talk to him again and never wanted to see him again...and for two years she hasn't done either. But no matter how much she now wants to believe that her parents' divorce is hers as well as her mother's, it is not so.

More than anything else, it will be the loving acts of her parents that will eventually help her find "the truth that will set her free"—set her free from her anger and set her free to grow. The truth is that children need both a mother and a father, and that mothers and fathers both need their children, and that when there is love, there is always hope of surviving even the hardest of times.

That this is so was confirmed for me again the other day by the words of a nine-year-old who reflected back on his parents' divorce. Among other things he wrote about his family nowadays were these words:

"I love my folks more than anything in the world. They have been separated for two and a half years, but it doesn't bother me very much, and I go see my father every other weekend and sometimes longer. . . . I have two parents that I think are just great, and I'm lucky to have that much. . . . I like everything we do together when I'm with my mom or my dad. But most of all we are together, and that's what counts.

"I have learned almost everything from my family. One thing is that when your parents are divorced, they love you just as much as if they were married. . . . My family is like my Whole Life. . . . My family means comfort, warmth, and love. They give me respect and things that a kid really needs. . . . My family really does mean everything to me, like what could mean more than a Family?"

One of the frequent outcomes of divorce is *step*-family, and when a child moves in with a stepparent, or a stepparent moves in with a child, we can be sure that everyone who's part of that family is going to have some new, strong feelings to deal with. In many cases, some of those feelings will be joyful and others will be painful and difficult, particularly for a young child. Whether through divorce or death, a stepparent usually arrives in a child's life following a loss, and such losses can give rise to a lot of grief and anger. While working on those feelings, a child may draw more dependently close to the parent he or she lives with. If it's the father who has gone, a child may see Mommy as more "mine" than ever. A home with grief, anger, and possessiveness would be a hard one for anyone to enter, let alone a stepparent, who is likely to introduce a new set of conflicts over loyalty.

JoAnn's parents separated when she was a baby. When she was four, her mother remarried. Her mother described her daughter's reactions like this: "JoAnn had a very hard time accepting my new husband into our family. She would tell him she hated him and that she wanted him to go away. We tried to acknowledge her feelings, but we also told her that my new husband was here to stay. I think in her own way she was testing my husband and me to our limits to see if he would really stay before she invested her love and trust into our new family arrangement."

What a natural reaction! But that may have been only part of it. She may also have been troubled by what would happen if she allowed herself to like or even love this new man. "If I get to like him," she may have felt, "that means I'll love real Daddy less. I'd never do that!" It may have seemed to her that there was another risk as well: that she would get close to this new man only to have him leave her just the way her daddy had done.

As it turned out, JoAnn, over time, was able to accept her stepfather. But as she did so, a new problem arose: It seems that when JoAnn started being more affectionate and trusting toward her stepfather, she started being more obstinate and mean to her dad. That may seem a strange turnabout for JoAnn to have made. How could she do it? We can't know for sure, but as she came to feel more secure in her stepfather's affection, she may also have been able to feel, for the first time, how angry she was at her father for having left. Like most children, she may have felt that she had caused the divorce—that she'd done something bad, lost her father's love, and that's why he'd gone away. When you feel "bad" and unlovable, it can be very hard to give love. Imagine what anguish her apparent rejection must have brought her father!

It's always remarkable to me that children can find their way through such complex and turbulent emotions, bring them to healthy resolutions, and turn out to be capable of forming loving and lasting relationships of their own. But children do it all the time—not all children, to be sure, but many, many children. How fortunate JoAnn seems to be to have a mother and stepfather who know how to listen to her, who aren't afraid to talk about important things or to help her talk about them, and who have the patience and understanding not to hurry her through her feelings but to let her take the time she needs. With that kind of care, children can make it through almost any storm.

Like nature's turbulences, the storms that blow through family life are of varying intensities and often unpredictable. Some simply buffet a family around for a while and then move on—like the storms of adolescence. Others, such as tragic accidents, come with swift and sudden destruction. Still others seem like huge, slow-moving weather fronts that settle in and persist. Illnesses can be like that, and not only illnesses of the body.

A parent's emotional illness, for instance, can push a whole family right up against the limits of its members' abilities to cope. . . . and keep on pushing. When we hear about a storm like that, it's usually through a letter from the "well" parent, and the central questions in these letters tend to be: How do I explain the situation to my child? What can I do so that it won't wreck my child's life? When these letters come, I'm reminded of Melanie.

Melanie was born to parents who both had bad histories of emotional disturbance. They had married at a time of seeming stability, but the frictions of learning to live together day by day proved too hard for them to handle. By then, though, Melanie's birth was imminent.

Both her parents loved Melanie. They tried to care for her as best they could. They were courageous enough to reach out for professional help for themselves, but this meant that during Melanie's first two years, one or the other of her parents was frequently away from home under medical care. For the partner who was left at home, the pressures and responsibilities of single parenthood were overwhelming.

Melanie's grandmother lived in the same city. She worried about Melanie but believed that the parents, so long as they possibly could, were the best people to raise their own child. It wasn't until Melanie began to have accidents—a burn on her arm, a broken leg—that she suggested Melanie come live with her. Her parents agreed.

For the next five years Melanie lived in a loving and stable home. But as she grew, she became aware that her family wasn't like others she knew, and she began asking why. Her questions were simple at first, such as, "Where are my mommy and daddy?" "They're at home," her grandmother would reply. "You'll be seeing them soon."

Then it became: "Why don't I live with my mommy and daddy?" To which her grandmother replied, "Your mom and dad love you a lot, Melanie, and they want you to have the kind of care they know that children need. They can't give you that kind of care right now, and so they've asked me to help look after you."

Then, one day when Melanie was older, she asked why her parents couldn't take care of her. Her grandmother explained that it was very hard for her parents to take care of themselves, and when they knew that Melanie was well taken care of, that made life a little easier for them.

By the time Melanie was eight, her mother was well enough to take care of her, but by then her mother and father were no longer living together. Melanie became used to visiting her father either in a clinic or in the small apartment where he lived, and her mother explained that her father might always need special help. She could help, too, her mother said, by giving him the affection he needed.

Melanie will be twenty-one this year. She's a bright young person who is living on her own and doing well at the design school she attends. Her grandmother is no longer alive, but Melanie is still very close to her mother and father, who continue to live apart. What seems different about Melanie is that she seems somehow wiser than other children her age. Perhaps it's the extra measure of compassion she shows toward people. She seems secure in the knowledge that her parents' problems were not of her making, and there was nothing she could have done to make them go away. She seems confident in knowing that she has been loved, truly loved.

If there's a moral to this story, I believe it's this: Anything human is mentionable, and anything mentionable can be manageable. In addition, Melanie's story confirms another belief of mine. Children who are consistently cared for and loved by *someone* when they are little always have the chance of weathering turbulence to grow into healthy, caring adults capable of passing on that love to others.

Some family struggles, because of their nature, are lifelong. Those of you who read *Mister Rogers Talks with Parents* will already have "met" Jonathan in the letter from his mother included in the book. At the time of that letter, Jonathan was almost three. He had cerebral palsy, braces for legs that wouldn't work, and glasses for eyes that had "quite a bit of astigmatism." But on good days, Jonathan was a "tiger" in the neighborhood and had calluses on his hands and knees to prove it. His doctors doubted that he'd ever walk, but his mother thought he would. "I'm sure that with or without crutches, some day Jonathan will walk," she wrote. "I only worry about what kind of person he will be when he does walk."

We heard from Jonathan's mother again and thought you might like to know how life has changed in that family. Where once there were five children in the family (four, including Jonathan, adopted), now there are six. And yes, with the help of crutches, Jonathan walks! In fact, at this time of writing, he's a junior high student, up to grade level, a swimmer, a horseback rider, a fisherman, a bowler, and a player of both the piano and the recorder. When he was little, his father made him hand-propelled tricycles, but now he rides an adult tricycle with a basket on the back for his crutches, his books, and the grocery bags. "Friends from school come over, and he visits them on his tricycle," his mother tells us. "He phones and writes notes to pretty girls. And they phone back!"

But Jonathan and his family have grown through much physical and emotional pain—"so many heartaches, tears, and struggles." He has endured many operations, complications, and setbacks. There will be more to come. He still has to battle his way through physical therapy and speech therapy, individual and family counseling. The road Jonathan and his family have traveled has been steep, and it looks like it's going to stay that way. Such climbs take their toll. "Jonathan has suffered in body and personality," his mother admits. "He is bright and very angry. Only a marvelous sense of humor and resilience keep him going. As a family we laugh and cry . . . and laugh again." Such climbs do bring strength as well.

There are so many things to think about in the letters from Jonathan's mother! One that strikes me forcefully is how anger is so much a part of love, and what a healthy and constructive feeling anger can be when it's expressed out of love. Through love, anger can even be transformed into healthy growth, creativity, and compassion.

That this is true is constantly reinforced in the letters people write us. One television friend writes: "I was abused sexually for years by an alcoholic, schizophrenic father and left unprotected by a frightened, resentful mother. Fortunately I survived and met warm, kindly people. . . . I like best of all now to pass on the warmth and kindness I received when I needed it." Who could have guessed that from such a sad and angry childhood would come an adult who would add an extra measure of caring to this world? How fortunate that friend was to find a "family" in those warm, caring people she mentions!

Many people must have learned a lot from Jonathan and his particular family constellation, and I'm sure that as the years go by, many more people will be touched by that family's continuing resolutions to their struggles. I hope Jonathan can feel a sense of pride in knowing how much hope he has engendered in other people just by dealing with his own struggles with such determination.

Gathering the Clan

There are many reasons families gather together: traditional holidays, someone's birthday, or some other special milestone in life's pas-

A child might wonder: Who am I to these people?

WORKING AND GROWING TOGETHER 199

sage that is either joyful or sad. Sometimes these "gatherings of the clan" take place for no reason other than Sunday dinner, but whatever brings them about, they're sure to raise questions for the young children who are there. They not only wonder about the meaning of adult rituals, but they also have deeper questions that children may feel rather than think—questions such as, Who am I to these people? What is my place among them? And what is love all about?

Those are hard questions for any of us to answer, and I believe that our uncertainty about them plays a large part in generating the mixed emotions many of us carry to, and take away from, family get-togethers. I feel sure, too, that the same uncertainty often underlies the fatigue and stress that children show as long family days wear on.

How to include very young children in these occasions, or even whether to include them, is perplexing for many parents. Because parents are the ones who know their children best, they are usually the first to sense that a child is beginning to feel overwhelmed by what's going on. It can be very helpful, when the early signs of stress appear, for a parent and child to move away from the group—just the two together. It might be a time to take a walk, to look at a book, or to lie down for a while. There are many times, as children grow, when they need to borrow from a grown-up's self-control, and knowing they can do so helps them develop greater self-control of their own. In the security of a parent's presence, children can often find the strength to regain the mastery of their feelings that they were about to lose . . . and to once again feel ready to go on coping.

Many families have found it helpful to set a space apart where children can go alone. It doesn't have to be a room; it might be just a corner behind a sofa, or a tent made by draping a blanket over the backs of two chairs. What matters is that children know it's a space for them, and that it's all right with the grown-ups for them to feel the need to go there, to find some solitude. Even adults in the family can wish for that kind of "breather" from time to time!

I can understand that some parents choose to excuse their children from long family affairs, particularly ones that are going to be hard. A friend of ours, whose father died, chose to leave her four-year-old daughter out of the actual funeral and burial services. She thought they'd be too oppressive and long and full of speeches that would be boring for her. But later, when she took her daughter to the cemetery to show her where Grandpa was buried, what her little girl wanted to know was, "Why wasn't I here then?" That mother isn't sure she would make the same decision again. She wonders now if feelings of exclusion may not be harder to bear than feelings of tedium and even sadness.

Most of us want our children to become part of the family and family traditions that we, ourselves, grew up with. Stressful though family gatherings may be, they are significant times for children to sense the values of their families and their cultures. They are important chances for children, in their own ways, to ponder who we are to one another and to wonder at love's mysterious capacity to grow fuller and stronger even as we give it away.

The regularity and intensity of the winter holiday season—the time that spans both Channukah and Christmas—makes it unique in the roster of family times. When that season nears, I always find myself thinking of grandparents. That's partly because my grandparents were so very important to me at holidays when I was young, but it's also because grandparents have a way of being the keepers of the old traditions—the festival of lights, the star in the east, as well as many others. Somehow I find it's grandparents who, in their age and endurance, most represent the hope and faith of the season.

It took me many years to think of grandparents this way. I was often bored when they insisted that all the children be very quiet for things like Bible readings. But my mother and dad told me they had to sit just the same way for just the same readings when they were little—and they survived. Anyway, when I got to be a parent, it fascinated me to see how much those same readings meant to me and how much I wanted our children to hear them.

Sometimes it works that way and sometimes it doesn't. One friend told me recently: "My wife and I observe some traditions around Christmas that come from our own growing up; but others we've chosen to leave behind. My wife's parents sing carols Christmas Eve, and everyone gets to open one present. We still do that with our children.

"My parents, on the other hand, play charades on Christmas Eve. I can't stand charades and never could. So that's 'out' in our family. Nevertheless, when we're visiting my folks, we still play charades, like it or not. It makes me feel like a school boy all over again, and our children don't seem any more comfortable with the game than I was."

Grandparents are both our past and our future. In some ways they are what has gone before, and in others they are what we will become. Just as the old traditions of spinning the dreidel and hanging up the stockings will continue long after our time, so, too, will the sequences of the generations as young children grow into grandparents with grandchildren of their own. My turn is coming to be a grandparent. I find comfort and joy in this knowledge that I have my place in the continual unfolding of the human family.

Birthdays are another significant family time, in some ways more perplexing than the holidays we share, because birthdays don't come with preestablished rituals. Birthdays are only what we make them, and many parents find that presents and parties alone don't necessarily make for happy ones. Presents can bring disappointments, and parties can end in chaos, tears, and grouchy grown-ups. In talking with parents, we found that their unease about childhood birthdays tended to reflect three main concerns: fulfilling wishes, continuing family traditions, and meeting social expectations.

One father told us: "By the time of our son's third birthday, my wife and I had already come to the conclusion that 'What do you want for your birthday?' was a really dangerous question. How could Mark know what was reasonable to ask for: How could he know what we'd be happy for him to have and what we wouldn't? We felt such an open-ended question just set us all up for trouble."

What those parents did was to start making birthdays "surprise days"—days when Mark suddenly finds a package somewhere when he isn't expecting it. The first one might turn up at the breakfast table, and then others in other places during the day. The last two are always on his pillow at bedtime, one from his mother and one from his father, and they are always small things his parents have made.

Some of Mark's presents are things he wanted; his parents look and listen for clues beforehand. But even these come as surprises, and I think that family's approach, besides lessening the chance of disappointments, helps avoid another of birthdays' pitfalls: too much all at once and over too soon.

When a friend of ours was little, family tradition always made birthdays a formal affair even for the children. Everyone was expected to be all dressed up and on best behavior. Her birthday guests were in good part relatives; she was allowed to invite just one special friend of her own age. She remembers feeling very important and special with so many grown-ups paying so much attention to her, but she has other memories as well: "I can't say those days were fun or comfortable, even though they were exciting. It was so difficult to stay good and polite and neat for so long! We've broken that family tradition with our children. For us it's blue jeans and a picnic or an outing with several children, and the cake and ice cream is a quick ceremony. I know my parents don't approve, and I feel awkward about that. All the same, my husband and I feel good about starting new traditions of our own—ones that seem right for us and our children."

I can understand that feeling of awkwardness; it can be hard to let go of family traditions—just as it can be hard to resist social pressure.

One pressure several parents mentioned is the seemingly growing custom to invite a whole classroom of children to a birthday celebration. For some families, this approach may work out fine, but many others clearly find it burdensome. It's too much work to have a party like that at home, some say, while noting that it's just too expensive to do it anywhere else. In addition, they point out that a large party crowd often leads young children into overexcitement, accidents, and unhappiness. And yet, if one family invites everybody in the class, shouldn't every family return the invitation?

I don't believe so. There are many ways to celebrate birthdays, and what works best for each family is what their celebration should be. After all, the reason for birthdays is to give our children a once-a-year, strong, and special confirmation of the importance of their lives in our family and among their friends. How to give children that gift of love is something that parents are the best ones to decide.

Reflections on that Four-Letter Word—Love

We heard a story from a friend, co-worker, and fine teacher (who, like many fine teachers, often taught through stories), and it went like this:

As a topic for his thesis, a student once chose—the Universe. His professor read the thesis ... and failed the student for not sticking to the subject.

Deciding to end this book with an essay on Love may run the same risks, but a note from a correspondent set off a sudden train of thought that we felt compelled to try to catch in words. "It isn't possible," our correspondent wrote, "for parents to love their children equally, and they should not feel guilty when they come to that realization."

The problem, of course, is, What is love? We can't hope to answer that here once and for all, but perhaps these thoughts will help you find answers of your own and put the problem of "equal love" in a slightly different light.

Love, whatever it is, is essential nourishment for human beings' healthy emotional growth. That nourishment has many, many ingredients. We couldn't list them all any more than we could list all the foods that give our bodies nourishment, but here are a few that might appear on such a list.

There's liking, feeling affectionate toward, needing to feel dependent on, needing to feel in control of. We'd want to put friendship and companionship on the list, as well as attachment, physical attraction, passion, and sexuality. Shared interests and contrasting interests can be important. Certainly respect and admiration. Then there's loyalty and fidelity, and the darker ingredients, such as possessiveness, jealousy, anger, grief, disappointment, yearning, emptiness, loss, and the like. And there are the brighter ones, such as fullness, tenderness, patience, compassion, concern, sympathy, empathy.

There's touching and being touched . . . and on and on.

Whatever "love" is, it is never all of these ingredients all at once. It doesn't even have to include *liking*; for some people, loving their enemies has real meaning. In fact, love does not even have to depend on *knowing* someone; some people can "love their neighbors" without ever having met them. And, of course, many people find a love of the un-meetable and unknowable when they say, in their own ways, that they love—and are loved by—God.

The love we feel at any given moment may be comprised of one, a few, many of love's possible ingredients. The ingredients that constitute love change as we change, as those we love change, as times and circumstances change. The combination of different ingredients produces different feelings, and when put together, the different ingredients change one another just as different combinations of foods produce different chemical reactions.

Love's ingredients have different intensities, durations, and depths —different "tastes" and effects. Some are sharp and biting . . . and may not last long. Some are spicy and can burn. Some are sweet or sour or bitter. Some are soothing and long-lasting. Some fill us quickly and soon leave us empty. Some fill us slowly and can sustain us on long journeys. Some are necessary, others self-indulgent.

Given the countless combinations of ingredients and intensities, it is inevitable that we feel differently about any two people that we say we "love." As our correspondent clearly knew, no parents ever feel exactly the same way about any two of their children . . . and no child ever felt the same way about both parents. As children, most of us wrestled at one time or another with which parent we loved the most. We probably jumped to the conclusion that the parent we felt we needed more right then was the parent we loved the most, and that had to mean we loved the other less, and so we felt guilty. As parents, we can feel once again those old pangs of guilt when we wonder whether we love one of our children more than another.

But if today I have a need, even a craving, for the nourishment that apples can bring, does that mean I've lessened my "love" for oranges? As parents and children work and grow together, it's natural for them to feel differently about one another at different times. I don't believe that recognizing our differing feelings needs to bring us guilt.

I find it helpful to think about love as separate from any of its possible ingredients. It's a different kind of thing. Love is like "infinity": You can't have more or less infinity, and you can't compare two things to see if they're "equally infinite." Infinity just *is*, and that's the way I think love is, too. That may be the most one can hope to say, but when love *is* there . . . well, that's saying more than enough!

INDEX

INDEX

About the Authors

FRED MCFEELY ROGERS, known to millions of American families as "Mister Rogers" of *Mister Rogers' Neighborhood*, was born in 1928. He graduated from Rollins College with a B.A. in music composition and became a creator and producer of television programming for children. In addition, he found time to complete his theological studies at the Pittsburgh Theological Seminary and was ordained as a minister in the United Presbyterian Church. He also took the Masters program in Child Development at the University of Pittsburgh. The Rogers family—his wife, who is a concert pianist, and their two sons and daughter-in-law—live in Pittsburgh.

BARRY HEAD, a freelance writer, has been associated with Fred Rogers for fifteen years. British by birth, he graduated from New College, Oxford, and spent several years as a journalist and magazine editor. His articles and short fiction have appeared in such national publications as *Harper's Magazine, Mademoiselle,* and *Redbook*. He is the co-author, with Neil Paylor, of *Scenes From a Divorce* (Winston Press). In addition to developing a wide range of media materials for children and families, he has worked in public affairs television and documentary film. He is the father of two sons, and makes his home in eastern Long Island.